THE ORIGINS OF THE NECESSARY AND PROPER CLAUSE

The Necessary and Proper Clause is one of the most important parts of the U.S. Constitution. Today this short thirty-nine-word paragraph is cited as the legal foundation for much of the modern federal government. Yet constitutional scholars have pronounced its origins and original meaning a mystery.

Through three independent lines of research, the authors trace the lineage of the Necessary and Proper Clause to the everyday law of the founding era – the same law that American founders such as Madison, Hamilton, and Washington applied in their daily lives. The origins of the Necessary and Proper Clause can be found in the founding-era law governing agency, public administration, and corporations. All of those areas were undergirded by common principles of fiduciary responsibility – reflecting the founders' view that a public office is truly a public trust. This explains the choice of language in the clause and provides clues about its meaning. This book thus serves as a reference source for scholars seeking to understand the intellectual foundations of one of the Constitution's most important clauses.

Gary Lawson is a professor of law and the Abraham and Lillian Benton Scholar at Boston University School of Law. Professor Lawson has authored (with Guy Seidman) *The Constitution of Empire: Territorial Expansion and American Legal History*, five editions of a casebook on *Federal Administrative Law*, and more than sixty articles in law reviews and other journals.

Geoffrey P. Miller is the Stuyvesant P. Comfort Professor of Law at New York University Law School. Miller is the director of NYU Law School's Center for the Study of Central Banks and Financial Institutions and is a founder of the Society for Empirical Legal Studies.

Robert G. Natelson is Senior Fellow in Constitutional Jurisprudence at Independence Institute, and formerly professor of law at the University of Montana. He is an expert on the framing and adoption of the United States Constitution, and on several occasions he has been the first to uncover key background facts about the Constitution's meaning.

Guy I. Seidman is an assistant professor of law at the Interdisciplinary Center in Herzliya, Israel. He is a former visiting scholar at the University of Chicago and Northwestern University. Dr. Seidman is primarily interested in administrative and constitutional law, and in comparative law and legal traditions.

The Origins of the Necessary and Proper Clause

Gary Lawson

Boston University School of Law

Geoffrey P. Miller

New York University School of Law

Robert G. Natelson

Independence Institute

Guy I. Seidman

The Interdisciplinary Center, Herzliya, Israel

CAMBRIDGE
UNIVERSITY PRESS

CAMBRIDGE UNIVERSITY PRESS
Cambridge, New York, Melbourne, Madrid, Cape Town, Singapore,
São Paulo, Delhi, Dubai, Tokyo, Mexico City

Cambridge University Press
32 Avenue of the Americas, New York, NY 10013-2473, USA

www.cambridge.org
Information on this title: www.cambridge.org/9780521119580

First published 2010

Printed in the United States of America

A catalog record for this publication is available from the British Library.

Library of Congress Cataloging in Publication data
The origins of the necessary and proper clause / Gary Lawson ... [et al.].
p. cm.
Includes bibliographical references and index.
ISBN 978-0-521-11958-0 (hardback)
1. Legislative power – United States. 2. United States. Congress.
3. Legislation – United States. 4. Legislators – United States.
5. Constitutional law – United States. I. Lawson, Gary, 1958– II. Title.
KF4930.075 2010
342.73'052–dc22 2010018051

ISBN 978-0-521-11958-0 Hardback

As with all things, to Patty, Nathaniel, and Noah.

Gary Lawson
March 2010

This book is dedicated in loving memory to my parents,
Ady Seidman (1930–2009) and Lea Seidman
(né Carmi, 1934–1999).

Guy Seidman
March 2010

Contents

Acknowledgments

Gary Lawson is grateful to Robert P. Smith for creating and funding the David Saul Smith Award, which was instrumental in producing this book. Professor Lawson is also grateful to the Abraham and Lillian Benton Fund for support and to participants at a workshop at Boston University School of Law for characteristically insightful comments. Portions of Chapter 6 are based on material from Gary Lawson and Guy I. Seidman, *The Jeffersonian Treaty Clause*, 2006 ILL. L. REV. 1 (2006), and other portions of that chapter exist only because of the prior scholarship of Professor Robert G. Natelson.

Gary Lawson and Guy I. Seidman
March 2010

A version of Geoffrey P. Miller's chapter was previously published in *The George Washington Law Review* and is available at 79 GEO. WASH. L. REV. 1 (2010). I wish to thank Sharae M. Wheeler for superb research assistance on this project.

Geoffrey P. Miller
March 2010

Among those deserving credit for my scholarship in general are my wife, Elizabeth J. Natelson, who over the years has supported my research in every way (including some sharp editing), and my parents, Dr. Sydney and Florence Natelson, who paid for my education. Most of this scholarship was conducted while I was a faculty member at The University of Montana, and thus was made possible through the generous support of Montana taxpayers.

A number of people provided assistance specific to this book – among them helpful and intelligent librarians, who located and guided me through the ancient sources: the staff and administration of the Bodleian Law Library, University of Oxford; Dr. Norma Aubertin-Potter, librarian-in-charge of the Codrington Library at All-Souls College, University of Oxford; Dr. Vanessa Hayward, keeper of the Middle Temple Library, London, and her staff; Ms. Virginia Dunn and the Archives Research Services staff at the Library of Virginia in Richmond; and Fritz Snyder, Stacey Gordon, Philip Cousineau, and Robert Peck, all at the Jameson Law Library at The University of Montana.

Finally, great credit goes to Gary Lawson, who conceived of this book, brought the contributors together, wrote much of it, and guided it to fruition.

Robert G. Natelson
Missoula, Montana
March 2010

I

Raiders of the Lost Clause

Excavating the Buried Foundations of the Necessary and Proper Clause

The U.S. Constitution creates a national government of limited and enumerated powers. More precisely, it creates a set of *institutions* of national governance of limited and enumerated powers. The Constitution never grants power to the "national government" or the "federal government" as an undifferentiated entity, but instead grants various aspects of governmental power to discrete actors. The president is vested with the "executive Power," the federal courts are vested with the "judicial Power," and Congress is vested with a range of specified "legislative Powers," primarily though not exclusively identified in Article I, section 8 of the document,[1] including the power to lay and collect taxes, borrow money, regulate various types of commerce, and provide for a military. The first seventeen clauses in Article I, section 8 identify (depending upon how one counts) roughly two dozen such legislative powers.

The eighteenth and last clause in Article I, section 8 grants Congress power "[t]o make all Laws which shall be necessary and proper for carrying into Execution the foregoing Powers, and all other Powers vested by this Constitution in the Government of the United States, or in any Department or Officer thereof."[2] Antifederalist critics of the Constitution pejoratively dubbed this provision "the Sweeping Clause," arguing that it granted dangerously broad and ill-defined powers to the new national

[1] Some non–Article I powers of Congress are the power to allow inferior federal officers to be appointed by the president, the federal courts, or federal department heads without Senate confirmation, U.S. CONST. art. II, § 2, cl. 2; the power to prescribe the manner in which state acts and judicial proceedings will be given full faith and credit by sister states, *id.* art. IV, § 1; the power to admit new states, *id.* art. IV, § 3, cl. 1; the power to make "Rules and Regulations respecting the Territory or other Property belonging to the United States," *id.* art. IV, § 3, cl. 2; and the power to propose constitutional amendments, *id.* art. V.

[2] *Id.* art. I, § 8, cl. 18.

government.[3] The defenders of the Constitution vigorously contested this construction of the clause, but generally accepted the Antifederalist label for "the sweeping clause, as it has been affectedly called."[4] In modern times, however, the clause is more typically known as the "Necessary and Proper Clause," and we employ the modern label throughout this book.[5]

The origins of the Necessary and Proper Clause have proven to be something of a mystery to constitutional scholars. Those who look to the clause's drafting history for clues about its origins have generally been disappointed, complaining that "the accounts of the 1787 Constitutional Convention are silent on the meaning of the necessary and proper power."[6] One of the leading modern scholars on the clause reports that "[t]he Necessary and Proper Clause was added to the Constitution by the Committee of Detail without any previous discussion by the Constitutional Convention. Nor was it the subject of any debate from its initial proposal to the Convention's final adoption of the Constitution."[7] As for the Committee of Detail, the scholarly verdict is that it "gave no hint why it chose the language it did. ..."[8] A broader look at the state ratifying conventions and early constitutional history seemingly provides no further guidance about the drafters' choice of language: Those sources contain considerable argument about the extent of

3 *See* John P. Kaminski, *The Constitution Without a Bill of Rights, in* The Bill of Rights and the States: The Colonial and Revolutionary Origins of American Liberalism 16, 29 (Patrick T. Conley and John P. Kaminski eds., 1992) (noting that Antifederalists "pointed to the general welfare clause and the necessary and proper clause to show that Congress possessed unlimited authority under the Constitution"). For example, a petition to the Pennsylvania ratifying convention warned that the clause "submits every right of the people of these states, both civil and sacred to the disposal of Congress, who may exercise their power to the expulsion of the jury trial in civil causes to the total suppression of the liberty of the press; and to the setting up and establishing of a cruel tyranny, if they should be so disposed, over all the dearest and most sacred rights of the citizens." *Cumberland County Petition to the Pennsylvania Convention*, Dec. 5, 1787, *reprinted in* 2 Documentary History of the Ratification of the Constitution 309, 310 (Merrill Jensen ed., 1976).

4 The Federalist No. 33, at 203 (Alexander Hamilton) (Clinton Rossiter ed., 1961).

5 The "sweeping clause" label, however, remained standard into the twentieth century. *See* 1 Francis Newton Thorpe, The Constitutional History of the United States 525 (1901).

6 Bernard H. Siegan, The Supreme Court's Constitution: An Inquiry into Judicial Review and Its Impact on Society 1 (1987).

7 Randy E. Barnett, *The Original Meaning of the Necessary and Proper Clause*, 6 U. Pa. J. Const. L. 183, 185 (2003).

8 Mark A. Graber, *Unnecessary and Unintelligible*, 12 Const. Commentary 167, 168 (1995).

the powers granted to Congress by the Necessary and Proper Clause, but the arguments were pitched at a very high level of generality, and it looks at first glance as though nothing in those materials explains the peculiar wording of the clause. Indeed, Philip Kurland and Ralph Lerner's *The Founders' Constitution*, an encyclopedic compilation of source material on the Constitution, contains some excerpts from these debates but nothing that appears to shed light on the clause's origins.[9] In particular, Kurland and Lerner's often-indispensable work contains no entries on the Necessary and Proper Clause's background that predate the ratification debates. If there are nuggets to be mined in the standard sources of constitutional history, they seem thus far to have escaped notice.

All of this has led one scholar to proclaim the Necessary and Proper Clause "a masterpiece of enigmatic formulation."[10] Mark Graber, one of the country's most eminent legal historians, aptly summed up the conventional wisdom on the Necessary and Proper Clause's provenance when he insisted that "no one, including the constitutional framers, knows the point of the phrase 'necessary and proper.'"[11]

It would be truly extraordinary if the Necessary and Proper Clause emerged from a late-eighteenth-century Committee of Detail with no intellectual antecedents. As the vigorous founding-era debates over the scope of the clause illustrate, the Necessary and Proper Clause is central to the constitutional scheme of enumerated powers. It is indisputably the source of congressional power to enact most criminal statutes and other enforcement mechanisms[12] and to create and structure federal offices beyond the very few directly created by the Constitution.[13] Historically, it was the alleged source of federal power to create instrumentalities such as the Bank of the United States,[14] and the New Deal Court relied upon the Necessary and Proper Clause – rather than, as

9 *See* 3 Philip B. Kurland & Ralph Lerner, The Founders' Constitution 238–277 (1987).

10 Joseph M. Lynch, Negotiating the Constitution: The Earliest Debates Over Original Intent 4 (1999).

11 Graber, supra note 8, at 168.

12 The Constitution specifically authorizes Congress to punish counterfeiting, U.S. Const. art. I, § 8, cl. 6, piracy and offenses against the law of nations, *id.* art. I, § 8, cl. 10, and treason, *id.* art. III, § 2, but those are the only express authorizations for the enactment of criminal laws.

13 Indeed, a Convention proposal to add the words "and establish all Offices" to the clause was rejected 9–2 on the stated ground that the clause already conferred such power. *See* James Madison, Notes of Debates in the Federal Convention of 1787, at 489 (1893).

14 *See* McCulloch v. Maryland, 17 U.S. (4 Wheat.) 316 (1819).

is often wrongly supposed, the Commerce Clause – to permit federal regulation of seemingly intrastate matters, such as the growing of wheat for home consumption.[15] More controversially, some scholars (including two of the present authors) have identified the Necessary and Proper Clause as the true source of the federal spending power,[16] and others (including one of the present authors) see it as the font of congressional power to create exceptions to the Supreme Court's appellate jurisdiction.[17] In modern Supreme Court jurisprudence, the Necessary and Proper Clause has been a central player in debates concerning federalism, including disputes over the ability of Congress to regulate seemingly noneconomic intrastate activities,[18] to control the actions of state legislatures and executives,[19] to abrogate state sovereign immunity,[20] and to construct a federal system of civil commitment for persons deemed sexually dangerous.[21] And because the Necessary and Proper Clause is the source of virtually all of the congressional power to structure the federal government, the clause is at the heart of almost any interdepartmental dispute about the separation of powers. There is a good argument that it is the most important clause in the Constitution. If the origins of such a vital provision are truly unknowable, then it is understandable why the Necessary and Proper Clause would prominently appear in a volume on "Constitutional Stupidities."[22]

The aim of this book is to challenge the conventional wisdom concerning the origins of the Necessary and Proper Clause – and indeed to do so three times over. Far from emerging immaculately from the Constitutional Convention, the Necessary and Proper Clause has a rich history, with numerous antecedents that would have been readily

[15] *See* Stephen Gardbaum, *Rethinking Constitutional Federalism*, 74 Tex. L. Rev. 795, 807–08 (1996).

[16] *See* Gary Lawson and Guy Seidman, The Constitution of Empire: Territorial Expansion and American Legal History 25–31 (2004).

[17] *See* Steven G. Calabresi and Gary Lawson, *The Unitary Executive, Jurisdiction Stripping, and the* Hamdan *Opinions: A Textualist Response to Justice Scalia*, 107 Colum. L. Rev. 1002, 1039–42 (2007); David E. Engdahl, *Intrinsic Limits of Congress' Power Regarding the Judicial Branch*, 1999 B.Y.U. L. Rev. 75, 119–26.

[18] Gonzalez v. Raich, 545 U.S. 1 (2005).

[19] Printz v. United States, 521 U.S. 898, 923–24 (1997).

[20] Alden v. Maine, 527 U.S. 706, 732–33 (1999).

[21] Comstock v. United States, 551 F.3d 274 (4th Cir. 2008), *cert. granted*, 129 S. Ct. 2828 (2008); United States v. Tom, 565 F.3d 497 (8th Cir. 2009).

[22] Mark Graber, *Unnecessary and Unintelligible*, *in* William N. Eskridge, Jr., and Sanford Levinson, Constitutional Stupidities, Constitutional Tragedies 43 (1998).

knowable (and were almost certainly known) by informed eighteenth-century drafters and ratifiers. These antecedents have thus far escaped notice because they are not found – or at least are not found without considerable interpretative background knowledge – in the sources to which constitutional scholars typically look for guidance: the Convention notes, the ratification debates, and early American constitutional history. Instead, the origins of the Necessary and Proper Clause are found in principles of agency law, administrative law, and corporate law that infused founding-era constitutionalism but are not generally consulted by constitutional scholars and courts. We thus say of those who despair about finding the origins of this clause precisely what Indiana Jones and Sallah said of the efforts of Belloc and the Nazis to excavate the Well of Souls using faulty calculations from the staff of Ra: "They're digging in the wrong place!"

This book combines three independent lines of research into the origins of the Necessary and Proper Clause. Professor Robert Natelson's research over several years tends to show that the private law of agency strongly informed the founding generation's theories of constitutionalism.[23] With specific reference to the Necessary and Proper Clause, he then traced the origins of the phrase "necessary and proper for carrying into Execution" to (primarily) private-law agency instruments that used similar language; his findings on the foundations of the Necessary and Proper Clause were published in 2004.[24]

At roughly the same time, without knowing of Professor Natelson's work, Professors Gary Lawson and Guy Seidman began exploring the relevance of British administrative law for founding-era constitutionalism, with particular emphasis on the so-called principle of reasonableness that required power delegated by Parliament to be exercised in an impartial, efficacious, proportionate, and rights-regarding manner. They principally sought to understand the background norms of administrative law that helped define the "executive Power," but the potential applications to understanding the genesis of the Necessary and Proper Clause were evident as a future project. This work was also first published in 2004.[25]

[23] *See* Robert G. Natelson, *Judicial Review of Special Interest Spending: The General Welfare Clause and the Fiduciary Law of the Founders*, 11 TEX. REV. L. & POLITICS 239 (2007); Robert G. Natelson, *The Constitution and the Public Trust*, 52 BUFF. L. REV. 1077 (2004): Robert G. Natelson, *The General Welfare Clause and the Public Trust: An Essay in Original Understanding*, 52 U. KANSAS L. REV. 1 (2003).

[24] *See* Robert G. Natelson, *The Agency Law Origins of the Necessary and Proper Clause*, 55 CASE WESTERN RESERVE L. REV. 243 (2004).

[25] LAWSON AND SEIDMAN, *supra* note 16, at 51–57 (2004).

Entirely independent of both of these projects, Professor Geoffrey Miller had begun researching founding-era corporate charters, which he discovered often employed provisions similar in phrasing to the Necessary and Proper Clause. Given the quasi-governmental status of founding-era corporations – and the more-than-quasi-corporate status of colonial governments – he thought it eminently sensible to ask whether corporate law (in this eighteenth-century sense) might have influenced the final form of the Necessary and Proper Clause. That work lay dormant for some years until the preparation of Professor Miller's chapter for this book, but the project was conceived roughly contemporaneously with the other lines of inquiry collected here.

None of these three lines of research is part of the standard account of the Necessary and Proper Clause, but all hold promise as potential intellectual influences on the founding generation's choice of language in constructing the clause. Once the authors of this book all became aware of the parallel projects, the thought occurred of combining them into a single resource for those interested in the origins of the Necessary and Proper Clause. That has always been, and remains, the *raison d'être* for this book. We hope to demonstrate that modern puzzlement about the Necessary and Proper Clause's antecedents is the product of limited vision rather than limited materials. Far from suffering from a paucity of materials on the clause's origins, researchers have an extensive menu of such materials, and we hope to make that menu conveniently accessible here.

After the projects were combined, it was natural to ask whether they had common themes. It is easily evident that they do. All three projects explore applications of what we call, for lack of a better phrase, *public agency law*: the application of agency law principles to public actors.

Professor Natelson explicitly links the Necessary and Proper Clause to agency law. The founding generation, he argues, viewed government largely through the lens of agency; founding-era figures often described the duties of public officials in fiduciary terms and even analogized the Constitution to a private power of attorney. The language used in the Necessary and Proper Clause tracks the language found in many founding- and pre-founding-era private agency instruments, which used the words "necessary and proper" or some equivalent to give fiduciary agents incidental powers beyond those expressly described in the instruments. When one adds together the prevalence of such agency instruments, the wide knowledge of agency law among founding-era individuals (including nonlawyers) and the broad-based eighteenth-century consensus in favor of viewing government through the lens of agency, it is natural to see the Necessary and Proper Clause as a vehicle for importing those fiduciary and agency principles to Congress.

Professors Lawson and Seidman see in the words "necessary and proper" a vehicle for incorporating into Article I fundamental background principles of eighteenth-century administrative law. By the time of the American founding, it was well established in English law that grants of discretionary authority to executive and judicial agents of Parliament carried the implied requirement that exercises of such authority be reasonable – that is, fair, efficacious, proportionate, and rights-regarding. This principle would unambiguously apply, even without specific reference, to the federal Constitution's grants of executive and judicial power; delegations of such power presumed that agents would have to exercise that power reasonably. It is less clear, however, whether such a principle would automatically apply to a constitutional delegation of legislative authority to Congress. Accordingly, if a drafter wanted the principle of reasonableness in the exercise of delegated power to apply to Congress, some kind of textual reference to the principle would be in order, and the language of the Necessary and Proper Clause is an ideal textual reference for this purpose. This approach to understanding the origins of the Necessary and Proper Clause, like that employed by Professor Natelson, has roots in an agency-oriented approach to governance.

Professor Miller's work studying corporate charters fits elegantly into this theme, because corporations in the eighteenth century, and indeed into the nineteenth century, were effectively public actors charged with essentially governmental tasks, such as constructing public works, schools, and poorhouses – or, less frequently but more grandly, extending governmental influence through exploration. Corporate charters in those days were not general authorizations to do business, as is typical of modern charters, but instead defined the powers and responsibilities of these quasi-public actors. Indeed, because corporations in this period frequently exercised monopoly privileges, the scope of "purposes and powers" clauses in their charters – the enumerations of power – was generally narrow. Clauses similar to the Necessary and Proper Clause were thus important to ensure that an organization with limited powers and purposes would not be frustrated in the essential conduct of its governmentally authorized activities but would still be confined to its assigned functions. This model of corporations as a form of governmental or quasi-governmental agents entrusted with specific tasks yet again sounds the theme of public agency law.

Thus, there are close, and even striking, connections among the agency law, administrative law, and corporate law explanations for the language of the Necessary and Proper Clause. There is enough convergence to permit reasonably confident assertions about the clause's actual origins. An obvious next question is whether there is enough convergence to support a general theory of the clause's actual meaning.

Although that may be an obvious next question, it is not one that this book seeks to pursue. We embarked on this project intending to avoid making any strong claims about the meaning of the Necessary and Proper Clause. Our mission in assembling and integrating our research has always been historical and descriptive, not interpretative. We (at least largely) hold to that intention here. In order to make claims, or even draw implications, about the meaning of the Necessary and Proper Clause, one must first set forth a theory of constitutional interpretation. We fervently wish to elide those kinds of broad issues in this book – if only because the authors do not necessarily agree about interpretative methodology. Professors Lawson and Seidman have elsewhere staked out a fairly strong position in favor of original meaning as the only appropriate tool of constitutional interpretation,[26] and they have a specific conception of original meaning in mind: They believe that constitutional interpretation must always take place from the standpoint of a hypothetical reasonable observer, both because that is what the Constitution commands and because it is the only possible form of interpretation for jointly authored documents. That approach structures some of their inquiries in this book. Professor Natelson, by contrast, believes that founding-era interpretative conventions establish that the subjective intentions of the ratifiers, *where discoverable*, determine the meaning of the Constitution, and when those intentions are not discoverable, one looks to objective meanings as they would be understood by a reasonable interpreter.[27] He employs that founding-era methodology – without necessarily declaring it "correct" or the only admissible methodology – in his contributions to this book. Professor Miller, for his part, is willing to say that he believes it important to consider the original understanding (however defined) when interpreting the Constitution, but further the deponent saith not. Given the range of disagreement, we

[26] *See id.* at 8–12; Gary Lawson and Guy Seidman, *Originalism As a Legal Enterprise*, 23 Const. Commentary 47 (2006).

[27] *See* Robert G. Natelson, *The Founders' Hermeneutic: The Real Original Understanding of Original Intent*, 68 Ohio St. L.J. 1239 (2007).

choose jointly to avoid such interpretative issues to the extent possible and concentrate instead on providing raw material on the Necessary and Proper Clause's origins, which interpreters of all stripes can do with what they will.

Of course, each of us has his own research agenda beyond this book, of which the material presented herein may be one component. Each of us, therefore, might (or might not) in our individual projects seek to draw interpretative implications from the material developed herein. Accordingly, it would be artificial, and indeed silly, to try to craft all of the contributions to this book to imply or infer nothing at all about the underlying meaning of the Necessary and Proper Clause. It would be particularly odd if and when those individual thoughts on interpretation are reinforced or extended by the research of others – and there is too much reinforcement and extension in this volume to ignore.

We navigate between the Scylla of grand interpretative theory and the Charybdis of interpretative silence by retaining and declaring individual authorship of the contributions to this project. Chapters 2, 3, and 6 are attributable to Professors Lawson and Seidman; Chapters 4 and 5 are authored by Professor Natelson; and Chapter 7 is the work of Professor Miller. We hasten to add that this book is *not* an edited collection of essays. To the contrary, this is an integrated volume: The various chapters take close account of each other, and we think that they collectively form a remarkably coherent intellectual structure. We simply mean that we have not reduced the entire book to one voice or forbidden individual authors from offering thoughts or speculations about the ultimate meaning of the Necessary and Proper Clause from whatever perspective they deem appropriate. But *none* of the basic claims made in this book about the intellectual origins of the Necessary and Proper Clause depends to any significant degree on the interpretative claims –and they prove to be relatively few and far between – that any of us have chosen to offer.

Chapters 2 and 3 clear the decks by identifying some dead ends in the search for the origins of the Necessary and Proper Clause. Language similar to that in the clause, and in other constitutional provisions that contain qualifications on granted power, appeared frequently in British statutes throughout the eighteenth century. Chapter 2 accordingly conducts an extensive study of the use of power-granting and power-qualifying language in these British statutes, which reveals no discernible patterns to the use of adjectives, singly or in combination, in these enactments. It is not an overstatement to say that the eighteenth-century

British Parliament used phrases describing or qualifying the powers of statutory grantees essentially at random. If these statutes served as models or inspirations for American constitutional drafters, it would be fruitless to look for deeper origins of the clause or to plumb the clause's meaning in any systematic way.

Chapter 3 reveals that there is no reason to think that American drafters followed, or even paid attention to, their British parliamentary counterparts. There were reasons specific to the legislative process in England that accounted for the sloppy draftsmanship evident in British statutes – a sloppiness that was widely recognized and derided inside and outside Parliament. American drafting did not suffer from the same pathologies; a study of the language used in pre-1788 state constitutions shows far more care and attention to nuance than was evident across the ocean. The path is accordingly clear to seek other, more potent influences on the drafting and adoption of the Necessary and Proper Clause.

In Chapter 4, Professor Natelson offers his evidence for locating the origins of the clause in agency law. Professor Natelson first shows that the founding generation almost uniformly viewed government through the lens of agency law: Public actors were seen as fiduciaries, subject to the same kinds of restrictions on their power as private fiduciaries such as executors, factors, and guardians. He further shows founding-era familiarity with the doctrine of principals and incidents, in which agents were understood to have power to exercise authority not expressly granted by the instruments of agency if that authority was subsidiary to the accomplishment of the specified ends. He concludes that the language "necessary and proper for carrying into Execution" neatly incorporates these two large principles of agency law: A "necessary" law is one that conforms to the doctrine of principals and incidents, and a "proper" law is one that conforms to fiduciary norms appropriate for public actors.

In Chapter 5, Professor Natelson (re)examines the Necessary and Proper Clause's drafting and ratification history – a history that has been found by prior scholars to yield little of value. Viewed through the lens of the agency law principles described in Chapter 4, however, the clause's history takes more structured shape and exhibits a "public agency law" understanding of the clause, as a matter of both the knowable subjective intentions of the ratifiers and of the reasonable understandings of an objective public observer.

In Chapter 6, Professors Lawson and Seidman reach similar conclusions through a different analytical route. Founding-era administrative law understood delegated power to carry with it the implied, unstated requirement that such power be exercised in an impartial, efficacious, proportionate, and rights-regarding fashion. Each of these elements of "reasonableness" (as post-founding-era law came to call it) finds expression in important preconstitutional British cases describing the power of executive and judicial agents. These elements are well captured by the requirement that laws be "necessary and proper for carrying into Execution" governmental powers – and they also track almost precisely the principles of fiduciary law that Professor Natelson has shown infused founding-era understandings of government. Furthermore, given the constitutional structure and the ways in which it vests power in different governmental institutions, there are good reasons why the Constitution would explicitly specify this kind of fiduciary requirement for Congress but not for the president or the federal courts, because the requirement of reasonableness was implicit in the very nature of delegations of executive or judicial power. Accordingly, from the perspectives of both agency law and administrative law, the Necessary and Proper Law Clause imposes (combining the two perspectives) fiduciary obligations of reasonableness on Congress when it passes laws implementing federal powers.

Professor Miller's research in Chapter 7 focuses on the role of clauses in founding-era corporate charters similar in structure and wording to the Necessary and Proper Clause. While he cautions against drawing strong interpretative conclusions from this material and notes that there is no direct proof that corporate charters influenced the actual construction of the Necessary and Proper Clause, he finds the usage of terms that qualify power grants in these charters to be, at the very least, consistent with the accounts of the Necessary and Proper Clause offered elsewhere in this book. The term "necessary" appears frequently in corporate charters in connection with important aspects of the organization's business (such as the hiring of key personnel in small corporations), which suggests that "necessary" requires a moderately close connection between means and ends. He finds the word "proper" suggestive of an obligation on the part of corporate managers to take account of the effects of their actions on all stakeholders in the corporation – a conclusion that reinforces the idea that the word "proper" conveys a fiduciary idea of nondiscrimination.

* * *

We do not claim in this book to have uncovered the Well of Souls, much less the Ark of the Covenant. We do claim, however, that we can provide tools for future excavators who regard the origins of the Necessary and Proper Clause as interesting, either in their own right or as part of a wider interpretative enterprise.

2

Discretionary Grants in Eighteenth-Century English Legislation

Gary Lawson and Guy I. Seidman

The U.S. Constitution uses a wide variety of formulations to describe the discretion granted to various actors. The Constitution often grants discretion without specifying any constraint on the exercise of the granted power. The Census Clause, for example, provides that enumerations of persons shall be made within ten-year intervals "as ... [the Congress] shall by Law direct,"[1] with no textual indication that such laws must direct the census in any particular manner.[2] Indeed, the vast majority of the power grants in the Constitution, including the principal grants of power to Congress in Article 1, section 8, simply describe the power granted without any adjectival prescription of the manner in which the power may be employed.

Sometimes those powers are to be exercised only when certain objective conditions have been satisfied: For example, Congress may not suspend the writ of habeas corpus "unless when in Cases of Rebellion or Invasion the public Safety may require it"[3] and states may not engage in war "unless actually invaded, or in such imminent Danger as will not admit of delay."[4] But the objective conditions in these clauses use nouns (rebellion, invasion, danger) rather than

1 U.S. CONST. art. I, § 2, cl. 3.

2 The requirement in the Census Clause that there be an "actual Enumeration" of persons places limits on the manner in which Congress can direct the census, perhaps by constraining the use of sampling techniques rather than strict counting methods, *see* Dep't of Commerce v. U.S. House of Representatives, 525 U.S. 316 (1999); Thomas R. Lee, *The Original Understanding of the Census Clause: Statistical Estimates and the Constitutional Requirement of an "Actual Enumeration,"* 77 WASH. L. REV. 1 (2002), but nothing in the general grant to structure the census as Congress "shall by law direct" contains an internal textual limitation.

3 U.S. CONST. art. I, § 9, cl. 2.

4 *Id.* art. I, § 10, cl. 3.

adjectives to describe the range of circumstances in which it is permissible to exercise the power.

On some occasions, the Constitution grants discretion to an actor, qualifies that discretion with an adjective, and expressly makes the actor's judgment the measure of the discretion. The Slave Trade Clause forbade Congress from prohibiting, before 1808, "[t]he Migration or Importation of such Persons as any of the States now existing *shall think proper* to admit. ..."[5] The Appointments Clause permits Congress to vest the appointment "of such inferior Officers, *as they think proper*, in the President alone, in the Courts of Law, or in the Heads of Departments."[6] The president is instructed to recommend to Congress "such Measures *as he shall judge necessary and expedient*"[7] and is empowered to adjourn Congress "to such Time *as he shall think proper*"[8] when the two houses cannot agree. Congress may propose constitutional amendments "whenever two thirds of both Houses *shall deem it necessary*."[9]

Four provisions of the Constitution use adjectives to describe the extent of a discretionary power while phrasing the adjective in objective terms. Congress is given power to govern federal territory that is purchased from states "for the Erection of Forts, Magazines, Arsenals, dock-Yards, and other *needful* Buildings. ..."[10] No state may, without congressional consent, impose import or export duties "except what may be *absolutely necessary* for executing its inspection Laws. ..."[11] Congress has the power to "make all *needful* Rules and Regulations respecting the Territory or other Property belonging to the United States. ..."[12] And finally (analytically, not sequentially), Congress is given power "[t]o make all Laws which shall be *necessary and proper* for carrying into Execution the foregoing powers, and all other Powers vested by this Constitution in the Government of the United States, or in any Department or Officer thereof."[13]

The Constitution thus employs, in various combinations, the terms "proper," "needful," "necessary," and "expedient." All of these terms, and several similar ones such as "fit," "requisite," and "effectual," were

[5] *Id.* art. I, § 9, cl. 1 (emphasis added).
[6] *Id.* art. II, § 2, cl. 2 (emphasis added).
[7] *Id.* art. II, § 2, cl. 3 (emphasis added).
[8] *Id.* (emphasis added).
[9] *Id.* art. V (emphasis added).
[10] *Id.* art. I, § 8, cl. 17 (emphasis added).
[11] *Id.* art. I, § 10, cl. 2 (emphasis added).
[12] *Id.* art. IV, § 3, cl. 2 (emphasis added).
[13] *Id.* art. I, § 8, cl. 18 (emphasis added).

used with some frequency in eighteenth-century British statutes. It is natural to ask whether those British uses of adjectives qualifying power grants reflected patterns that might have served as models for American drafters in the later part of the century. More specifically, it is natural to ask whether the phrase "necessary and proper" had a distinctive meaning in eighteenth-century British statutory law that would have been widely known and available to the American legal community.

The answer appears to be "no": The phrase "necessary and proper" was used in eighteenth-century British legislation more or less interchangeably with a range of other phrases to describe the discretion granted to actors, and it does not appear that any of those phrases had a distinctive or specialized meaning. As we shall see in Chapter 3, that answer turns out to be unsurprising given the realities of eighteenth-century parliamentary drafting that made it unlikely that any clear patterns of usage in statutes would emerge.

In this chapter, we survey the evidence concerning the language of British statutes during the eighteenth century. We break up the century into four time periods for convenience and ease of exposition; we do *not* maintain that there were distinct periods for any analytical or historical purposes. After tracing the development of this statutory language, in the next chapter we assess its significance, if any, for American law. It turns out that there were enormous differences between American constitutional drafting and British statutory drafting in the late eighteenth century that make it very unlikely that the latter strongly influenced the former. But the English statutory usages existed nonetheless, and we accordingly present them as at least potentially part of the back story of the Necessary and Proper Clause.

I. PARLIAMENTARY DRAFTING, 1705–1743

The precise phrase "necessary and proper" in connection with grants of discretion seems to make its first eighteenth-century appearance in English statutory law in an enactment of 1736 dealing with watchmen in London. The mayor and council of London were authorized "to order and appoint what Number of Watchmen and Bedels *they shall judge necessary and proper* to be kept within each of the several Wards of the said City and the Liberties thereof. ..."[14] It seems evident that the phrase was not meant to describe a specific substantive limitation on the

[14] 10 Geo. 2, C A P. XXII (1736) (emphasis added).

discretion of the city officials to appoint watchmen. Not only does the statute authorize such hiring as the city officials "shall judge necessary and proper," but the remainder of the statute confirms, using slightly different language, that it was designed to grant the same kind of very broad discretion for related functions: After appointing watchmen, the city officials "shall then and there direct how they ought to be armed, and how long they are to watch, what Wages and Allowances shall be given to the said Watchmen and Bedels for their Attendance; and shall also order and direct what Number of Constables shall attend every Night in each respective Ward; and shall make all such other Orders and Regulations as the Nature of each particular Service shall seem to them to require."[15] There is no obvious difference in function between the language "shall seem to them to require" and "they shall judge necessary and proper," nor is there such an obvious difference between choosing the number of watchmen and determining their duties and wages to lead one to expect different grants of discretion for the different functions.

The text of the London watching act expressly declared the judgment of the city officials the measure of what was required or necessary and proper. That was a common form for discretion-granting clauses in such early eighteenth-century statutes, but it was hardly the only form. Many statutes granting discretion made no such express reference to the judgment of the actor to whom power was delegated. A survey of acts prior to 1736 strongly indicates that such choice of language was *not* generally understood to make a difference in the scope of the granted authority.

While the precise phrase "necessary and proper" does not show up in a statute until 1736, the phrase "proper and necessary" was frequently used in statutes in the first four decades of the eighteenth century. We have found nearly two dozen usages of the phrase between 1705 and 1736.

In 1705, a statute authorized courts of record to order viewings of evidence by jurors "where it shall appear to the Court ... that it will be proper and necessary. ..."[16] Two years later, a statute dealing with coinage in American colonies stated that it did not prevent the queen from regulating such coinage "as her Majesty ... shall from time to time judge proper and necessary. ..."[17] As with the London watchmen act, both of these statutes expressly committed the determination of propriety and necessity to the actor to whom power was delegated.

15 *Id.*
16 4 & 5 Ann. c. 3, § 8 (1705). For more on jury-viewing statutes, see *infra* XXX.
17 6 Ann. c. 57, § IV (1707).

There quickly followed, however, a raft of statutes that contained no such express commitment to the judgment of the actor. A series of statutes provided for the appointment of officers "as shall be proper and necessary" for stated purposes. Precisely the same phrase "as shall be proper and necessary" was used to authorize the appointment of "Commissioners of the Customs and Excise,"[18] "Justices of the Peace, Commissioners of the Customs, Receivers General, Collectors, Surveyors, and other Officers,"[19] "[Revenue] Commissioners and Officers,"[20] and "Commissioners of Customs and Excise, Receivers General, Collectors, Surveyors, and other judicial and ministerial Officers."[21]

Two features of these statutes bear mention. First, while these statutes make no explicit reference to the judgment of the appointing authorities as the measure of what is "proper and necessary," it seems remarkably unlikely that there could be some objectively correct number of such officers but no objectively correct number of bedels for the London watch – which strongly suggests that the presence or absence of specific mention of an actor's judgment had no substantive significance. Second, the statutes authorizing the appointments of officers followed a standard form into which the particular authorizations were plugged. All of these statutes dealt in one manner or another with revenue. Each statute opened with a statement of purpose in one of two similar forms: that all monies "may be duly and certainly raised and brought into the said Receipt of Exchequer for the Purposes aforesaid"[22] or that all monies "may be duly and certainly raised, and the same … may be justly and duly brought into the said Receipt of Exchequer, according to the true Meaning hereof."[23] Each of the statutes using the first formulation of purpose added that the appointed officers "shall perform their several Duties therein, as to them respectively shall appertain, under such and the like Penalties, Forfeitures, and Disabilities, for any Offence or

[18] 8 Ann. c. 12, § XXIV (1709); 6 Geo. 1 c. 11, § XXIII (1719); 10 Geo. 1 c. 10, § XLV (1723).

[19] 8 Ann. c. 10, § XII (1709).

[20] 9 Ann. c. 12, § XLVIII (1710); 9 Ann. c. 13, § XXIX (1710); 9 Ann. c. 16, § XLVIII (1710); 10 Ann. c. 18, § CXXIV (1711); 10 Ann. c. 19, § LXXVII (1711); 13 Ann. c. 18, § XXIX (1713).

[21] 9 Ann. c. 6, § XX (1710).

[22] 8 Ann. c. 12, § XXIV (1709); 8 Ann. c. 10, § XII (1709); 9 Ann. c. 6, § XX (1710); 6 Geo. 1 c. 11, § XXIII (1719).

[23] 9 Ann. c. 12, § XLVIII (1710); 9 Ann. c. 16, § XLVIII (1710); 10 Ann. c. 19, § LXXVII (1711); 10 Ann. c. 18, § CXXIV (1711); 13 Ann. c. 18, § XXIX (1713); 10 Geo. 1 c. 10, § XLV (1723).

Neglect therein, or for detaining, diverting or misapplying any Part" of the monies collected under the acts. Each statute employing the second formulation of purpose contained this same proviso, but with the phrase "in relation to the Premisses" substituted for the word "therein." The key point for the moment is that early eighteenth-century legislative drafters adopted certain standard forms for certain kinds of acts, so that subsequent enactments of similar character could be fitted into the appropriate form rather than have to be written from scratch. But there is nothing to suggest that the different forms conveyed any material difference in the scope of granted discretion or that there was anything notably significant about the precise language of the forms.

Other statutes confirm that the phraseology chosen to indicate discretion did not appear to convey any definite meaning. The master of any cod fishing vessel headed for the North Seas was allowed to take on board "such Quantities of *British* Salt, as he shall judge proper and necessary for his said Voyage. ..."[24] The governors of a corporation were authorized "to consider, consult, advise, agree upon, draw up, prepare and propose in Writing to her said Majesty, her Heirs and Successors, such proper and necessary Rules, Methods, Directions, Orders and Constitutions, as the said Governors, or any seven or more of them, with such *Quorum* as is therein directed, should in their Discretions judge most convenient to be observed. ..."[25] A statute authorizing a Scottish court to suspend application of a law limiting the importation of food into Scotland called for the court to examine grain prices and market conditions by holding hearings, taking testimony from knowledgeable landowners, "and by such other Ways and Means as to them shall be proper and necessary."[26] A statute governing naval prizes noted that "nothing in this Act shall be construed to restrain his Majesty, his Heirs and Successors, from giving such further Rules and Directions to his respective Courts of Admiralty ... as by his Majesty ... should be thought necessary or proper."[27] The prize statute uses the phrase "necessary or proper" rather than the more common phrase "proper and necessary." If the different formulations are

24 13 Ann. c. 13 (1713).

25 1 Geo. 1 St. 2 c. 10, § III (1714).

26 14 Geo. 2 c.7 (1740). To the same effect three decades later, see 13 Geo. 3 c. 43, § XIV (1772).

27 17 Geo. 2 c. 34, § XXIV (1743). Identical or near-identical statutes confirming royal power over admiralty courts were enacted throughout the eighteenth century. *See* 29 Geo. 2 c. 34, § XXXII (1756); 16 Geo. 3 c. 5, § XXXIV (1776); 19 Geo. 3 c. 67, § XIX (1779); 33 Geo. 3 c. 66, § XXXV (1793).

meant to convey different degrees or kinds of discretion, that meaning is not obvious.

The cavalier use of discretion-defining language in early-eighteenth-century statutes is best illustrated by the Edinburgh Beer Duties Act of 1722. The statute appropriated funds for a list of city purposes, ranging from the salary for the professor of the Civil Law to the "causeying or laying with Free Stones (in such Places where it may be found proper and necessary) the High Streets, Areas, Courts or Squares, Lanes and By-Streets that are or shall be within the said City. ..."[28] One specified purpose was "making a Communication, Street or Way to the Fields and Grounds belonging to the said City, on the North-side thereof," and another was to construct official buildings. To those ends, it would likely have been necessary to acquire private property, and the statute accordingly authorized the use of appropriated monies

> for purchasing such Houses and Grounds, as shall be by the said Magistrates and Council with the Approbation of the Overseers *judged proper and necessary* to be bought and purchased for making the said Street or Communication Way ..., and likewise for purchasing such Houses and Grounds, *as may be thought proper and necessary* as aforesaid, for making a *convenient* Area for building the said new Church, and for building a *proper* Hall or other Conveniencies, for accommodating the Court of Justiciary, and what Conveniencies may be *found necessary* for accommodating the other Courts of Justice, that meet in the said City. ...[29]

There is no obvious pattern to the use of language, the functions to which the language is attached, or the extent to which exercises of discretion are tied to objective conditions. The statute simply identifies a number of administrative functions, confers discretion on relevant actors, and does not appear to be overly concerned with the precise form in which that discretion is conferred. The written statutes of the era, in other words, do not seem to be constructed to control discretion in distinct, calibrated fashions.

II. PARLIAMENTARY DRAFTING, 1744–1769

The British statutes in the next quarter-century displayed the same variations in language, with the same evident absence of specifically intended

28 9 Geo. 1 c. 14, § III (1722).

29 *Id.* (emphasis added). The statute also refers to "convenient" records offices.

meaning, as was seen in the first four decades of the eighteenth century. For example, a 1756 statute, continuing and expanding a series of prior acts, empowered a commission to provide grants for proposals for discovering longitude.[30] The prior acts, in order to encourage development of "a proper Method for finding the said Longitude," had authorized commissioners to allot such money as they "shall think necessary" for proposals that they "think it proper to make Experiment thereof"; and finding it "absolutely necessary" to chart the shores of England and Ireland, had further authorized the commissioners to fund surveys of the shores "as they should think necessary." Prior to 1756, all but a small percentage of the previously appropriated funds had been spent by the commissioners, leaving "no more ... towards making any further Experiments which they may think proper and necessary to be made." Accordingly, to enable the commissioners to fund further research "as they shall think proper for the Purposes aforesaid," additional money was appropriated to fund proposals that the commissioners shall "think it proper to make Experiment, thereof" in such amounts as they "shall think necessary." The statute employs the terms "necessary," "proper," "absolutely necessary," and "proper and necessary" with no indication that those terms are meant to have different meanings.

Statutes for building and widening bridges also used a variety of terms, often in the same sentence, to describe grants of discretion. The 1756 Westminster Bridge Act described (in one long sentence) the powers of the commissioners with respect to opening new streets "as they shall find proper to be opened," purchasing "such Houses and Grounds as they shall find necessary for them to be possessed of," acquiring and removing "such Buildings, Houses, Grounds and Estates ... as they should think proper and necessary," and purchasing from owners buildings and grounds "as they shall think necessary to be removed."[31] Three different phrases – "shall find necessary," "should think proper and necessary," and "shall think necessary" – are used to describe power to purchase buildings and grounds.[32] The same year, another statute authorized the mayor and Common Council of London to improve and widen

30 Every naval power at that time, and before, was engaged in similar efforts to establish more accurate means of determining locations at sea. *See* http://query.nytimes.com/mem/archive-free/pdf?_r=1&res=9B0oEFD91330E633A25755C1A9649D94699FD7CF (visited May 4, 2009).

31 29 Geo. 2 c. 38 (1756).

32 The same terms appear in a 1757 statute authorizing the commissioners to widen a street "in such Manner as they shall think proper." 30 Geo. 2 c. 34 (1757).

London Bridge. The statute noted that it was "absolutely necessary" to widen the bridge, and it empowered the city officials to acquire buildings that they "shall judge necessary to be taken down and removed" and then separately empowered them to take down those buildings that they "shall deem necessary and proper to be taken down. ..."[33] It seems highly implausible that there was meant to be a material difference between the power to acquire buildings to be taken down and the power to take them down once acquired.

Another series of statutes during this period dealt with the power of commissions authorized to implement drainage projects. One statute from 1757 authorized such drainage works as the commissioners "thought fit, necessary and convenient" and (in the very next phrase) provided for taking and using earth "as shall be necessary" for making or strengthening river banks "as the said Commissioners ... shall think necessary and proper."[34] The pairing of the phrase "as shall be necessary" with the phrase "as the said Commissioners ... shall think necessary and proper" in connection with precisely the same function of the commission[35] is as direct evidence as one will find that statutory drafting in that era did not clearly distinguish either the word "necessary" from the term "necessary and proper" or grants of power that expressly made the judgment of the actor the measure of compliance from those written in seemingly objective terms. Furthermore, one year later, another statute provided for payments by landowners for drainage projects, stating that the sums collected "shall be applied towards defraying the Expence of erecting, making and maintaining such Works, as the said Commissioners, or any five or more of them shall judge necessary or proper, for the draining and improving the Lands and Grounds. ..."[36] The use of "necessary and proper" as opposed to "necessary or proper" does not appear to have any substantive significance. Finally, another drainage act from 1762 provides for commissioners to impose taxes

33 29 Geo. 2 C A P. XL. (1756).

34 31 Geo. 2 c. 18 § VII (1757).

35 So that there is no question about the context of these terms, the full clause grants the commissioners power "to take and use such Earth and Ground, near or adjoining to the said Banks, as shall be necessary for the making, raising, strengthening and maintaining thereof, as the said Commissioners, or the major Part of them assembled at such Meeting or Meetings, as aforesaid, shall think necessary and proper." *Id.* Exactly the same language was employed again in the same context ten years later. *See* 7 Geo. 3 c. 53 § VI (1767).

36 32 Geo. 2 c. 13 § IX (1758).

> as shall by them *be judged necessary* for the making, erecting and preserving any private Works, Banks, Drains or Engines ... in such manner as to them shall *appear necessary and proper* for the Purposes of private Drainage; which said Works, Banks, Drains and Engines the said Commissioners are hereby empowered to raise and erect in such Places, and in such Manner, as to them, or any five or more of them, shall *seem most proper and convenient* for the said Purposes....[37]

Another section of the same statute provided for a gowt (a sluice in the embankments) "of such Headway as the said Commissioners shall think proper," and if that project did not produce sufficient drainage, it authorized "such further Works as they shall think necessary and proper."[38] It does not appear as though the terms "proper" and "necessary and proper" are performing different functions.

A miscellany of other statutes reinforced the pattern of patternlessness. The governors of Magdalen Hospital were empowered – all in the same clause of the statute – to enter into such contracts as they "shall think proper," to transact any matters that "to them ... appear to be necessary or proper," and to delegate powers to a committee "as they shall think necessary."[39] Another corporate board was empowered "to meet as often as they shall think necessary or proper," to nominate and appoint officers "as shall be any ways necessary," to change the number of officers or employees as they "shall from time to time think proper," and to direct the affairs of the corporation "as they shall think proper."[40] Trustees were authorized to make "all such Orders, Rules, and Regulations, as to them shall seem necessary and proper."[41] All "proper and necessary Materials" were to be provided for fortifications at Milford.[42] Duties could be combined into a single stamp "as shall by the said Commissioners be thought proper or necessary."[43] Watchmen could be appointed in such number as commissioners "shall judge necessary and proper."[44] Colonial duties could be applied to the

37 2 Geo. 3 c. 32 § XVIII (1762) (emphasis added).

38 *Id.* § XL.

39 9 Geo. 3 c. 31 § III (1769).

40 4 Geo. 3 c. 37, § VI (1763).

41 9 Geo. 3 c.21, § VII (1769).

42 32 Geo. 2 c. 26, § III (1758).

43 2 Geo. 3 c. 36, § III (1762). To the same effect, see 5 Geo. 3 c. 47, § III (1765).

44 6 Geo. 3 c. 24, § XXI (1766). To the same effect, see 9 Geo. 3 c. 32, § XIV (1769). Six years later, another statute granted power to appoint watchmen in such numbers as the commissioners "shall judge necessary or proper." 12 Geo. 3. c. 68, § LXXVI (1772).

expenses of colonial governance as the king "shall think proper or necessary."[45] Glasgow city officials were authorized to build a bridge and "to erect, build, and make, all necessary and proper Abutments, Ramparts, Wings, Walls, Banks, Ways, and other Works, for the Use, Support, Preservation, of the said intended Bridge; and to make all proper Streets, Passages, and Communications thereto, as they shall judge necessary. ..."[46]

One of the most compelling indicators of language usage during this period, and indeed throughout the century,[47] is a large group of statutes providing for the calling of witnesses. A 1751 statute provided for eminent domain to acquire land for a royal hospital. In the event of dispute over transfer of the property or the amount of compensation paid to landowners, a jury would be summoned and the corporate commissioners or governors could "call before them all and every Person and Persons whatsoever, who shall be thought proper and necessary to be examined as a Witness or Witnesses before them. ..."[48] Throughout the eighteenth century, this became a standard provision in statutes delegating power to commissioners, governors, trustees, guardians, and other persons. The authorization to call witnesses often included all persons "who shall be thought proper and necessary," as in the 1751 act.[49] But sometimes the language referred to persons thought "proper or necessary,"[50] "necessary or proper,"[51] or "necessary and proper."[52] If there is a pattern or significance to these differing formulations, it is not evident. The statutes also generally authorized the relevant

45 7 Geo. 3 c. 46, § V (1766).

46 8 Geo. 3 c. 16, § XVIII (1768).

47 For convenience, we include in the next ten footnotes statutes extending beyond 1769 that use the identical or near-identical language from the earlier statutes.

48 25 Geo. 2 c. 42 (1751).

49 *See*, e.g., 31 Geo. 2 c. 25, § VI (1757); 7 Geo. 3 c. 37, § XII (1766); *cf.* 14 Geo. 3 c. 45, § XXIII (1774) (authorizing courts to order jury viewing of evidence "where it shall appear to the Court ... that it will be proper and necessary").

50 *See*, e.g., 33 Geo. 2 c. 30, § III (1759); 7 Geo. 3 c. 51, § VII (1767); 8 Geo. 3 c. 33, § LX (1768); 11 Geo. 3 c. 21, § LXVII (1771); 11 Geo. 3 c. 44, § XXIV (1771); 14 Geo. 3 c. 91, § V (1774); 15 Geo. 3 c. 33, § VI (1775); 17 Geo. 3 c. 18, § II (1776); 19 Geo. 3 c. 33, §§ IX, XIX (1779).

51 *See*, e.g., 4 Geo. 3 c. 39 (1763); 5 Geo. 3 c.50, § XIV (1765); 10 Geo. 3 c. 23, § XXXIII (1770); 10 Geo. 3 c. 25, § LIX (1770); 10 Geo. 3 c. 28, § II (1770); 11 Geo. 3 c. 33, § XXVIII (1771); 11 Geo. 3 c. 54, § XLV (1771); 11 Geo. 3 c. 46, § LXII (1771); 12 Geo. 3 c. 68, § LXXXII (1772); 12 Geo. 3 c. 69, § XXIII (1772); 18 Geo. 3 c. 17, § VI (1778).

52 *See*, e.g., 9 Geo. 3 c. 32, § XLVII (1769); 11 Geo. 3 c. 19, § XXX (1771).

tribunals or officials to provide for jury views "if they think fit"[53] or "as they the said Commissioners ... shall think fit"[54] or if the commissioners "shall think it necessary" in such a manner as they "shall think fit"[55] or "in case they think the same proper"[56] or occasionally with no qualifications at all.[57]

III. PARLIAMENTARY DRAFTING, 1770–1787

During this period, which perhaps has the most potential relevance for understanding the drafting background of the American Constitution, the number of English statutes vesting discretion in commissioners or other agents grew enormously; we found more such statutes in this period of less than two decades than in the rest of the eighteenth century put together. The discretion-granting language in these statutes does not appear to have been chosen with any more care than in the preceding part of the eighteenth century.

We have already noted the large number of statutes providing for the calling of witnesses that employed differing formulations to describe the circumstances under which witnesses should be called.[58] Several statutes enacted between 1772 and 1774 are even more intriguing. The statutes authorizing the summoning of jurors and the calling of witnesses generally provided as well for holding those persons in attendance until matters were completed. The formulation in the Greenwich Hospital Act of 1751 simply noted that the commissioners "shall have power ... to command such Jury, Witnesses and Parties, to attend until all such Affairs for which they were summoned shall be concluded,"[59] with no

53 25 Geo. 2 c. 42 (1751); 33 Geo. 2 c. 30, § III (1759); 7 Geo. 3 c. 37 § 12 (1766); 8 Geo. 3 c. 33, § LX (1768); 14 Geo. 3 c. 91, § V (1774); 15 Geo. 3 c. 33, § VI (1775); 17 Geo. 3 c. 18, § II (1776).

54 26 Geo. 2 c. 36, § XI (1753); 4 Geo. 3 c. 39, § XIX (1763); 9 Geo. 3 c. 32, § XLVII (1769); 11 Geo. 3 c. 19, § XXX (1771); 11 Geo. 3 c. 21, § LXVII (1771); 19 Geo. 3 c. 33, § IX (1779).

55 5 Geo. 3 c. 50, § XIV (1765); 10 Geo. 3 c. 23, § XXXIII (1770); 11 Geo. 3 c. 33, § XXVIII (1771); 11 Geo. 3 c. 54, § XLV (1771); 12 Geo. 3 c. 69, § XXIII (1772).

56 7 Geo. 3 c. 51, § VII (1767).

57 *See*, e.g., 10 Geo. 3 c. 28, § II (1770) ("such Justices shall, by ordering a View, or otherwise, use all lawful Ways and Means, as well for their own as for the said Jury's Information"); 11 Geo. 3 c. 44, § XXIV (1771) (commissioners "may order and authorise the said Jury ... to view the Place or Places, or Matters in question").

58 *See supra* notes 49–53 and accompanying text.

59 25 Geo. 2 c.42 (1751).

adjectival qualification on that power – a formulation that continued to be employed at times throughout the century.[60] A few statutes, however, employed the "proper or necessary" formulation for the calling of witnesses, but then added in the next clause that courts could hold juries and witnesses in attendance "as shall be necessary or proper."[61] In none of these cases does it appear that the differing language serves any purpose or makes any difference, or indeed that the presence or absence of adjectival language serves any purpose or makes any difference.

Wide variations in language often appeared in the same statute addressing similar or identical subjects and seemingly granting similar or identical powers. In 1770, commissioners of Southampton were authorized to sell soil or rubbish "as they shall think proper or necessary" and to buy or rent land for disposing of soil or rubbish "in case they shall think proper so to do"[62]; and were further empowered to construct sewers and other public works and in so doing to enter any lands "which shall be deemed necessary for that Purpose" and to repair those projects "whenever it shall be requisite," and to cut through walls or into old projects "if the same shall be found necessary and proper."[63] Another statute enacted the next year gave the same powers to commissioners in Winchester, except that they were authorized to repair works projects "whenever it shall be necessary"[64] rather than "whenever it shall be requisite"; the power-granting language was otherwise identical.

A series of improvement acts from 1771 is also instructive. The South Leith Improvement Act gave commissioners general power to make rules and perform acts that to them "shall seem proper and necessary for putting this Act in Execution"[65] and also gave them power to lay pipe wherever it shall to them "appear necessary and proper."[66] The Wakefield Improvement Act granted power to acquire property that the commissioners "shall judge necessary or proper to be pulled down, removed, cut, digged, altered, or used, for the Purposes of this Act"[67] and permitted the commissioners to authorize town inhabitants to make enclosures

60 *See*, e.g., 14 Geo. 3 c. 91, § V (1774); 15 Geo. 3 c. 33, § VI (1775); 17 Geo. 3 c. 18, § II (1776).

61 12 Geo. 3 c. 73, § XIV (1772); 14 Geo. 3 c. 78, § XXXIII (1774).

62 10 Geo. 3 c. 25, § X (1770).

63 *Id.* § XXXIV.

64 11 Geo. 3 c. 9, § XLI (1771).

65 11 Geo. 3 c. 30, § VII (1771).

66 *Id.* § IX.

67 11 Geo. 3 c. 44, § XXIII (1771).

"as may be proper and necessary."[68] The Winchester Improvement Act authorized the disposition of soil as the commissioners "shall think proper and necessary."[69]

Three preambles from harbor acts from 1772 provide an equally intriguing combination of language. The Port Glasgow Harbour Act authorized commissioners to provide "highly necessary" piers and quays of "proper" dimension, as well as "proper and necessary" and "other necessary" works as the commissioners "shall judge to be necessary and expedient."[70] The Aye Harbour Act allowed improvements "and other necessary Works ... as shall be proper and necessary" for safe shipping to the extent that the local officials "shall judge to be necessary."[71] The Aberdeen Harbour Act dealt with "necessary Works," improvements "as shall be found necessary," maintenance of navigation aids "as shall be judged necessary," and other works "as shall be deemed ... proper and necessary for the Improvement of the said Harbour."[72]

Four canal acts passed between 1774 and 1776 are even more dramatic in their cavalier use of qualifying terms. The Calder Canal Act authorized Sir John Ramsden to construct a canal, with the following powers: "to make all necessary Cuts, Trenches, Passages, and Works" to supply the canal with water; "to make, maintain, and repair all such Trenches, Passages, Gutters, and Watercourses, as shall be necessary and proper" for conveying water to the canal; "to make such Back Drains, Gutters, or Trenches, as shall be necessary or proper" to prevent damage to the lands near the canal; to enclose land near the canal "as shall be necessary or proper" for docks and other buildings; to set up fences or other dividers "as he or they shall think necessary and proper"; to obtain soil, stones, or other materials "proper, requisite, or convenient, [f]or making, carrying on, continuing, or repairing the said Canal, and all other Matters and Works proper and necessary" for maintaining navigation; and to do all other matters "necessary or proper for the making, carrying on, completing, maintaining, and using, the said Navigation, as he the said Sir John Ramsden, his Heirs or Assigns, shall, from Time to Time, think fit."[73] Moreover, a later section of the statute provides that, in case of damage from flood or other accidents, Sir John could

68 *Id.* § XLVIII.
69 11 Geo. 3 c. 9, § VIII (1771).
70 12 Geo. 3, c. 16 (1772).
71 12 Geo. 3. c. 22 (1772).
72 13 Geo. 3 c. 29 (1772).
73 14 Geo. 3 c. 13 (1774).

enter adjoining lands and remove soil, stones, or other materials "as may be necessary or proper" for repairs.[74] The statute's preamble already authorized the removal of materials "proper, requisite, or convenient" for repairing the canal; the later section repeats the same authority with the language "necessary or proper."

The Stafford Canal Act authorized the cutting and repairing of such watercourses "as shall be necessary and proper" to convey water to the canal and then immediately thereafter authorized the making of trenches or drains "as shall be necessary or proper" to prevent damage to adjoining lands.[75] The statute then adds, in two separate clauses, the power to construct bridges, tunnels, locks, roads, and a long list of other ancillary projects that the builders "shall think requisite and convenient for the Purposes of the said Navigation" and the general power "to construct, erect, make, and do all other Matters and Things which they shall think necessary and convenient for the making, effecting, extending, preserving, improving, completing, and using the said Navigation."[76] It seems unlikely that the power to construct mechanisms for conveying water to the canal was meant to be narrower than the power to construct mechanisms for protecting neighboring lands, or that either power was meant to be narrower than the general power to provide ancillary works to the canal or to do anything else to promote the canal's effectiveness.

The Stourbridge Canal Act granted commissioners powers to establish reservoirs and aqueducts to feed the canal "as to them shall seem necessary or proper"; to identify lands "as they shall think necessary and proper for making the said Canal and collateral Cuts, and all other such Matters and Conveniences as they shall think proper and necessary" for navigation; to dig and take any soil or stone "which may be proper, requisite, or convenient" for constructing or repairing the canal; to put in "Bridges, Tunnels, Aqueducts, Sluices, Locks, Weirs, Pens for Water, Stanks, Reservoirs, Drains, Wharfs, Quays, Landing-places, Weigh-beams, Cranes, Fire-engines, or other Machines, and other Works, Ways, Roads, and Conveniencies" as the authorities "shall think requisite and convenient" for navigation; to construct "Roads, Towing-paths, Banks, and Ways" as the authorities "shall think convenient"; and to do "all other Matters and Things which they shall

74 *Id.* § XXX.
75 15 Geo. 3 c. 16 (1775).
76 *Id.*

think necessary and convenient."[77] The Trent and Mersey Canal Act contained identical power grants with respect to bridges, tunnels, and other ancillary works ("shall think requisite and convenient"), towing-paths and roads (as the authorities "shall think convenient"), and the catch-all power to do all other "Matters and Things" ("which they shall think necessary and convenient"), but employed slightly different power grants in other contexts. The statute authorized such watercourses to feed the canal "as shall be necessary and proper," while the equivalent provision in the Stourbridge Act used the phrase "as to them shall seem necessary or proper", and it provided for taking soil and stone "proper, requisite, and convenient," while the Stourbridge Act provision used the slightly different formulation "which may be proper, requisite, or convenient." Both statutes move from phrase to phrase, and from references to the judgment of the officials to purely objective descriptions of the granted power, without evident rhyme or reason.

The era's drainage acts were of a piece with the other statutes from this period. The Market Weighton Act created a commission with power "for executing and completing all and singular the Works, Matters, and Things which shall be necessary or proper for the carrying [of] those Purposes into full and perfect Execution."[78] The contemporaneous Bedford Level Drainage Act empowered a commission to implement the statute "as the said Commissioners ... shall think necessary or proper."[79] It is difficult to envision how the phrases "necessary or proper" and "shall think necessary or proper" are meant to be different empowerments. The Cambridge Drainage Act authorized the commissioners to strengthen certain banks "as they ... shall think proper" and to maintain other banks "as the said Commissioners ... shall think necessary or proper."[80] It is implausible to suppose that the commissioners' powers varied from bank to bank. The 1775 Fen Drainage Act authorized the commissioners to "heighten, strengthen, widen, make, maintain, and support, or cause to be heightened, widened, strengthened, made, maintained, and supported" banks "as they ... shall think proper" and also to "cleanse, widen, make, cut, build, erect, purchase, and support, alter, or remove, all such Banks, Bridges, Headings, Cuts, Drains, Dams, Outlets, Mills, Engines, and other Matters and Things already

77 16 Geo. 3 c. 28 (1776).

78 12 Geo. 3 c. 37 (1772).

79 13 Geo. 3 c. 45, § XIX (1772).

80 12 Geo. 3 c. 26, § XLIV (1772).

made, built, or erected, or hereafter to be made, built, or erected, by virtue of this Act ... as the said Commissioners respectively ... shall think necessary or proper."[81] The commissioners of the fourth district were "authorised and impowered to erect and make, or cause to be erected and made, two or more Mills, and such Drains as they shall agree upon and judge necessary or proper for ... effectual draining,"[82] while the commissioners of the second district were "authorised and impowered to erect and make, alter or remove, or cause to be erected, made, altered, or removed ... a Mill or Mills ... as they shall agree upon and judge proper for sufficiently draining and preserving the said second District" and to make drains or banks "as they shall think proper or necessary for effectually draining and preserving the same."[83] The Isle of Ely Drainage Act empowered the commissioners to set up any drainage works or remove any earth "as they shall think necessary and convenient" and to repair or improve existing drainage works "as they shall think proper and necessary."[84] The statute further ordered abutting landowners to maintain dikes "as the said Commissioners ... shall judge proper and necessary," and if the landowners fail in this duty, the commissioners were authorized "to cause the same to be done in a proper and effectual manner."[85] The Lancaster Drainage Act authorized the commissioners to meet "as often as they shall think proper" and to adopt such rules "as they shall deem necessary" for executing the act[86] and to remove obstructions to channels "as they ... shall from Time to Time think proper or necessary."[87]

A large number of statutes from this period dealt with the power to appoint and supervise officers or employees, and the language chosen to express that power seems entirely random. The trustees of the Watford Churchyard and Workhouse could appoint "One or more fit and skilful Persons (if they shall think proper so to do) ... that may be necessary and proper to execute" the act and may discharge such officers "when they shall think proper so to do."[88] The Tyne Bridge Act authorized the appointment of "One or more fit and skilful Person

[81] 15 Geo. 3 c.65, § XLI (1775).
[82] *Id.* § LXIII.
[83] *Id.* § LV.
[84] 15 Geo. 3 c. 66, § VII (1775).
[85] *Id.* § XXIX.
[86] 19 Geo. 3 c. 33, § XIV (1779).
[87] *Id.* § XXXVII.
[88] 12 Geo. 3 c. 28, § V (1772).

or Persons (if he or they shall think proper so to do) as may be necessary and proper."[89] London authorities could appoint "what Number of Watchmen they shall judge necessary or proper" and erect watch stands "as they shall think proper."[90] The statute further empowered the authorities to prescribe the clothing, arms, duties, and wages of the watchmen, without any adjectival limitation ("shall likewise direct and appoint").[91] Hampstead commissioners were authorized to appoint watchmen in such numbers as the commissioners "shall from Time to Time direct and appoint" and to promulgate rules for the watchmen as they "shall think proper."[92] Another statute preserved the right of the king to appoint judges in Quebec as he "shall think necessary and proper for the Circumstance of the said Province."[93] Governors of penitentiary houses were authorized to employ such assistants as they "shall think proper and necessary."[94] Nothing suggests that the differing formulations had any significance.

Many statutes also dealt with building or construction of some sort, again with no evident pattern to the authorizations. Commissioners could erect lamps "as they shall judge necessary and proper."[95] Trustees were authorized to receive proposals and make contracts for any materials or matters "necessary and proper" for repairing or improving a bridge.[96] Other authorities were empowered to construct a bridge using whatever means they "shall think necessary and proper" and to perform other acts "requisite and necessary, useful or convenient" for erecting the bridge.[97] The Earl of Thanet was authorized to make reservoirs "as shall be found necessary" for a canal and (in the same phrase) "as shall be proper and necessary" for conveying water to and from the canal, and also to do anything else which he "shall think convenient and necessary" for the project.[98] Trustees were authorized to build and equip a church as "shall be deemed proper or necessary,"[99] and to contract for any materials "necessary or proper for effectually performing

89 12 Geo. 3 c. 62, § VII (1772).
90 12 Geo. 3 c. 17, § XXXIV (1772).
91 *Id.*
92 15 Geo. 3 c. 58, § X (1775).
93 14 Geo. 3 c. 83, § XVII (1774).
94 19 Geo. 3 c. 74, § XX (1779).
95 15 Geo. 3 c. 58, § X (1775).
96 12 Geo. 3 c. 62, § XII (1772).
97 12 Geo. 3. c. 41 (1772).
98 13 Geo. 3 c. 47 (1772).
99 14 Geo. 3 c. 12, § II (1774).

the Purposes of this Act."[100] A bridge could be constructed using any materials "proper and necessary."[101] Another bridge could be built by cutting river banks "as shall be necessary and proper" and by doing all other acts "necessary and convenient."[102] Commissioners could pay all sums "which shall be proper and necessary" for maintaining bridges and mooring posts.[103] Trustees could erect poorhouses "as they shall think proper and necessary."[104] Commissioners were authorized to construct an outfall drain "in such Manner as the said Commissioners ... shall think necessary and proper"[105] and could obtain or remove any materials "proper, requisite, and convenient" for making a drain, and could perform all other works or acts "as the said Commissioners ... shall from Time to Time think proper and necessary for carrying the Purposes of this Act into Execution."[106]

The last-mentioned authorization to carry an act into execution appeared in some form in many statutes (and would seem to be among the stronger candidates for an antecedent to the Necessary and Proper Clause). Churchyard trustees were empowered "to make Contracts for, or purchase or provide any other Materials, Matters, or Things, necessary and proper for the effectually carrying into execution the Purposes of this Act."[107] Trustees of a lighthouse could pay all charges "that shall be proper and necessary for executing the Trusts of this Act."[108] A committee of wool manufacturers could "do all other Matters and Things which may be deemed necessary and proper for carrying this Act into Execution, in such Manner as the said Committee ... shall judge and think best. ..."[109] Sewer commissioners were empowered to "do and perform all such other Works, Matters, and Things, as the said Commissioners of Sewer ... shall from Time to Time think proper

[100] *Id.* § XIV.

[101] 16 Geo. 3 c. 17, § XXIV (1776). To the same effect, see 17 Geo. 3 c. 12, § XXX (1776).

[102] 16 Geo. 3. c. 17 (1776). To the same effect, see 17 Geo. 3 c. 12 (1776); 18 Geo. 3 c. 44, § III (1778); 20 Geo. 3 c. 27 (1780).

[103] 16 Geo. 3 c. 23, § XXXIV (1776).

[104] 17 Geo. 3 c. 5, § XV (1776).

[105] 23 Geo. 3 c. 13 (1783).

[106] *Id.* § III.

[107] 12 Geo. 3 c. 28, § X (1772).

[108] 16 Geo. 3 c. 61, § XXV (1776). To the same effect, with marginal differences in language, see 26 Geo. 3 c. 101, § XV (1786).

[109] 17 Geo. 3 c. 11 (1776). To the same effect, see 25 Geo. 3 c. 40 (1785); 31 Geo. 3 c. 56 (1791).

and necessary for carrying the Purposes of this Act into Execution."[110] Corporate governors had power "to do, manage, transact, and determine, all such Matters and Things as shall to them ... appear to be necessary or proper."[111] The formulations sometimes do and sometimes do not specifically mention the judgment of the empowered actors, and the formulations of the granted authority are not consistent. There is nothing to indicate that the different formulations reflected different grants of power.

Parliament during this period also enacted a miscellany of statutes employing a miscellany of formulated grants of discretion. Persons involved with licensed madhouses could be summoned and examined "as often as shall be thought necessary and proper."[112] Poor rates were to be set as relevant officials "shall think necessary and proper"[113] or "shall think proper and necessary."[114] Trustees did not have to light or watch certain places "unless the said Trustees ... think it necessary and proper."[115] Buoys could be laid as trustees "shall find necessary and proper."[116] A sheriff was authorized to move prisoners to a new facility "as he shall think necessary or proper."[117] Hospital governors could, "when and so often as they shall think proper and expedient," grant mineral leases "as they shall deem necessary and proper."[118] Discharged prisoners were to be given clothing "as shall be judged necessary and proper."[119] The Court of King's Bench could authorize the publication of depositions "when the same shall appear to them to be proper and necessary."[120] The East India Company directors could sell capital stock "as they shall from Time to Time think fit, and find it necessary and proper to sell."[121]

If American drafters of this era looked to British statutes for guidance, they would find very little.

[110] 23 Geo. 3 c. 13, § III (1783).
[111] 15 Geo. 3 c. 24, § II (1775).
[112] 14 Geo. 3 c. 49, § XXIX (1774).
[113] 15 Geo. 3 c. 23, § IX (1775).
[114] 23 Geo. 3 c. 44, § III F(1783).
[115] 16 Geo. 3 c. 26, § VI (1776).
[116] 16 Geo. 3 c. 61, § XXIX (1776).
[117] 18 Geo. 3 c. 17, § III (1778).
[118] 18 Geo. 3 c. 29, § V (1778).
[119] 20 Geo. 3. c. 27, § XXXVII (1779).
[120] 24 Geo. 3 c. 25, § LXXXI (1784).
[121] 26 Geo. 3 c. 62, § V (1786). To the same effect, see 33 Geo. 3 c. 47, § XI (1793); 37 Geo. 3 c. 31, § IV (1797).

IV. PARLIAMENTARY DRAFTING, 1788–1799

The last twelve years of the eighteenth century produced a modest number of statutes that tracked the usages of the first eighty-eight. The king was authorized to give orders to the governor of Newfoundland as he "shall deem proper and necessary" to fulfill a treaty.[122] Ministers receiving requisitions could "take such Steps as to them may seem proper or necessary" for executing them.[123] The chief justice of Newfoundland could establish court procedures "as shall seem necessary and proper for expediting Matters with the most Convenience and least Expence to the Parties concerned therein."[124] The chancellor could break the seal of patent specifications when "it may be judged by the said Lord High Chancellor necessary or proper to inspect the same."[125] Bankruptcy factors were authorized to perform acts "which may be deemed necessary or proper for the Recovery of the Estate and Effects situated in Foreign Parts. ..."[126] The surveyor general should include in reports on Crown lands any matters which "shall seem proper and necessary to be contained and set forth in such Reports."[127] Commissioners could put the militia into readiness "as it shall seem to them requisite and necessary" and could order inspections "so often as they shall think proper and necessary."[128] Commissioners could extend repayments of loans and accept substitute securities "as to them the said Commissioners shall seem proper and necessary" and could require new securities "whenever they shall think the same necessary."[129] The directors of the East India Company could draft noncommissioned officers for service abroad "as they shall think proper and necessary."[130]

If American constitutional drafters in the late eighteenth century used contemporaneous British statutes as a model, one would likely conclude that the differing formulations for grants of discretion in the U.S. Constitution had little or no substantive meaning. As it happens,

[122] 28 Geo. 3 c. 35 (1788).
[123] 32 Geo. 3 c. 34, §§ XVII, XIX, XXI (1792).
[124] 32 Geo. 3 c. 46, § XIV (1792). To the same effect, see 33 Geo. 3 c. 76, § XIV (1793).
[125] 32 Geo. 3 c. 73, § II (1792).
[126] 33 Geo. 3 c. 74, § XV (1793).
[127] 34 Geo. 3 c. 75, § XXI (1794).
[128] 34 Geo. 3 c. 81, § XLIV (1794); 35 Geo. 3 c. 27, § XVIII (1795).
[129] 39 & 40 Geo. 3 c. 13 (1799).
[130] 39 Geo. 3 c. 109, § VI (1799).

however, there is no reason to think that the British statutes actually served as guideposts or models across the Atlantic. Parliamentary drafters constructed discretionary grants as they did because of certain background assumptions and drafting techniques that were not representative of the American constitutional drafting process.

3

An Ocean Away

Eighteenth-Century Drafting in England and America

Gary Lawson and Guy I. Seidman

I

In 1795, after spending twelve years as a barrister, Charles Abbott (1757–1829) was elected to the House of Commons. He quickly became the leading figure urging the systematization and promulgation of the burgeoning mass of British statutes in the late eighteenth and early nineteenth centuries; indeed, one modern scholar calls him "the hero of statute promulgation."[1] In 1796, at Abbott's instigation, the House of Commons appointed a committee to study the many expiring and temporary statutes that had accumulated over the years.[2] The committee's report, building on material gathered by Abbott, roundly decried the volume of, lack of systematization concerning, and publication practices respecting these statutes. More pointedly for our purposes, the report described the drafting style that was characteristic of these laws as "for the most part verbose, tautologous, and obscure; all of which circumstances seem to have engaged the attention of Parliament at successive periods, but not to have produced any improvement, in the degree which their importance demands."[3]

[1] David Lemmings, *Introduction, in* THE BRITISH AND THEIR LAWS IN THE EIGHTEENTH CENTURY 1, 17 (David Lemmings, ed. 2005). Abbott eventually became, inter alia, Chief Secretary of Ireland and Speaker of the House of Commons.

[2] For a detailed examination of Abbott's key role in initiating and executing investigations and reforms of statutory practices, see SHEILA LAMBERT, BILLS AND ACTS: LEGISLATIVE PROCEDURE IN EIGHTEENTH-CENTURY ENGLAND 180–82 (1971); Simon Devereaux, *The Promulgation of the Statutes in Late Hanoverian Britain, in* THE BRITISH AND THEIR LAWS IN THE EIGHTEENTH CENTURY, *supra*, note 133, at 80, 89–95.

[3] *Report from the Committee upon Temporary Laws, Expired or Expiring, in* 14 REPORTS FROM THE COMMITTEES OF THE HOUSE OF COMMONS 34, 35–36 (1803).

The committee's study was limited to expired or expiring laws, but it seems quite clear that the drafting defects identified by the report were characteristic of a broad pattern in eighteenth-century English statutory design. Indeed, critics who were not commissioned by the House of Commons were even less charitable about England's legislative work product than was Abbott and the committee that he inspired. Contemporary observers of eighteenth-century parliamentary drafting practices decried "the poor formulation, careless drafting, glaring inaccuracies and disturbing inconsistencies to be found in the statute book."[4] Jeremy Bentham (who, as it happens, was Charles Abbott's half-brother) wrote in the 1770s:

> In no book that ever saw the light of day will the reader find examples of nonsense so unfathomable as what is frequently to be met with in our Statute book. Because there is no Style so repugnant to every purpose of language as that which distinguishes and disgraces the work of our Legislature.[5]

In a lengthy essay on statutory drafting published after his death, more than half a century later, Bentham added:

> The English lawyer, more especially in his character of parliamentary composer, would, if he were not the most crafty, be the most inept and unintelligent, as well as unintelligible of scribblers. Yet no bellman's verses, no metrical effusion of an advertising oil-shop, were ever so much below the level of genuine poetry, as when, taken for all in all, are the productions of an official statute-drawer below the level of the plainest common sense.[6]

In sum, said Bentham, "[i]t required the union of professional industry and ingenuity with supreme power, to create and preserve, in the country that claims in respect of psychological endowments of all sorts, intellectual and moral, the superiority over every other, a mode and habit of literary intercourse between governors and governed, so peculiarly and manifestly adverse to every honest purpose."[7]

Subsequent observers have concurred with these contemporary criticisms of eighteenth-century British statutory design. In 1938, William Holdsworth opined that "Bentham's criticism upon the draftsmanship

[4] David Lieberman, The Province of Legislation Determined: Legal Theory in Eighteenth-Century Britain 18 (1989).

[5] Jeremy Bentham, The Manuscripts of Jeremy Bentham in University College London, box 95, at 1 (quoted in Lieberman, *supra* note 135 at 18).

[6] Jeremy Bentham, *Nomography or the Art of Inditing Laws*, *in* The Works of Jeremy Bentham 231, 242 (John Bowring, ed. 1838).

[7] *Id.* at 241.

of the statutes was thoroughly well justified"[8] and that the crafting of eighteenth-century statutes "often left much to be desired."[9] The problems actually began a century earlier, when "the style of legal draftsmanship, which was used in the drawing of pleadings, conveyances, and other documents, was tending to become more verbose, [and] the statutes which these lawyers drew exhibited the same quality. ..."[10] Holdsworth noted that "all of these tendencies were aggravated in the eighteenth century."[11]

The subset of statutes that we surveyed in the previous chapter, containing "necessary," "proper," "proper and necessary," "necessary and proper," and related adjectives and combinations, turns out to have been particularly likely to have been poorly drafted. Accordingly, the randomness with which those statutes used adjectives and adjectival phrases is not surprising; given what we know about eighteenth-century British law, one would not expect much else.

Although the statutes in our survey in Chapter 2 cover a wide range of subjects, a very high percentage of those statutes deal with such matters as bridges, drainage, canals and other construction projects (often accompanied by provisions for viewing evidence in connection with just compensation determinations), roads, watchmen, corporations, and other matters of a – for want of a better phrase – local character. They generally involve matters of particular concern to a limited number of persons and localities. While even seemingly local laws can have national consequences, and their approval by Parliament could, therefore, be an integral part of a centralized legislative strategy,[12] it would not be surprising if less attention was paid to the crafting of these local laws than of laws of more visibly general character.

To be sure, there is no sharp line to be drawn among classes of eighteenth-century British statutes. The law distinguished between public and private acts for purposes of the form of royal assent[13] and the extent and form of publication by the royal printer,[14] but the public/private

8 11 WILLIAM HOLDSWORTH, A HISTORY OF ENGLISH LAW 376 (1938).

9 *Id.* at 373.

10 *Id.* at 370.

11 *Id.* at 370–71.

12 Joanna Innes, *The Local Acts of a National Parliament: Parliament's Role in Sanctioning Local Action in Eighteenth-Century Britain*, 17 PARLIAMENTARY HIST. 23, 25–26 (1998).

13 LAMBERT, *supra* note 2, at 172 ("Public acts received the [royal] assent in the form 'le roi le veult' and private in the form 'soit fait comme il est desiré'.").

14 The general principle was that public acts would be officially distributed while private acts would not, but that principle, and the grounds for distinguishing between public

line was elusive and often turned on nothing more than the presence or absence of an introductory clause declaring an act to be public.[15] A more substantive distinction between general laws with a "national provenance" and local laws that were "highly particular or personal in their concerns"[16] developed late in the eighteenth century; the legal significance of this distinction was essentially that local acts had to originate in petitions.[17] Because this distinction was not formalized until 1798, it is treacherous to try to read too much of the distinction back into the earlier eighteenth-century practice. "When we speak of 'local acts' therefore we speak nontechnically of a category of legislation whose boundaries historians may define as they see fit (though the category of 'local legislation' as subsequently employed suggests guidelines)."[18]

If, however, one takes as the general thrust of local legislation "such matters as the paving, lighting, or watching of streets, construction and regulation of market places, rebuilding of churches, improvement of roads, bridges and harbours, establishment of theatres, county halls and prisons, of small debt courts, workhouses and boards of poor law guardians,"[19] it is evident that most of the laws that we encountered in the previous chapter fall into this loose category. And the eighteenth-century drafting practices for local laws, so understood, were fraught with problems.

Unsurprisingly, local laws normally originated from the affected locality. As David Lemmings explains:

> In these cases legislation followed a request from the locality. Typically the promoters of a river navigation project, a turnpike, or some other 'Improvement' would organize a petition from the magistrates and leading inhabitants assembled at the assizes or quarter sessions setting out the advantage to be gained from the project and explaining why legislation was necessary to accomplish it. The petition would subsequently be presented in the House of Commons by a local member, who would move to bring in a bill and pilot it through the various stages of discussion and debate.[20]

and private acts, shifted considerably in the course of the eighteenth century. *See id.* at 172–77.

[15] *See* LIEBERMAN, *supra* note 4, at 22–23; Julian Hoppit, *Patterns of Parliamentary Legislation, 1660–1800*, THE HISTORICAL J. 109, 116 (1996); Innes, *supra* note 12, at 23. ("Acts were not assigned to these [public and private] categories in a consistent fashion.")

[16] Hoppit, *supra* note 15, at 116.

[17] *See* Innes, *supra* note 12, at 24.

[18] *Id.*

[19] *Id.*

[20] Lemmings, *supra* note 1, at 10.

These laws were thus initially drafted by local promoters, and for a variety of reasons, that practice was a recipe for incoherence and inconsistency.

First, where drafting responsibility is diffused in this fashion, one would expect "a large amount of individuality"[21] in the statutes unless there was some powerful force encouraging consistency among the acts. There was no such force: "the idea that some measure of symmetry in the arrangement and contents of the statutes should be attempted, seems to have occurred only occasionally to the Legislature."[22] Indeed, this lack of systematization was one of the major spurs to Charles Abbott's reform efforts in the late eighteenth and early nineteenth centuries. It was thus left up to individual drafters to borrow (or ignore) the language of prior acts as they saw fit. Thus, as our survey in Chapter 2 graphically illustrates, one sees in these laws "the same provisions ... repeated over and over again ..., with such variations in phraseology as seemed good to their individual draftsmen."[23] There is nothing in this process that suggests a consistent meaning to any particular usage.

Second, this individuating tendency was unlikely to be countered by serious efforts to secure uniformity within Parliament. The sheer mass of legislation proposed in and emanating from Parliament grew dramatically during and just before the eighteenth century. "In the 203 years between the accession of Henry VII in 1485 and the flight of James II in 1688 the Westminster parliament passed nearly 2,700 acts, excluding the constitutionally troubled years 1642 to 1660. In the 112 years from the Glorious revolution to union with Ireland over 13,600 acts were passed."[24] The growth in local legislation tracked, if it did not largely drive, this trend:

> In the 1690s, local acts passed at the rate of about five a session, a total which rose gradually to a level of about 15 a session by the 1730s and [17]40s, and then, in the 1750s, jumped to 30 or more, chiefly as a result of an upsurge in turnpike legislation. In the 1770s, numbers rose further, to some 50 to 70 a session, this rise reflecting an increase in numbers of acts across a broader range of fields. Numbers of acts passed decreased during the American war and subsequent political crisis, but recovered thereafter.[25]

21 HOLDSWORTH, *supra* note 8, at 372.
22 *Id.* at 373.
23 *Id.* at 372.
24 Hoppit, *supra* note 15, at 109.
25 Innes, *supra* note 12, at 26.

With an increase in workload volume of that magnitude, the likelihood that significant attention would be given to a local bill, whose impact would be at best indirect on most communities, was quite remote. Indeed, committee attendance at meetings to discuss these bills was typically very low, which "could prevent serious criticism from occurring at the committee stage."[26] There was thus not much reason to expect the review and enactment process in Parliament to secure uniformity of language across acts, much less across local acts.

Third, the general thrust of legal drafting in the eighteenth century, in all contexts, tended towards technicality and verbosity in legal instruments, "and for that reason the length and verbiage of legal documents tended to increase."[27] Indeed, the excerpts that we have provided in Chapter 2 from eighteenth-century statutes do not begin to communicate the verbal complexity, redundancy, and sheer length of these statutes. Moreover, if one assumes that the persons asked to draft local acts were likely to be lawyers, whose principal activity was conveyancing, there was a very potent economic reason to expect to see statutes in which language is heaped upon language in repetitious clauses: "[W]hen conveyancers were paid according to the length of their conveyances, and when conveyancers were employed to draft Acts, they naturally used the same style which they found it profitable to employ in the drafting of their conveyances."[28] This explanation at least makes it easier to understand why any thinking person would draft statutes to read as did the British local acts in the eighteenth century.

Accordingly, there are multiple reasons to expect eighteenth-century British statutes generally, and local acts specifically, to be inconsistent in their use of language and to employ multiple phrases and adjectives without giving serious thought to their relationship to the rest of the legal world. The drafting of statutes, especially those drafted at the local level and enacted with little debate or discussion, was not attentive to subtleties of language, and so it would make little sense to try to glean meaning from the different phraseologies employed across, or even within, these statutes. Sloppy statutes are simply a brute fact of eighteenth-century parliamentary practice.

What can we say about late eighteenth-century American drafting practice? It is obvious – so obvious that it requires little or no

[26] Lieberman, *supra* note 4, at 21.

[27] Holdsworth, *supra* note 8, at 373.

[28] *Id.*

elaboration – that the drafting of the American Constitution was very different from the drafting of British canal acts. It may, however, be helpful to trace, however briefly, the evolution of American constitutional drafting through the ratification of the Constitution of 1788 to see how the American and British experiences differed in the extent to which careful use of language was an accepted norm of legal drafting, especially of constitutions.

II

Once the states declared their independence from England, they had to govern themselves, which required choosing some method for establishing the governmental structures of the new nation-states. One possibility was simply to allow the preexisting colonial documents to remain in force and provide the machinery of government – as was done in Massachusetts until 1780. Another possibility, employed by Rhode Island and Connecticut, was formally to recognize and readopt the royal charters as governing documents for nationhood. Yet another possibility, however, was to construct a new State (and here the capitalization reflects the internationally sovereign status of each State) constitution that would provide governance mechanisms, perhaps including mechanisms unlike any from the colonial period. Such a constitution could be a brief document that incorporated large portions of preexisting British law, as with the New Hampshire Constitution of January 5, 1776, or it could be a lengthy construct setting out in considerable detail the blueprint for a new form of governance, as with the Massachusetts Constitution of 1780.

In any case, the construction of a constitution was a significant intellectual and political event. England famously had, and has, no single written document containing all of its basic governance mechanisms; the British constitution is an accumulation of documents, practices, and traditions developed over long periods.[29] A brand new nation-state could not rely on such a combination of documents, traditions, and practices, unless it was prepared simply to incorporate those of England (or conceivably some other country that had enough governmental history

[29] It is commonplace to describe the British constitution as "unwritten." That is somewhat misleading: "The English had developed the concept of a written constitution, but the writing was scattered over thousands of documents and no one was quite sure which documents should be included." DONALD S. LUTZ, COLONIAL ORIGINS OF THE AMERICAN CONSTITUTION: A DOCUMENTARY HISTORY 21–22 (1998).

to provide a foundation for a new order). By substituting centralized written texts for scattered or unwritten norms and practices, were the Americans committing themselves to striving for a clarity and consistency of language markedly different from that of their British counterparts? And if so, did they deliver?

Although the state constitutions crafted from 1776–1788 had many substantive similarities in the kinds of structures that they created,[30] it is difficult to generalize across these documents with respect to drafting. Not only did they differ widely in their length, detail, and novelty, but they were drafted and replaced at a fairly rapid pace; "[b]etween 1776 and 1798 the first sixteen states wrote a total of twenty-nine constitutions. ..."[31] Thus, there really is not a unitary set of pre-1788 state constitutions from which one can draw broad generalizations. Instead, there were several distinct "waves" of constitutional development,[32] with variation and experimentation within each wave.

Nonetheless, the differences between these state constitutions, even casually lumped together, and the British local acts from the same period are dramatic enough to provide a useful basis for comparison. The state constitutions from 1776–1788 made frequent use of the adjectives "necessary" and "proper," and less frequent but still noticeable use of "convenient," "fit," and "requisite." The most striking difference between these documents and the contemporaneous British statutes, even on a casual reading, is that the former do not contain the repetitious strings of adjectives that characterize the latter. British statutes generously employed phrases such as "proper, requisite, or convenient."[33] The American state constitutions contained no such equivalent conjunctions of adjectives; the closest equivalent, which in fact uses nonredundant adjectives, is the declaration that "[a] well regulated militia is the proper, natural, and sure defense of a state."[34] Indeed, the American constitutions contained very few conjunctions of adjectives at all. The phrase "proper and necessary" that appears so frequently in eighteenth-century British statutes does not appear at all, as far as we call tell, in pre-1788 American

30 For a detailed discussion of these substantive similarities, see Donald S. Lutz, The Origins of American Constitutionalism 104–05 (1988).

31 *Id.* at 97.

32 *See id.* at 103–04.

33 15 Geo. 3 c. 16 (1775).

34 N.H. Const. of 1784, art. XXIV. *See also* Md. Const. of 1776, art. XXV (the militia is the "proper and natural defence of a free government"); Va. Const. of 1776 (militia is the "proper, natural, and safe defence of a free State").

state constitutions. The phrase "necessary and proper" appears only once, in a provision of the Massachusetts Constitution of 1780 devoted to emergency powers of the legislature:

> The general court [the legislature] shall have full power and authority for prompt and temporary succession to the powers and duties of public offices, of whatever nature and whether filled by election or appointment, the incumbents of which may become unavailable for carrying on the powers and duties of such offices in periods of emergency resulting from disaster caused by enemy attack, and to adopt such other measures as may be necessary and proper for insuring continuity of the government of the commonwealth and the governments of its political subdivisions.[35]

Apart from a few references to appointment of "a fit and proper person"[36] or the "equitable and proper" adjustment of representation,[37] drafters of state constitutions chose to employ single adjectives to describe the various powers and responsibilities of political actors.

That, of course, does not mean that the early American constitutional drafters chose their words with great precision. Indeed, it proves to be quite difficult to determine the extent to which specific wording in these constitutions was generally understood to convey specific meaning. But there is a marked difference in the use of language in legal instruments on the two sides of the Atlantic Ocean in the late eighteenth century.

The word "necessary," for example, was used in a variety of ways in state constitutions. Sometimes it was specifically qualified by adjectives, as in the several provisions declaring that "frequent recurrence to fundamental principles is absolutely necessary, to preserve the blessings of liberty,"[38] that such recurrence is "indispensably necessary,"[39] that government of some form is "absolutely necessary"[40] or "indispensably necessary,"[41] and that virtue is "absolutely necessary to preserve the

[35] Mass. Const. of 1780, art. LXXXIII.

[36] Md. Const. of 1776, arts. XIII, XLI, XLII, XLVII.

[37] N.J. Const. of 1776, art. III.

[38] N.C. Const. of 1776, Decl. of Rights &c XXI. For similar declarations, see Pa. Const. of 1776, Decl. XIV; Vt. Const. of 1777, Rights XVI; Ma. Const. of 1780, Part the 1st, art XVIII.

[39] N.H. Const. of 1784, art. XXXVIII.

[40] Pa. Const. of 1776, Preamble; Vt. Const. of 1777, Preamble. Vermont's constitution tracked that of Pennsylvania, and we will henceforth not give parallel references to the former.

[41] S.C. Const. of 1776, Preamble. *Cf.* N.C. Const. of 1776, Preamble (stating that "it becomes necessary that government should be established in this State").

advantages of liberty."[42] When used by itself, the term "necessary" often meant something fairly strong, such as "essential." Every citizen was expected to "yield his personal service when necessary."[43] The New Jersey Speaker could convene the legislature "whenever any extraordinary occurrence shall render it necessary."[44] Delegates to the Continental Congress would be chosen "while necessary."[45] No matters could be annexed or added to a money bill "not immediately relating to, and necessary for the imposing, assessing, levying, or applying the taxes or supplies, to be raised for the support of government, or the current expenses of the State."[46] Many formal procedures of government were identified as "necessary" in this strict sense: "[T]he consent of both Houses shall be necessary to every law";[47] a majority of senators "shall be necessary to constitute a senate sufficient to proceed upon business";[48] for impeachment, "it shall always be necessary that two-thirds parts of the members present shall concur";[49] and in matters requiring secrecy, oaths would be administered to "officers necessary to carry the business into execution."[50]

Other uses of "necessary," sometimes in the same document with the unambiguously strict usages, were less clear about the degree of urgency required. Legislatures were declared to have "all other powers necessary for the legislature of a free and independent State."[51] Executives could appoint "all necessary civil officers not hereinbefore mentioned"[52] and were instructed to "transact all necessary business."[53] Citizens could not, without the consent of themselves or the legislature, be forced to leave the border of the commonwealth "except so far as may be necessary"

42 MA. CONST. OF 1780, Part the First, art. XVIII.

43 PA. CONST. OF 1776, Decl. of Rights VII; VT. CONST. OF 1777, Rights IX; MA. CONST. OF 1780, Part the 1st art. X; N.H. CONST. OF 1784, art. XII.

44 N.J. CONST. OF 1776, art. V.

45 N.C. CONST. OF 1776, art. XXXVII; PA. CONST. OF 1776, § 11.

46 MD. CONST. OF 1776 at § XI.

47 *Id.* art III.

48 N.Y. CONST. OF 1777, art. XII.

49 *Id.* art. XXXIII. *See also* S.C. CONST. OF 1778, art. XXIII.

50 GA. CONST. OF 1777, art. XXX.

51 DEL. CONST. OF 1776, art. 5; PA. CONST. OF 1776, § 9; *cf.* MA. CONST. OF 1780, Ch. 1, art. 4 (legislature has general power "for the necessary support and defence of the government thereof").

52 DEL. CONST. OF 1776, art. 16. *See also* S.C. CONST. OF 1776, art. XXV (executive may appoint "all other necessary officers").

53 N.Y. CONST. OF 1777, art. XIX; *cf.* PA. CONST. OF 1776, § 20 (executive transacts "such business as may appear to them necessary to lay before the General Assembly").

for defending otherwise inaccessible parts of the state.[54] Constitutional amendments could be proposed "as are necessary for the preservation of the rights and happiness of the people."[55] It is "necessary" that the governor have a fixed salary to avoid influence.[56] Houses of hard labor were established "to make sanguinary punishments less necessary."[57] The executive could convene the legislature "if necessary"[58] or "when necessary"[59] – but without a specific reference to "extraordinary occurrence[s]," as with the New Jersey Speaker's similar power. Election judges were permitted to adjourn "from day to day, if necessary."[60] Trial by jury was preserved, except in maritime cases when "the legislature shall hereafter find it necessary to alter it."[61] The legislature must meet annually "and if necessary, oftener."[62] The governor of Massachusetts may "kill, slay, and destroy, if necessary, and conquer, by all fitting ways" enemies of the commonwealth.[63] It would certainly be possible to give the term "necessary" a very strict reading in these contexts, but it is not obvious that such a reading is required.

There was no usage of the term "necessary" in state constitutions in which the term unambiguously means nothing more than "helpful" or "related to in a rational fashion." The usages closest to such a meaning are from the Massachusetts Constitution of 1780, whose preamble declares that people have a right "to take measures necessary for their safety, prosperity, and happiness"[64] and whose Part the First states that the people have a right and duty to expect virtue in their government officials "in the formation and execution of the laws necessary for the good administration of the commonwealth"[65] – and the meaning of "necessary" in these settings is hardly unambiguous. The Massachusetts

54 MA. CONST. OF 1780, ch. 2, § 1, art. VI.

55 PA. CONST. OF 1776, § 47. *Cf.* MA. CONST. OF 1780, ch. 6, art. X (preparing for "such alterations as from experience shall be found necessary").

56 MA. CONST. OF 1780, ch. 2, § 1, art. XIII.

57 *Id.* § 39.

58 MD. CONST. OF 1776, § XXIX; S.C. CONST. OF 1776, art. VIII; VA. CONST. OF 1776.

59 PA. CONST. OF 1776, § 20.

60 MD. CONST. OF 1776, art. III.

61 MA. CONST. OF 1780, art. XV; N.H. CONST. OF 1784, art. XX (substituting "think" for "find" but otherwise using identical language to that of the Massachusetts provision).

62 MD. CONST. OF 1776, § 23.

63 MA. CONST. OF 1780, ch. 2, § 1, art. VII.

64 *Id.* Preamble.

65 *Id.* Part the First, § XVIII.

constitution also provided that expired commissions of justices of the peace "may, if necessary, be renewed, or another person appointed, as shall most conduce to the well-being of the commonwealth."[66] The provision could be read to embody a very loose understanding of necessity or a presumption against reappointment of judges. All of the other uses of "necessary" in these documents connote some connection or requirement stronger than mere convenience or helpfulness.

There are, however, a number of provisions in which various actors are made the judges of the necessity of some action, and in those contexts the word "necessary" appears to have a looser meaning. The legislature was authorized to create counties and districts "as to them shall appear necessary."[67] Courts may have "such other powers as may be found necessary by future general assemblies."[68] The legislature shall assemble "at such other times as they shall judge necessary."[69] The government shall contain such officers "as may be judged necessary to be immediately appointed."[70] The legislature "may call for all public or official papers and records, and send for persons, whom they may judge necessary in the course of their inquiries."[71]

When British statutes of this era used express discretion-granting language, it was doubtful whether the language was meant to have substantive effect; certainly, there is no pattern that one can detect in the British laws indicating any such intention. The effect of discretion-granting language in American state constitutions is less clear. It is certainly plausible, however, given the usages just surveyed, to suppose that actors were given express discretion to determine necessity when a looser rather than a stricter standard for necessity was contemplated.

The patterns of usage of "necessary" are especially intriguing given the fact that the adjective "convenient" was consistently used in these constitutions to mean (for want of a better word) "convenient." The executive could convene the legislature "at such place as he shall think most convenient,"[72] and the legislature's meeting place "ought to be fixed,

66 MA. CONST. OF 1780, ch. 3, art. III.

67 N.Y. CONST., art. XII. *Cf.* MA. CONST. OF 1780, Ch. 1, § 2, art. I (counties shall be election districts "until the general court shall determine it necessary to alter the said districts").

68 PA. CONST. OF 1776, § 24.

69 MA. CONST. OF 1780, Ch. 1, art. I.

70 VA. CONST. OF 1776.

71 MD. CONST. OF 1776, art. X.

72 DEL. CONST. OF 1776, art. 8.

the most convenient to the members thereof."[73] Election officials "shall provide a convenient box for receiving the said ballots,"[74] and elections shall be held "at some convenient place."[75] Schools should be established "for the convenient instruction of youth."[76] The legislature shall select places of election "at some convenient time."[77] When there is danger, the governor can change the seat of government to "a more secure and convenient place of meeting."[78] The contrast between the evident meanings of "necessary" and "convenient" in these documents is actually quite striking.[79] At a maximum, it suggests a widespread practice of using "convenient" to describe a looser requirement of fit than "necessary." At a minimum, it at least suggests a care in drafting that sets these instruments far apart from the statutes across the ocean.

It is less clear how to deal with the numerous usages of "proper" in the state constitutions. On some occasions, the word "proper" is used to mean something quite strict, such as "distinctively fitted to or suited for." The Virginia and Georgia constitutions both proclaimed, in identical language, that "[t]he legislative, executive, and judiciary departments shall be separate and distinct, so that neither exercise the powers properly belonging to the other."[80] Other provisions referred to the "proper qualifications" for voting or holding office,[81] the necessity for "proper forms of government,"[82] "proper laws" for creating districts and counties,[83] the "proper form for submission to the people" for initiatives[84] and the "proper identification and certification of signatures" on petitions,[85] the "proper" role of the militia in state defense,[86] and the "proper divisions

[73] Md. Const. of 1776, art. IX.

[74] Ga. Const. of 1777, art. XIII.

[75] Va. Const. of 1776.

[76] N.C. Const. of 1776, art. XLI.

[77] S.C. Const. of 1776, art. XI.

[78] S.C. Const. of 1778, arts. XII–XIII.

[79] The usage of "convenient" that most fails to fit the pattern was the provision in the Pennsylvania constitution noting that, with frequent elections, "the danger of establishing an inconvenient aristocracy will be effectually prevented." Pa. Const. of 1776, § 19. One suspects that a reasonable observer at the time would regard the prospect of the establishment of an aristocracy as a bit more than inconvenient.

[80] Va. Const. of 1776; Ga. Const. of 1777, art. I.

[81] N.H. Const. of 1784, art. XI.

[82] Pa. Const. of 1776, Preamble.

[83] S.C. Const. of 1778, art. XXXIX.

[84] Ma. Const. of 1780, art. XLVIII.

[85] *Id.*

[86] Md. Const. of 1776, art. XXV; Va. Const. of 1776, § 13; N.H. Const. of 1784, art. XXIV.

of the militia" into units.[87] In other usages, however, "proper" seems to mean something more like "conveniently appropriate." New York's constitution called for "a proper magazine of warlike stores" in every county,[88] and Pennsylvania's provided that "all persons at proper times shall be admitted to see the prisoners at their labour."[89] In the case of special elections, South Carolina's legislature "shall appoint proper days" for such elections.[90] The Massachusetts legislature could take property "for the purpose of securing and promoting the proper conservation, development, utilization and control thereof."[91] In Maryland, taxes and fines "may properly and justly be imposed or laid,"[92] and the governor may appoint "a fit and proper person" to fill various vacancies.[93]

Finally, a wide range of provisions expressly identified an actor who was to judge the propriety of some action. In all of these usages, the word "proper" appears to mean something like "conveniently appropriate." The legislature can create more justices of the peace "if the legislature shall think proper to increase their number,"[94] and sheriffs and coroners may serve in office "provided the freemen think proper to reelect them."[95] Criminal trials may be moved to another county if "the assembly shall think proper to direct the trial in the nearest county in which an impartial trial can be obtained."[96] The legislature can adjust county representation when they "judge it equitable and proper."[97] The New York Council of Revision could veto bills "when it should appear improper to the said council or a majority of them, that the said bill should become a law."[98] The legislature may "naturalize all such persons, and in such manner, as they shall think proper."[99] Judicial salaries can be raised "as the general court shall judge proper."[100] As with the usages

[87] MA. CONST. OF 1780, ch. 1, art. X.
[88] N.Y. CONST. OF 1777, art. XL.
[89] PA. CONST. OF 1776, § 39.
[90] S.C. CONST. OF 1776, art. XXVII.
[91] MA. CONST. OF 1780, art. XLIX.
[92] MD. CONST. OF 1776, art. XIII.
[93] *Id.* arts. XIII, XLI, XLII, XLVII.
[94] DEL. CONST. OF 1776, art. 12.
[95] *Id.* art. 27. *See also* PA. CONST. OF 1776, Decl. of Rights VI ("the people have a right, at such periods as they may think proper, to reduce their public officers to a private station").
[96] N.H. CONST. OF 1784, art. XVII.
[97] N.J. CONST. OF 1776, art. III.
[98] N.Y. CONST. OF 1777, art. III.
[99] *Id.* art. XLII.
[100] MA. CONST. OF 1780, ch. 1, art. XIII.

of "necessary" which do and do not expressly commit the determination of necessity to the judgment of some particular actor, the usages of "proper" that do and do not make such express commitments appear to be conveying different meanings in some respects, at least across some cases in which "proper" assumes its strictest guise.

The Articles of Confederation were drafted and ratified during this period of state constitutional development, so for the sake of completeness, they should also be included in this chapter's survey of American drafting practices. The Articles add little, if anything, to what can be gleaned from the state constitutions with respect to the use of power-qualifying adjectives, because it used very few. With respect to "necessary": The Articles provided that no state should keep naval vessels in time of peace "except such number only, as shall be deemed necessary by the United States in Congress assembled,"[101] and a similar restriction was placed on troop levels, which must be "such number only, as in the judgment of the United States in Congress assembled, shall be deemed requisite to garrison the forts necessary for the defense of such state."[102] The Congress could appoint "committees and civil officers as may be necessary for managing the general affairs of the United States"[103] and could "ascertain the necessary sums of money to be raised for the service of the United States"[104] (but only by majority vote[105]). With respect to "proper": Each state was obliged to have "a proper quantity of arms, ammunition and camp equipage,"[106] and each state's quota of troops could be lowered "if the United States in Congress assembled shall, on consideration of circumstances[,] judge proper that any State should not raise men. ..."[107] And just for completeness: Delegates were to be appointed annually "[f]or the most convenient management of the general interests of the United States,"[108] and postage could be charged "as may be requisite to defray the expenses of the said office."[109] There is nothing to suggest that great weight should be given to the precise adjectival terminology of any of these clauses.

101 ARTICLES OF CONFEDERATION art. VI, cl. 4.
102 *Id.*
103 *Id.* art. IX, cl. 5.
104 *Id.*
105 *Id.* art. IX, cl. 6.
106 *Id.* art. VI, cl. 4.
107 *Id.* art. IX, cl. 5.
108 *Id.* art. V, cl. 1.
109 *Id.* art. IX, cl. 4.

While it would be rash to conclude from this brief survey that American drafters of state constitutions carefully considered each word that they wrote, it seems very clear that the process of American constitution-drafting was not subject to the pathologies that afflicted local acts in Parliament in the eighteenth century. One doubts whether Jeremy Bentham or Charles Abbott would have been quite as harsh on the American state constitutions as they were on their own legislature's work product. At the very least, these documents make it unlikely in the extreme that the use of adjectives in legislative drafting in England had any appreciable influence on the American constitutional drafting process.

III

It would be pointless, and well beyond the scope of this book, to explain in detail how the drafting and reading of the American Constitution of 1788 differed from the drafting and reading of British statutes during the same century. The history of the drafting of the American Constitution is a subject well trod by scholars, and we do not intend here to try to add anything of great weight to the scholarly corpus beyond our specific contribution to an understanding of the Necessary and Proper Clause. We have sought to demonstrate in this chapter merely that there is no reason to think that the drafting methods, or the use of the phrase "necessary and proper," in eighteenth-century England had any influence on the language that ultimately appeared in the Necessary and Proper Clause. We are not at this point drawing any strong lessons for the American Constitution from the state constitutions that preceded it. That would be a fruitless task, in view of the fact that only one provision in one state constitution used the phrase "necessary and proper." But it is important to clear the decks, so to speak, by eliminating possible influences on or models for the creation of the Necessary and Proper Clause, and one can now safely rule out British statutory drafting practice as an influence or model.

It is enough for the modest purposes of this chapter that the crafting of the American Constitution was so unlike the crafting of contemporaneous local acts in England that the latter can safely be disregarded in the study of the former. That much, we think, quite literally goes without saying. Even a casual glance through the convention notes, the ratification debates, and the early episodes in government is enough to show that the language of the American Constitution was universally understood as something to take very seriously. When Hamilton, Marshall, Jefferson, and Madison clashed about the meaning of the word "necessary" in the Necessary and Proper Clause,[110] they all assumed that the language mattered, and they constructed arguments – quite elaborate ones – on that assumption. Chief Justice Marshall's famous bit of "[i]ntratextualism"[111] in *McCulloch v. Maryland*,[112] in which he compared the word "necessary" in the Necessary and Proper Clause with the phrase "absolutely necessary" in the Imposts Clause, is just one example of the obvious proposition that the American Constitution was viewed from the outset as a carefully constructed instrument. Given the founding generation's awareness of the historic magnitude of their opportunity and responsibility,[113] one could not expect anything else.

But if British statutes did not influence the framing generation's choice of language, could there have been some other influence, perhaps one that was more a part of the daily life of the educated lawyer of the late eighteenth century, that might account for the ultimate shape of the Necessary and Proper Clause? Perhaps instead of looking to public law models, the answer can be found in the mundane world of private law.

[110] *See* Randy E. Barnett, *The Original Meaning of the Necessary and Proper Clause*, 6 U. PA. J. CONST. L. 183 (2003).

[111] Akhil Reed Amar, *Intratextualism*, 112 HARV. L. REV. 747 (1999).

[112] 17 U.S. (4 Wheat.) 316, 414–15 (1819).

[113] *See* FORREST MCDONALD, NOVUS ORDO SECLORUM: THE INTELLECTUAL ORIGINS OF THE CONSTITUTION 6–7 (1985).

4

The Legal Origins of the Necessary and Proper Clause

Robert G. Natelson

A key to the Necessary and Proper Clause is the founding generation's conviction that government officials ought to conform their conduct to the rules governing private fiduciaries. Also important is the specific content of those rules as they existed at the time. Our conclusion is that the Necessary and Proper Clause granted Congress powers incidental to the powers elsewhere granted in the Constitution, to be exercised in accordance with fiduciary principles – and in particular, in accordance with the principles of agency. The remainder of this book explains and defends that conclusion.

Numerous extant eighteenth-century documents reflect both fiduciary law and the belief that government should conform to fiduciary standards. Although many British statutes contained language similar to that in the Necessary and Proper Clause, British statutes were far less influential on the American public than other kinds of instruments by which one person or other granted power to another.

This chapter first documents the widespread founding-era conviction that government officials are, or should be, subject to fiduciary standards. Next, it focuses on one aspect of founding-era agency law: the doctrine of incidental powers. It then identifies some of the adjectives that accompanied power grants during the two centuries prior to the founding and explains their relationship to the incident power doctrine. Finally, it compares different forms of power-granting clauses available to eighteenth-century drafters and locates the Necessary and Proper Clause within this universe.

I. OF FOUNDERS AND FIDUCIARIES[1]

The Constitution should be read through a fiduciary lens. A central purpose of the document was to adopt for America a federal

[1] Detailed source citations for the following discussion of the founders' ideal of fiduciary government can be found in Robert G. Natelson, *The Constitution and the Public Trust*, 52 BUFF. L. REV. 1077 (2004).

government whose conduct would mimic that of the private-law fiduciary. Specifically, the purpose was to erect a government in which public officials would be bound by fiduciary duties to honor the law, exercise reasonable care, remain loyal to the public interest, exercise their power in a reasonably impartial fashion, and account for violations of these duties. This was to be accomplished both by the manner in which the government was structured and by imposing on public officials obligations comparable to those owed by their private-sector counterparts.

The founders did not invent this governmental ideal. Elements of it extend back to Aristotle and Cicero; during the English constitutional struggle of the seventeenth and eighteenth centuries, it emerged as a principal criterion of free government. By the time of the American founding, this view of government was accepted almost universally among British and American Whigs and among many Tories.

Eighteenth-century statemen absorbed the fiduciary ideal from both Greco-Roman classics and English Whig philosophers such as John Locke. As elaborated by Locke, the terms of the social compact were that citizens conveyed to government certain powers (alienable rights) so those citizens could enjoy more fully the powers retained (inalienable rights), *and that the government had a fiduciary obligation to manage properly what had been entrusted to it.*[2] Popular eighteenth-century essayists echoed Locke's fiduciary theme. For example, in the early 1720s, John Trenchard and Thomas Gordon published "Cato's Letters," an influential series of essays provoked by government policies leading to the speculative South Sea Bubble. Relying explicitly on Aristotle's Nicomachean Ethics, "Cato" wrote that, "Power in a free state, is a trust committed by all to one or a few, to watch for the security, and pursue the interest, of all," and that "[t]he administration of government is nothing else, but the attendance of the trustees of the people upon the

[2] John Locke, The Second Treatise of Civil Government: An Essay Concerning the True Origin, Extent, and End of Civil Government in Two Treatises of Government (Thomas I. Cook ed., 1947) (1690) § 136, at 190 ("[T]he community put the legislative power into such hands as they think fit with this trust, that they shall be governed by declared laws, or else their peace, quiet, and property will still be at the same uncertainty as it was in the state of nature."); *see also id.* § 139, at 192 ("But government, into whatsoever hands it is put, being, as I have before shown, entrusted with this condition, and for this end, that men might have and secure their properties...."); *id.* § 156, at 200 ("The power of assembling and dismissing the legislative, placed in the executive, gives not the executive a superiority over it, but is a fiduciary trust placed in him for the safety of the people....").

interest and affairs of the people."[3] Like Locke, Trenchard and Gordon argued that breaches of public trust were greater than merely private breaches, so standards imposed on public trustees ought to be high:

> [Government] is therefore a trust, which ought to be bounded with many and strong restraints, because power renders men wanton, insolent to others, and fond of themselves. Every violation therefore of this trust, where such violation is considerable, ought to meet with proportionable punishment; and the smallest violation of it ought to meet with some, because indulgence to the least faults of magistrates may be cruelty to a whole people.[4]

Another entry in the literary canon of the founding generation was Henry St. John Bolingbroke's *Dissertation Upon Parties*.[5] Bolingbroke listed four principal duties arising from the trust reposed in the King and in members of Parliament: The first two were to preserve liberty and to preserve the Constitution – obligations analogous to the duty of an agent to follow the instructions set forth in the instrument granting him his powers. The third principal duty was to prevent the sort of "corruption" of the legislature by the executive against which John Locke had inveighed. The fourth was the obligation to exercise care – that is, to administer the government competently.

In the same genre was James Burgh's 1774 *Political Disquisitions*. Burgh focused on the trust duty of legislators to represent faithfully the interests of their constituents. His work is particularly notable for its emphasis on the duty of public trustees to account for their conduct. Like Locke, he pointed out that private trustees have a duty to account for their conduct and that the far greater power of public trustees suggested that the standard regulating them ought to be higher rather than lower. Similar were the sentiments of the famed British clergyman Richard Price: "[Parliaments] possess no power beyond the limits of the trust for the execution of which they were formed. If they contradict this trust, they betray their constituents and dissolve themselves."[6]

3 1 JOHN TRENCHARD & THOMAS GORDON, CATO'S LETTERS 179 (Ronald Hamowy ed., 1995); *id.* at 111. *See also id.* at 179 ("Men who have a trust frankly bestowed upon them by the people, to frequently betray that trust, become conspirators against their benefactors, and turn the sword upon those who gave it").

4 *Id.* at 267.

5 *See, e.g.*, Henry St. John Bolingbroke, *A Dissertation Upon Parties*, in 2 THE WORKS OF LORD BOLINGBROKE 45–46, 95, 100–02, 106–07, 117–18, 158 (1967) (1844).

6 RICHARD PRICE, OBSERVATIONS ON THE NATURE OF CIVIL LIBERTY, THE PRINCIPLES OF GOVERNMENT, AND THE JUSTICE AND POLICY OF THE WAR WITH AMERICA (1776), *available at* http://www.constitution.org/price/price_3.htm (last visited Oct. 25, 2009).

Founding-era political figures agreed. At the federal constitutional convention, many of the delegates enunciated ideals of fiduciary government, among them James Madison, Alexander Hamilton, Pierce Butler, Nathaniel Gorham, Gouverneur Morris, Elbridge Gerry, Luther Martin, Rufus King, and John Dickinson. During the ensuing public debate over the Constitution, leading proponents of the new government repeatedly characterized officials as the people's servants, agents, guardians, or trustees. Among these were Madison, Dickinson, John Jay, Tench Coxe, George Washington, James Kent (the future New York chancellor and treatise-writer), Roger Sherman, James Iredell, and Alexander Hamilton. This was a subject on which there was no disagreement from the Constitution's opponents. They very often used the same kind of language, and based their own arguments on fiduciary principles as well.[7]

The same can be said for the delegates to the state ratifying conventions.[8] Indeed, the delegates at the Maryland convention described themselves formally as "trustees of the public."[9] The Virginia convention narrowly approved the Constitution, but with a recommendation that a "declaration or bill of rights" be added, including the proclamation, "That all power is naturally invested in, and consequently derived from, the people; that magistrates therefore are their trustees and agents, at all times amenable to them." The new federal Constitution itself referred in several places to "public Trust" and to public offices being "of Trust."

Thus, the Constitution was drafted in an environment in which the fiduciary metaphor was almost universal. That metaphor seems to rank just below "liberty" and "republicanism" as an element of the ideology of the day.

In the debates over the Constitution, people praised or criticized it according to how well they thought it would serve the fiduciary ideal. By approving the proposal, the ratifiers brought into being, in James Iredell's words, a "great power of attorney" – an instrument erecting a new fiduciary relationship between governors and governed.

7 For detailed listings of Federalist and Anti-Federalist appeals to public trust principles, see Natelson, *supra* note 1.

8 For detailed listings, see *id.*

9 Maryland Convention (Apr. 21, 1788), in 2 The Documentary History of the Ratification of the United States, 556 (Merrill Jensen ed., 1976); *cf. Reports of the Constitutional Convention Proceedings*, Penn. Herald, July 28, 1787, *reprinted in* 13 A Documentary History of the Ratification of the United States, 125 (John P. Kaminski & Gaspare J. Saladino eds., 1981) (describing the federal convention as an "important trust").

One might fairly inquire as to whether such talk was anything more than rhetoric or fancy.[10] The historical record makes this improbable. The reason members of the founding generation found the fiduciary analogy so powerful was that fiduciary law and management had an immediate, real-world impact upon them. In a way in which most people today do not, they knew what being a fiduciary actually meant, and they understood the implications of applying fiduciary standards to government.

A majority of those who drafted the Constitution and guided it to ratification were lawyers who were, or had been, in private practice. Most of the others were men of affairs of the sort who employed fiduciaries – managers, factors, and so forth – in their personal business enterprises. For example, planters made wide use of commodity factors (brokers) to sell their crops abroad, and the larger planters served as factors themselves.

Members of the founding generation who were neither lawyers nor businessmen often gained personal knowledge of the relevant standards by serving as fiduciaries themselves, particularly in family affairs: Family relationships were warmer in the eighteenth century than in some eras, and family obligations were honored accordingly. Among those obligations was service as guardians, executors, administrators, and trustees. There is reason to believe that people had significantly more exposure to that fiduciary service than is true today, both because the shorter life expectancy of the time left far more estates to administer per capita and because guardians and executors typically served in teams rather than singly. Certainly, general knowledge of the law was more widely spread among the public than it is today, as one can see from the records of the public debates, very often carried on in explicitly legal terms.

In sum, when the founding generation spoke about government officials as fiduciaries, they knew what they were saying, and there is every reason to think that they meant what they said.

Eighteenth-century fiduciary law was somewhat fragmented, encompassing a wide spectrum of actors – administrators of estates, attorneys (both public and private), bailiffs, executors, factors, guardians, servants,

[10] Detailed citation for the portions of this chapter discussing the founders' fiduciary experience and contemporaneous rules of fiduciary conduct can be found at Robert G. Natelson, *Judicial Review of Special Interest Spending: The General Welfare Clause and the Fiduciary Law of the Founders*, 11 TEX. R. OF L. & POLITICS 239 (2007).

stewards, and trustees. Nevertheless, English and American lawyers understood that common principles underlay the law governing different fiduciaries. To a certain extent, we see witness to this in the occasional use of the term "fiduciary" to fiduciaries of various descriptions. More important was the persistent generalization of all fiduciary obligations as obligations of "trust." Thus, a person who presumed to be an infant's guardian was "look'd upon as Trustee for the Infant."[11] A servant who stole his master's goods was said to be guilty of a "breach of trust."[12] An executor or administrator was characterized as a kind of trustee, and his default as a breach of trust. The records contain many other instances of this usage.

A full discussion of contemporaneous fiduciary duties is beyond the scope of this book, but in general they were similar to those imposed today. Of particular significance were those discussed in the following sections.

A. *The Duty to Follow Instructions and Remain Within Authority*

Fiduciaries were required to honor the rules creating their power and, therefore, had an absolute obligation to remain within their authority. If a fiduciary did not act within his power, it was irrelevant whether or not he acted reasonably.

The meaning of the instrument creating the fiduciary relationship – including the scope of authority – was interpreted according to the intent of the person or persons who executed it. A fiduciary's authority was said to be construed strictly; but to effectuate the intent of the persons who granted it, that authority also included incidental powers. The doctrine of incidental powers is central to the Necessary and Proper Clause, and is discussed later in this chapter.[13]

[11] A TREATISE OF EQUITY 164 (1756); *see also* 2 A GENTLEMAN OF THE MIDDLE TEMPLE. A GENERAL ABRIDGMENT OF CASES IN EQUITY ARGUED AND ADJUDGED IN THE HIGH COURT OF CHANCERY, & C. 484 (4th ed., 1756) ("Guardians appointed by Will ... are only Trustees. ...").

[12] TIMOTHY CUNNINGHAM, *A New and Complete Law Dictionary, or, General Abridgment of the Law* (3rd ed., 1783) (unpaginated) (stating, in discussion of "apprentice," "if a man had delivered goods to his servant to keep, or carry for him, and he carried them away animo furandi; this was considered only a breach of trust, but not felony.").

[13] *Infra* pages 60–68.

B. *The Duties of Loyalty and Good Faith*

Fiduciaries were to represent their beneficiaries honestly and with undivided loyalty and not act in a way prejudicial to them. Self-dealing was a breach of trust.

C. *The Duty of Care*

Fiduciaries were not insurers of everything that might go wrong under their administration, that is, for "meer [sic] accident"[14] or for cases in which the beneficiary was at fault. There was, nonetheless, a basic duty of care or diligence. The duty was expressed as an obligation not to neglect the business nor to be guilty of "folly or negligence"[15] or, in some cases, as an obligation to avoid "supine" or "extreme" negligence, or *crassa neglegentia* (gross negligence).

A fiduciary had to apply good business sense. Thus, if authorized to hire agents, the fiduciary had to exercise care in doing so. For example, when a factor was authorized to sell on credit, extending credit for an unreasonable time rendered the factor liable to his principal.

D. *The Duty to Exercise Personal Discretion*

When not authorized in the instrument creating the relationship, fiduciary duties were nondelegable. The applicable rule was *delegatus non potest delegare* – the delegate cannot delegate. As Matthew Bacon phrased it in his *A New Abridgment of the Law*, "One who has an Authority to do an Act for another, must execute it himself, and cannot transfer it to another; for this being a Trust and Confidence reposed in the Party, cannot be assigned to a Stranger."[16] In England, positions whose holders could assign them to others were designated "offices of

[14] 3 Matthew Bacon, A New Abridgment of the Law 565.

[15] *Id.*, at 564–65 (stating that where a servant got a bank bill from another and not from Sir Stephen as instructed [although still drawn on Sir Stephen], the servant was not liable when Sir Stephen failed, as this was "meer Accident," not folly or negligence); George Duke, The Law of Charitable Uses 25 (1805) (stating that, in the context of charitable trusts, breaches of duty included "Abuses, breaches of Trusts, Negligences, Misemployments, not [E]mploying, Concealing, Defrauding, Mis-converting, or Mis-government of the same Lands" (emphasis added)); A Treatise of Equity, *supra* note 11, at 146 (describing liability of joint trustees due to negligence).

[16] 1 Bacon, *supra* note 14, at 203 (pointing out that for that reason, an executor with authority to sell cannot sell by attorney).

profit," but positions that were unassignable without prior authorization were "offices of trust."

When the instrument specifically authorized delegation, the fiduciary was expected to follow appropriate standards, including the standard of care, in choosing agents. If delegation was authorized but an agent violated his own duties, the fiduciary was liable if the choice of agent was made negligently or otherwise in breach of duty. If delegation was authorized and the agent breached, the fiduciary was not liable if not at fault.

E. *The Duty to Account*

Fiduciaries, then as now, were expected to account to those for whom they worked. This could involve accounting for profits or repairing from the fiduciary's own assets any damage arising from a breach of his obligations.

F. *The Duty of Impartiality*

In absence of a specific rule to the contrary (such as the rule permitting a creditor executor to pay himself before he paid other creditors), the common law courts favored impartiality among members of the same class.[17] The bias of the High Court of Chancery – the source of most fiduciary law – toward impartiality was even stronger. In the absence of instructions to the contrary, the chancellor required fiduciaries who represented more than one beneficiary to treat them all fairly. For example, a broker acting for both the purchaser of stock and the creditor who financed the purchase was a trustee for both and could not sell prematurely for the benefit of the creditor and the prejudice of the purchaser.[18]

In the event of loss to the parties, the same principle of impartiality governed. If an executor found an estate insufficient to pay all general legacies, he was to abate all in proportion. Similarly, in the absence of a

[17] *E.g.*, Letheullier v. Tracey, Amb. 221, 221, 27 Eng. Rep. 146, 146 (Ch. 1754) (recounting the argument of counsel, including the later Lord Mansfield, that in the absence of the testator's direction to the contrary, great-grandchildren not in being should be treated equally).

[18] *See, e.g.*, 2 General Abridgment, *supra* note 11, at 746 (citing an example of a broker acting as trustee for two parties and affirming the nature of his independent fiduciary duty to each); 21 Charles Viner, A General Abridgment of Law and Equity, 511 (1742) (affirming that under English law, a broker acting on behalf of two parties to a transaction is trustee for both and thus has an independent fiduciary duty towards each party).

direction to the contrary, when the value of the estate of a fiduciary fluctuated, those for whom the estate was administered were all to benefit or lose in fair proportion.

II. THE DOCTRINE OF INCIDENTAL POWERS IN THE EIGHTEENTH CENTURY

A. *Principal-and-Incident Law: In General*

To determine whether a fiduciary was honoring, or had honored, his duty to remain within authority, it was, of course, necessary to determine the scope of the fiduciary's authority. That authority was defined, not only by the express provisions of the authorizing document, but also by the fiduciary's implied, incidental authority. The doctrine of implied, incidental authority is central to the meaning of the Necessary and Proper Clause.

Maxims were an important component of eighteenth-century Anglo-American law. After a court had acknowledged and approved a maxim, the common law ascribed to that maxim legal authority on a par with an act of Parliament; as Giles Jacob wrote in 1775, "Maxims are one of the Grounds of the law of *England*, and are of the same Weight in Law as the Statutes, and the general Customs of the Realm are their Strength and Warrant."[19] One of the more prominent maxims was *Quando aliquis aliquid concedit, concedere videtur & id sine quo res ipsa esse non potest*,[20] – "When someone grants something, he is seen to grant also that without which the thing itself cannot be."

The *Quando aliquis* maxim served as a foundation for four related bodies of jurisprudence. Those were appendants, appurtenance, fixtures,[21] and principal and incident. The first three were real property

[19] Giles Jacob, A Law Grammar 77 (5th ed., 1775).

[20] 14 Viner, *supra* note 18, at 346 (reporting the maxim under the heading of "incidents"); Saunders' Case (C.P. 1599) 5 Co. Rep. 12a, 12a, 77 Eng. Rep. 66, 67; Kennycott v. Bogen (K.B. 1613) 2 Bulst. 250, 252, 80 Eng. Rep. 1098, 1100.

[21] The term "fixtures" seems not to have come into vogue until a few years before the American founding. *E.g.*, Ex Parte Quincy (Ch. 1750) 1 Atk. 477, 477, 26 Eng. Rep. 305, 305, and earlier in the century, William Salkeld had reported a fixture case under the title, "Incident, Appendant, and Appurtenant." Poole's Case (N.P. 1703) 1 Salk. 368, 91 Eng. Rep. 320. Further evidence of the primacy of principal-incident law comes from a passage in Coke: "... but all things ... appendant, and appurtenant to the mannor [*sic*], as incidents or adjuncts to the same." 1 Edward Coke, Institutes of the Lawes of England, at *121b (1628).

relationships. Principal-and-incident law was of more general application, although important in real property law as well.[22]

Contemporaneous legal dictionaries did not define "principal," but their definitions of "incident" all followed the description of the same word in Coke's *Institutes*: "a thing appertaining to or following another as a more worthy or principall [*sic*]."[23] The 1782 edition of Giles Jacob's popular[24] law dictionary, for example, defined an incident as "a thing necessarily depending upon, appertaining to, or following another that is more worthy or principal,"[25] while the *Student's Law-Dictionary* of 1740 stated that an incident "is any Thing that necessarily depends on, or appertains to another, which is principal or more worthy."[26] What those definitions called "things," we would today call "interests."

Thus, to qualify as an incident, an interest had to be less important or less valuable than its principal.[27] The term "merely" was often applied to incidents,[28] as was the word "only."[29] An incident was always subordinate to or dependent on the principal. The courts sometimes phrased the latter requirement by stating that an incident could not comprise

[22] An example of the continued coexistence of three of these subjects in the law of real estate appears in Matthew Bacon's, *Abridgment*, which included as a subject heading under the general category of grants: "Where a Thing shall be said to pass as appendant, appurtenant, or incident." 2 BACON, *supra* note 14, at *669.

[23] 1 COKE, *supra* note 21, at *151b (1628). This, in turn, was closely related to Coke's definition of "appendant." *Id.* at 121b.

[24] On the popularity of various works, including Jacob's *New Law-Dictionary*, see HERBERT A. JOHNSON, IMPORTED EIGHTEENTH-CENTURY LAW TREATISES IN AMERICAN LIBRARIES 1700–1799 59–64 (1978).

[25] GILES JACOB, A NEW LAW-DICTIONARY (10th ed., 1782) (unpaginated). Jacob followed this definition with examples. This definition was similar to Coke's found in Coke's *Institutes*.

[26] THE STUDENT'S LAW-DICTIONARY (1740) (unpaginated).

See also 2 RICHARD BURN & JOHN BURN, A NEW LAW DICTIONARY 9 (1792); THOMAS BLOUNT, A LAW-DICTIONARY AND GLOSSARY (3d ed., Nutt & Gosling, London, 1717) (unpaginated) ("a Thing appertaining to, or following another, that is more worthy or principal"); JOHN COWELL (or "Cowel"), A LAW DICTIONARY: OR THE INTERPRETER OF WORDS AND TERMS USED EITHER IN THE COMMON OR STATUTE LAWS OF GREAT BRITAIN AND IN TENURES AND JOCULAR CUSTOMS (1727) (unpaginated) ("a Thing necessarily depending upon another as more principal"); 1 CUNNINGHAM, *supra* note 12, (unpaginated) ("a thing necessarily depending upon another as more principal"); WILLIAM RASTALL, LES TERMES DE LA LEY 404 (1742) ("a Thing necessarily depending upon another as more principal").

[27] Ex parte Duke of Ancaster (H.L. 1781) 2 Bro. P.C. 153, 159, 1 Eng. Rep. 855, 859; Bevil's Case (K.B. 1583) 4 Co. Rep. 8a, 8b, 76 Eng. Rep. 862, 865.

[28] Barnard v. Garnons (H.L. 1797) 7 Bro. P.C. 105, 115, 3 Eng. Rep. 69, 75.

[29] Ibgrave v. Lee (C.P. 1556) 2 Dy. 116b, 117a, 73 Eng. Rep. 256, 257.

a subject matter independent of its principal[30] nor could it change the nature of the grant.[31] For example, in the 1618 case of *Lord Darcy v. Askwith*,[32] the question was whether an eighty-year lease that permitted coal mining carried with it the power to use timber for mining purposes. The court held it did not because a grant took with it only "things incident and directly necessary," and that "the lessee hath no power to change the nature of the thing demised."

By the founding era, the jurisprudence of principals and incidents had become a prominent and well-developed branch of the law. Numerous cases had specified which lesser interests were incident to which greater interests. In the realm of real property law, one owning a reversion enjoyed the incidental benefits of fealty[33] and rent.[34] Ownership of a fee simple[35] or of personal property[36] was principal to an incidental power of disposal. Ownership of a manor carried with it the power to hold court.[37] The owner of trees on another's ground enjoyed the right to show them to a prospective buyer.[38] Title to a mineral gave one the right to dig for it.[39] Ownership of a pump on another's land carried the power to repair.[40]

There were many principal-incident relationships in other areas of law as well. For example, the privilege of holding a fair implied the

[30] Atty. Gen. v. Rigby (Ch. 1732) 2 Eq. Ca. Abr. 201, 201, 22 Eng. Rep. 172, 172 (holding that a right to nominate beneficiaries of a rent-charge did not pass with the rent-charge since the latter was "a Thing independant [sic] and collateral" to the rent); Hill v. Grange (K.B. 1556) 1 Pl. Com. 164, 168, 75 Eng. Rep. 253, 260 (reporting counsel as noting, and the other side as admitting, that land is "another sort of a thing" from a messuage [house and yard] and does not therefore pass as an incident to it; nor does another edifice pass as an incident to conveyance of a house, for the same reason).

[31] Smith v. Stapleton (K.B. 1573) 2 Pl. Com. 426, 432, 75 Eng. Rep. 642, 650.

[32] Lord Darcy v. Askwith (K.B. 1618) Hob. 234, 80 Eng. Rep. 380.

[33] 2 WILLIAM BLACKSTONE, COMMENTARIES ON THE LAWS OF ENGLAND, *176 (1765–69); 1 COKE, *supra* note 21, at *93a, *143a & *150b.

[34] 2 BLACKSTONE, *supra* note 33, at *176; 1 COKE, *supra* note 21, at 148a, 319a; Smith v. Stapleton (K.B. 1568) 2 Pl. Com. 426, 432–33, 75 Eng. Rep. 642, 650–51; Casus Incerti Temporis (K.B. n.d.) Keil. 102, 108–09, 72 Eng. Rep. 266, 274; Read v. Lawnse (K.B. 1661) 2 Dy. 212b, 212b, 73 Eng. Rep. 469, 470. It was, however, unlike fealty, severable from the reversion. 1 COKE, *op. cit.*, at 93a.

[35] Hungerford v. Wintor (Ch. 1735) Amb. 839, 841, 27 Eng. Rep. 525, 526.

[36] Fettiplace v. Gorges (Ch. 1789) 3 Bro. C.C. 8, 10, 29 Eng. Rep. 374, 375.

[37] Marsh v. Smith (C.P. 1585) 1 Leo. 26, 27, 74 Eng. Rep. 24, 25; Rex v. Stafferton (K.B. 1610) 1 Bulst. 54, 55, 80 Eng. Rep. 756, 757.

[38] Liford's Case (K.B. 1614) 11 Co. Rep. 46b, 52a, 77 Eng. Rep. 1206, 1217.

[39] Case of Mines (Exch. 1568) 1 Pl. Com. 310, 317, 75 Eng. Rep. 472, 483.

[40] Pomfret v. Ricroft (K.B. 1669) 1 Wms. Saund. 321, 322, 85 Eng. Rep. 454, 455.

privilege of conducting any court customarily associated with the fair,[41] and one convicted of crime suffered from the legal incidents of conviction.[42] Central for our purposes are the many cases holding that one or more subsidiary powers were incident to a greater. For instance, capacity to operate as a corporation included the incidental powers to make bylaws[43] and remove corporate officers who had failed in their duties.[44] A grant of the right to fish carried with it the right to do so with nets.[45] One granted authority to make war enjoyed the incidental power to make peace.[46]

B. *Principal-and-Incident Law in Conveyances*

Many principal-and-incident cases arose as a result of one party conveying the principal – whether real estate, a power, or something else – to another. The courts established that if one had power to dispose of the principal, one had power to dispose of the incident,[47] and that (in absence of a proviso to the contrary) conveyance of the principal carried the incident even without express reference to the latter.[48] Indeed, if the

[41] *E.g.*, 4 Thomas Wood, An Institute of the Laws of England 490 (1772) ("The *Court of Pie-Powders* [*Curia Pedis Pulverizati*, because for Contracts and Injuries done in the Fair or Market, Justice shall be done as speedily as the Dust can fall from the Foot] is incident to every Fair and Market, for by Grant of the Fair or Market it shall pass.").

[42] 1 William Hawkins, A Treatise of the Pleas of the Crown 169 (6th ed., 1787).

[43] Rex v. Major (K.B. 1720) 1 Str. 385, 386, 93 Eng. Rep. 583, 584; Sutton's Hosp. Case (K.B. 1613) 10 Co. Rep. 23a, 30b, 77 Eng. Rep. 960, 970; The King v. Mayor of Durham (K.B. 1757) 1 Keny. 512, 523, 96 Eng. Rep. 1074, 1078 (reporting counsel as agreeing that corporations have an incidental power of making by-laws and where a charter states a general power to do so, the statement is superfluous).

[44] Lord Bruce's Case (K.B. 1728) 2 Str. 819, 819–20, 93 Eng. Rep. 870, 870.

[45] Randal v. Harvey (K.B. 1623) Godb. 358, 358, 78 Eng. Rep. 211, 211

[46] Nabob of Arcot v. E. India Co. (Ch. 1793) 4 Bro. C.C. 180, 194, 29 Eng. Rep. 841, 847 (holding that in 1781 the East India Company had a power to make treaties as an incident to its power to make war).

[47] Butler v. Baker (K.B. 1591) 3 Co. Rep. 25a, 32b, 76 Eng. Rep. 684, 702 (holding, "for inasmuch as the statute enables him by express words to devise the manor, by consequence it enables him to devise the manor, with all incidents and appurtenances to it").

[48] Thus, a royal pardon also restored "all the dependencies, penalties, and disabilities incident unto" the offense. Cuddington v. Wilkins (K.B. 1615) Hob. 81, 82, 80 Eng. Rep. 231, 232; Portington's Case (C.P. 1613) 10 Co. Rep. 35b, 39a, 77 Eng. Rep. 976, 982. Or as Blackstone wrote: "The incident passes by the grant of the principal, but not e converso: for the maxim of law is, '*accessorium non ducit, sed sequitur, suum principale*.'" 2 Blackstone, *supra* note 33, at *176 (emphasis in original). *See also* 1 Coke, *supra* note 21, at 93a.

grant included words expressly mentioning the incident, those words did not have independent legal effect. The applicable maxim was *Expressio eorum quae tacite insunt nihil operatur* – "The expression of those things that are silently inherent has no effect."[49]

Although transfer of the principal automatically included the incident, grant of an incident, without more, did not carry the principal with it. "*Accessorium non ducit, sed sequitur suum principale*," wrote Lord Coke[50] – the accessory does not lead, but follows its principal.

Courts sometimes had to decide whether a greater interest and a lesser interest stood in the relation of principal and incident without the guide of controlling statute or precedent. This process usually arose in the context of a conveyance or grant. It was referred to as one of determining whether the lesser interest was "necessary" to the greater. As Blackstone put it, "[a] subject's grant shall be construed to include many things, besides what are expressed, if necessary for the operation of the grant."[51] "Necessary" was a term of art, referring to any of three different situations. The first situation was when the putative incident was *indispensable* to the use of the principal. Blackstone observed that the grazing rights known as "commons appendant" were inseparable incidents of certain lands because:

> [W]hen lords of manors granted out parcels of land to tenants ... these tenants could not plough or manure the land without beasts; these beasts could not be sustained without pasture; and pasture could not be had but in the lord's wastes, and on the un[e]nclosed fallow grounds of themselves and the other tenants. The law therefore annexed this right of common,

[49] Boroughe's Case (K.B. 1596) 4 Co. Rep. at 72b, 76 Eng. Rep. at 1044 (reporter's commentary). *See* Case of Mines (Exch. 1568) 1 Pl. Com. 310, 317, 75 Eng. Rep. 472, 483 (stating that the king had incidental power to dig gold and silver ore he owned and the clause of licence is but matter of curtesy, and serves only to give notice to the possessor of the soil, and is not of necessity to be had); The King v. Mayor of Durham (K.B. 1757) 1 Keny. 512, 523, 96 Eng. Rep. 1074, 1078 (reporting counsel as agreeing that corporations have an incidental power of making by-laws and where a charter gives a general power, it is superfluous).

See also 1 WOOD, *supra* note 41, at 9 ("General Words of an Act shall not take away necessary Incidents").

[50] 1 COKE, *supra* note 21, at 152a.

[51] 2 BLACKSTONE, *supra* note 33, at *347; *see also* 1 COKE, *supra* note 21, at *268b ("all necessary incidents are to be supplyed [*sic*]"); GILES JACOB, THE STUDENT'S COMPANION: OR, THE REASON OF THE LAW 241 (3d ed., 1743) (citing 2 Coke, *Institutes*, at 235) ("And where a thing is granted by Statute, all necessary Incidents are granted with it.").

as inseparably incident, to the grant of the lands; and this was the original [*sic*] of common appendant.[52]

Other examples involved the power to dig and carry ore as incident to ownership of a mine,[53] a power to remove corporate officers as incidental to the corporation because it was "as necessary for the well governing [of] a corporation as an incidental power to make by-laws,"[54] and the power of each chamber of Parliament to evict members as an incident because it was "necessary to preserve" authority.[55]

The second situation in which a subordinate interest was deemed "necessary," and therefore incident to, the principal was if the absence of the subordinate interest would impair the value of the principal seriously enough that the owner of the principal would suffer "great prejudice." For example, a general bailiff of a manor, who usually had no authority to make leases for years, could grant a lease at will "because being to collect and answer the Rents of the Manor to his Lord, if he could not let Leases at Will, the Lord might sustain great Prejudice by Absence, Sickness, or other Incapacity to make Leases, when any of the former Leases were expired."[56] Again from Blackstone: "But deer in a real authorized park, fishes in a pond, doves in a dove-house, &c, though in themselves personal chattels, yet they are so annexed to and so necessary to the well-being of the inheritance, that they shall accompany the land wherever it vests. ..."[57] We shall call the "great prejudice" situation *reasonable necessity*.

The third kind situation in which an interest was "necessary," and therefore incident to, the principal was if it was *customary to the use of the principal*,[58] even if, objectively considered, there was little actual necessity. Blackstone cited the fact that a seal and by-laws were

[52] 2 BLACKSTONE, *supra* note 33, at *33.

[53] The Case of Mines (Exch. 1568) 1 Pl.l Rep. 310, 75 Eng. Rep. 472.

[54] The King v. Richardson (K.B. 1757) 2 Keny. 85, 119, 96 Eng. Rep. 1115, 1127 (Mansfield, C.J.).

[55] Colonel Pitt's Case (K.B. 1734) Ridg. T.H. 91, 106, 27 Eng. Rep. 767, 773. *See also* Randal and Harvey's Case, (K.B. 1623) Godb. 358, 78 Eng. Rep. 211 (ruling that arrest was not incident to debt-enforcement, since not necessary); Tyrringham's Case (K.B. 1584) 4 Co. Rep. 36b, 37a, 76 Eng. Rep. 973, 978 (holding that a right of common was incident "as a thing necessary and incident" to land).

[56] 3 BACON, *supra* note 14, at *406.

[57] 2 BLACKSTONE, *supra* note 33, at *427–28.

[58] *E.g.*, Neal & Jackson's Case (C.P. 1595) 4 Co. Rep. 26b, 26b, 76 Eng. Rep. 938, 938 (containing reporter's comment that "[a] steward, as incident to his office, may, by the general custom of all manors, take a surrender out of court").

considered incident to a corporation sole.[59] Custom might rise to the level of prescription,[60] but more often it was merely a device for construing the scope of the conveyance of the principal. For example, the courts were asked to construe powers of attorney given to factors, who were agents for the sale of goods or services, often overseas. One case held that a factor enjoyed implied authority to extend credit on behalf of his principal if such was the custom in the factor's business.[61] Another ruled that a power of attorney authorizing a factor to "receive all freights and profits due for such ship, and to compare and transact with the Commissioners of the Navy"[62] granted the factor the capacity to sell to a third party a Navy bill of exchange payable to the principal, since that power customarily followed such a grant. This inclusion of custom and hardship within the scope of "necessity" paralleled similar developments in the law of fixtures.[63]

It was established early that the role of principal-and-incident law, at least in the context of grants and other conveyances, was to effectuate the probable intent of the parties.[64] Accordingly, parties could disclaim a relation of incidence by expressly excluding it, as the Continental Congress did when drafting the Articles of Confederation.[65]

The practical effect of applying the jurisprudence of principals and incidents in *grants of power* was to contradict the maxim that delegated

[59] 1 Blackstone, *supra* note 33, at *464 (stating that for corporations sole the incidents of seal and by-laws might be severable). *See also* Dudfeild v. Andrews (C.P. 1689) 1 Salk. 184, 184, 91 Eng. Rep. 168, 168); Swayne's Case (C.P. 1608) 8 Co. Rep. 63a, 64a, 77 Eng. Rep. 568, 570 (discussing incidents by custom in copyhold tenure); Heddy v. Wheelhouse (K.B. 1597) Cro. Eliz. 558, 558, 78 Eng. Rep. 803, 803 (discussing customary incidents of fairs); Howard v. Bartlet (C.P. 1614) Hob. 181, 181, 80 Eng. Rep. 328, 328 (holding that customary incidents adhere to a life estate).

[60] On incidents created by prescription, see, *e.g.*, Cowper v. Andrews (K.B. 1612) Hob. 39, 44, 80 Eng. Rep. 189, 194; Heddy v. Wheelhouse (K.B. 1597) Cro. Eliz. at 558, 78 Eng. Rep. 803, 803 (reporting argument of counsel).

[61] *See* Anonymous, 12 Mod. 514, 88 Eng. Rep. 1487 (K.B. 1701).

[62] Elkins v. MacKlish (Ch. 1753) Amb. 184, 27 Eng. Rep. 125.

[63] *E.g.*, Poole's Case (N.P. 1703) 1 Salk. 368, 91 Eng. Rep. 320 (Holt, C.J) (considering "convenience of trade"); Lawton v. Lawton (Ch. 1743) 3 Atk. 13, 26 Eng. Rep. 811 & Lawton v. Lawton (K.B. 1782) 3 Atk. 17, 26 Eng. Rep. 813 (Mansfield, C.J.) (considering financial hardship and custom in a case with the same name as the chancery case arising 39 years previously).

[64] Hill v. Grange (K.B. 1556) 1 Pl. Rep. 164, 168, 75 Eng. Rep. 253, 260 (reporting as argued and admitted that land is not incident to a messuage because it is not intended to be granted with it).

[65] Art. Confed. art. II.

authority must be strictly construed.[66] Rather, the sum of the authority granted was defined by the intent of the parties. Making up that sum were (1) power to undertake acts within a strict construction of the grant plus (2) incidental power to undertake acts not within a strict construction but within the scope presumptively intended by the parties.[67]

C. *Distinguishing Incidental Authority from Discretionary Exercise Within Express Powers*

The doctrine of incidental powers granted authority to undertake acts not within the strict construction of the grant. One must distinguish this from power to choose means that *were* within a strict construction of the grant. Suppose the lord of a manor granted his steward (land manager) power to "manage my estate, including overseeing crops and hiring laborers," but did not specify which laborers the steward should hire. In this case, the steward's choice was within his good-faith discretion in carrying out an expressly granted power,[68] and that choice was therefore an exercise of express rather than implied authority.[69]

By contrast, incidental authority was *outside* the scope of the strictly construed wording of grants. Consider the issue of whether a steward hired to "manage" an estate could lease a portion of it for a term. This was arguably part of "managing" the estate, but strictly construed, it was not: A stricter definition of "manage" would comprise only raising crops, caring for the land, overseeing the workforce, and the like, rather than leasing, which could be seen as delegating management responsibilities to a tenant.

66 1 JOHN COMYNS, A DIGEST OF THE LAWS OF ENGLAND 458 (1780) (using the word "pursued" for "construed").

67 This was also how John Marshall understood the matter. JOHN MARSHALL'S DEFENSE OF MCCULLOCH V. MARYLAND 92 (Gerald Gunther ed., 1969) [hereinafter MARSHALL, DEFENSE] (discussing the difference between strict and intent-based construction of powers, and advocating the latter). *Cf. id.* at 167–69 ("All instruments are to be construed fairly, so as to give effect to their intention ...The object of language is to communicate the intention of him who speaks, and the great duty of a judge who construes an instrument, is to find the intention of its makers.").

68 Moore v. Mourgue (K.B. 1776) 2 Cowp. 479, 98 Eng. Rep. 1197 (Mansfield, C.J.). I previously treated this as an incidental powers case, Robert G. Natelson, *The Agency Law Origins of the Necessary and Proper Clause*, 55 CASE W. RES. L. REV. 243, 281–82 (2004). I was mistaken.

69 John Marshall relied in this distinction in his defense of the Supreme Court's holding in *Marbury*. MARSHALL, DEFENSE, *supra* note 67, at 162 & 171–73.

English courts resolved this issue by holding that a power to lease part of an estate for short terms was incident to a steward's management authority, apparently because stewards customarily exercised it,[70] and custom (in the absence of contrary evidence) suggested that the subsidiary power was within the intended scope of the grant. However, the courts held that stewards did not have power to sell portions of the fee – an activity considered a different kind from, or perhaps as "worthy" as, management.[71]

A public law analogue was cited by Virginia governor Edmund Randolph during the ratification debates. Unless limited to express powers (as Congress had been under the Articles of Confederation), a governmental entity granted authority to make war and peace enjoyed the incidental power to issue passports – even though passport-issuing was outside the scope of the language of the grant, strictly construed.[72]

III. "NECESSARY AND PROPER" DOCUMENTS IN THE EIGHTEENTH CENTURY

Given the special meaning of "necessary" in the law of agency and other fiduciary relationships, it is not surprising that power-conveying documents featuring the word were common in the eighteenth century. Moreover, the word was frequently coupled with its synonyms and with variations on "proper." In this section, we trace some of the history of those documents, describe how phrases of this type were commonly constructed, and examine a pair of cases illustrating how "necessary and proper"-style language interacted with the incidental powers doctrine.

A. *Some History*

Forerunners of the phrase "necessary and proper" appeared in British Latin-language documents long before the American founding.

[70] 3 VINER *supra* note 20, at 538–40 (listing powers within and without the implied authority of the bailiff of a manor). Also, a conveyance to "trustees, to preserve contingent remainders" conveyed the grant of certain additional powers. Thong v. Bedford (Ch. 1783) 1 Bro. C.C. 313, 313–14, 28 Eng. Rep. 1154, 1154. For an example of another incidental management power, see Howard v. Baillie (Ch. 1796) 2 H. Bl. 618, 126 Eng. Rep. 737 (discussed below).

[71] 3 VINER, *supra*, note 20.

[72] 3 THE DEBATES IN THE SEVERAL STATE CONVENTIONS ON THE ADOPTION OF THE FEDERAL CONSTITUTION 29 (Jonathan Elliot, 2d ed. 1891) [hereinafter ELLIOT'S DEBATES) (quoting Randolph at the Virginia ratifying convention).

Burdet's Case,[73] decided by Queen's Bench in 1586, construed a term in an agreement granting power to a steward *et ulterius ad faciendum et exequendum quantum in me est* – "and furthermore to do and carry out as much as I could do personally." The court deciding *Burdet's Case* held that while the steward may have exceeded his authority by taking a conveyance on condition instead of an absolute conveyance, his act nevertheless was valid by reason of the very broad wording in his deputation. The court might have been following the Roman law on the question, which upheld an agent's receipt of payment for the benefit of the principal if the agency agreement was unclear or multifaceted and if the payment "*mandatori expedierit*" (was expedient for the principal).

Other instruments conferring discretionary powers relied on the words "*necessaria*" and "*opportuna*" – the latter term renderable as "fit" or "proper." For example, Elizabeth I, who reigned from 1559 to 1603, promulgated statutes for the governance of St. John's College, Cambridge, which enabled the bishop to discipline the master and faculty of the college in certain ways and *caeteraque omnia et singula facere et exercere, quae ad eorum correctionem et reformationem sunt necessaria, aut quovismodo opportuna*[74] – "to do and exercise other things, all and singular, that may for their correction or reform be necessary or in any way fit [proper]." Early in the succeeding reign of James I (1603–1625), an appointment of a church officer authorized that officer to do "*ceteraq[ue] omnia et singula faciund[a] et exercend[a] in ea parte qu[a]e necessar[ia] forent seu quomodolibet opportuna*"[75] – all other things to be done or exercised in that regard that will be necessary or any way fit [or proper]. In 1724, a British form book was published featuring two Latin powers of attorney authorizing actions either "*necessaria*" or "*opportuna*."[76]

73 Cro. Eliz. 48, 48, 78 Eng. Rep. 311, 311 (Q.B. 1586).

74 *Quoted in King v. Bishop of Ely*, 1 Bl. W. 71, 74, 96 Eng. Rep. 39, 41 (K.B. 1756); also quoted in *St. John's College v. Todington*, 1 Burr. 158, 187, 9 Eng. Rep. 245, 262 (K.B. 1757).

75 *Quoted in Acton v. L'evesq* de Sarum, 2 Lutw. 1645, 1654, 125 Eng. Rep. 904, 909 (1702).

76 1 Nicholas Covert, The Scrivener's Guide 153 (4th ed., 1724) ("*ad faciend' exsequend' et expedend' omnia et singula et necessaria fuer' aut opportuna in vel circa executionem presentium secun' tenorem et veram intentionem earundem*); *id.* at 153–54 ("*omnia alia et singula que necessaria sunt aut opportuna in vel circa executionem presentium secundum tenorem et vera intentionem earundem*").

As the eighteenth century proceeded, however, such forms increasingly appeared in English. *Necessaria* became "necessary" or "needful," and *opportuna* was rendered "fit," "expedient," "convenient," "useful," "meet," or "proper."[77] Some documents relied only on a single standard, such as "necessary," "needful," "proper," and "fit." Others employed "necessary and proper," "necessary or proper," "needful and necessary," "necessary or useful," "necessary and convenient," "necessary and expedient" – and so on. These documents included private instruments, such as powers of attorney (then usually called "letters of attorney"), trust instruments, conveyances, and contracts. They also included public instruments, such as corporate charters, royal commissions, English and American statutes, judicial orders from the House of Lords to lower courts, ordinances of the Continental and Confederation Congresses – and, in five separate locations, in the Constitution itself.[78]

B. How Clauses of the "Necessary and Proper"-Type Were Structured

1. Express-Power Discretion Clauses vs. Further-Powers Clauses

Some variations on the "necessary and proper" theme communicated that the actor would have a choice of means within the scope of express authority. We can group these variations together as *express-power discretion clauses*. In the foregoing illustration involving the steward of a manor, the agreement employing the steward might provide that the steward could hire such laborers as he "deemed necessary, fit, or proper." The standard commission by which the British Crown invested new colonial governors authorized the governor to prorogue colonial assemblies "as [he] shall judge it necessary."[79] This clarified that the

[77] A LATIN DICTIONARY 1271 (Charlton T. Lewis, ed., 1879 (repr. 1980) [This dictionary is customarily known as "Lewis & Short," and accordingly is cited hereinafter as LEWIS & SHORT] (defining the masculine singular form, *opportunus* as fit, meet, convenient, suitable, seasonable, opportune; advantageous, serviceable, useful, and adapted to any end); ELISHA COLES, A DICTIONARY, ENGLISH-LATIN, AND LATIN ENGLISH (17th ed., 1764) (unpaginated) (including "proper" among the definitions of *opportunus*).

[78] In addition to the Necessary and Proper Clause, they are U.S. CONST. art. I, §8, cl. 17 ("and other needful Buildings"); art. II, §3 ("as he shall judge necessary and expedient"); art. IV, §3, cl. 2 ("all needful Rules and Regulations"), and art. V ("whenever two thirds of both Houses shall deem it necessary"). They are discussed below.

[79] ANTHONY STOKES, A VIEW OF THE CONSTITUTION OF THE BRITISH COLONIES 156 (1783) (setting forth a form for a royal governor's commission).

governor had discretion to select the time and occasion for exercising the express power to prorogue. Postindependence delegations issued by states[80] and by the Continental and Confederation Congresses likewise employed "necessary,"[81] "necessary and proper,"[82] and "proper and necessary" phrases to communicate that the agent would enjoy a choice of means within the scope of express authority.[83]

The Constitution's Property Clause,[84] authorizing Congress to "make all *needful* Rules and Regulations" for the governance of federal territories and "other Property" is an express-power discretion clause.[85] Also in this category are the Constitution's grants to the president of power to recommend to Congress "such Measures as he shall judge necessary

80 *E.g.*, 17 J. CONT. CONG. 636 (Jul. 17, 1780) (quoting from the South Carolina legislature's authorization to the governor and executive council to do all things "as may be judged expedient and necessary to secure the Liberty, Safety and Happiness of this State." *Cf.* 32 *id.* at 72 (Feb. 21, 1787) (instructions from New York to move for a federal convention to recommend changes in the Articles of Confederation "as the representatives met in such convention shall judge proper and necessary to render [the Articles] adequate to the preservation and support of the Union").

81 *E.g.*, 7 *id.* at 236 (Apr. 7, 1777) (authorizing appointment of "such a number of surgeons, nurses, or orderly men, as the director general ... shall judge necessary").

82 *E.g.*, 5 *id.* at 823 (Sep. 25, 1776) (empowering committee to "employ such [persons] as they may think necessary and proper"); 10 *id.* at 222 (Mar. 4, 1778) (directing the Board of War to "give such orders thereon as they may judge necessary and proper respecting the plans of forts and batteries and other matters incidental thereto"); *cf.* 29 *id.* 723 (suggestion that each consul general be "directed to nominate such and so many Consuls, for Ports within his District, as he may from Time to Time think necessary and proper").

83 *E.g.*, 2 *id.* at 208 (Jul. 26, 1775) (granting postmaster general the power to appoint "so many deputies as to him may seem proper and necessary"); 6 *id.* at 1032 (Dec. 21, 1776) (creating a committee with "powers to execute such continental business as may be proper and necessary to be done at Philadelphia); 10 *id.* at 168 (Feb. 14, 1778) (granting power to regulate provisions and location of magazines according to what is judged "proper and necessary"). *See also* 10 *id.* at 184; 19 *id.* at 314; 22 *id.* 122 (reproducing similar language).

Congress sometimes used similar terms in defining the scope of its recommendations to states, e.g., 5 *id.* at 564 (Jul. 16, 1776) (recommendation based on what the Pennsylvania convention "may deem proper and necessary"); 27 *id.* at 375 (May 12, 1784) (request to governor of Connecticut for "proper and necessary assistance"); *id.* at 606 (a recommendation for certain "proper and necessary" laws); 34 *id.* at 207 (Jun. 6, 1788) (recommendation that the executive of Virginia communicate "such Information on the Subject as may appear to him proper and necessary"). However, recommendations were not deputations of power and, therefore, did not create agency relationships.

84 U.S. CONST. art. IV, §3, cl.2.

85 Italics added. *See also* NORTHWEST ORDINANCE, §7 (1787) ("[T]he governor shall appoint such magistrates and other civil officers in each county or township, *as he shall find necessary.*") (italics added).

and expedient"[86] and to Congress of the power to recommend a constitutional amendment "whenever two thirds of both Houses shall deem it necessary."[87]

Further-power clauses granted *additional* authority to the express enumerations, strictly construed. For example, the typical royal governor's commission authorized the governor to "appoint Judges ... Commissioners ... Justices of the Peace *and other necessary* Officers and ministers ..."[88] Depending on the language adopted, the additional powers might be greater, less, or coterminous with incidental authority.

The structure and placement of the Necessary and Proper Clause suggest that it would have been understood as a provision granting (or recognizing) authority beyond strict construction of express powers rather than merely recognizing a choice of means within strictly construed express powers. The Clause occupies its own paragraph, and it is set off from the express powers by the word "And."

2. Formulae for Further-Powers Clauses

With some exceptions,[89] further-powers clauses may be described by five principal formulae. I shall call these by the creative names of Formula One, Formula Two, Formula Three, Formula Four, and Formula Five.

Formula One was very permissive. In essence, it was an English-language version of the Latin expression construed in *Burdet's Case.*

[86] U.S. CONST. art. II, §3, cl.1 (emphasis added).

[87] *id.* art. V (emphasis added).

[88] STOKES, *supra* note 79.

[89] Some documents mixed different formulae together. *See e.g.*, ORLANDO BRIDGMAN, CONVEYANCES: BEING SELECT PRECEDENTS OF DEEDS AND INSTRUMENTS CONCERNING THE MOST CONSIDERABLE ESTATES IN ENGLAND 23 (1702) (and to do all and every Act, Matter, and thing whatsoever, that may be necessary and convenient for making as many good and lawful entries, as he shall think fit); 10 STATUTES AT LARGE FROM THE FIFTH YEAR OF THE REIGN OF KING GEORGE THE THIRD TO THE TENTH YEAR OF THE REIGN OF KING GEORGE THE THIRD, INCLUSIVE 16 (1771) (granting commissioners the power to make proper installations as they may deem necessary); GILES JACOB, LEX MERCATORIA: OR, THE MERCHANT'S COMPANION 171 (2d ed., 1729), setting for the following from a letter of attorney:

> *And I give*, and by these Presents grant unto my said Attornies, my full Power and Authority to sue, arrest, &c. and upon Recovery, Acquittances in my Name to make, seal, and deliver, and one Attorney under them to substitute, and generally to do and execute all and every other Act or Acts, Thing and Things whatsoever needful and necessary in the Premisses, as fully and effectually as I myself might or could do personally."

Formula One clauses granted the actor all powers that the principal might execute if he or she were present.[90] This would appear to contemplate a grant of discretion broader than that encompassed by the doctrine of incidental powers.

Formula Two was perhaps as permissive. It conveyed the power to act *as the actor deemed* needful, necessary, fit, proper, or meet.[91] By this

See also 22 J. CONT. CONG. 347 (Jun. 24, 1782) (quoting Connecticut commission to delegates in Congress, giving them variously the power to do what was "necessary," "necessary and proper," and, as to hiring legal counsel, "as they shall judge needful").

90 *See, e.g.*, NEW PRECEDENTS IN CONVEYANCING 321 (John Worrell, ed., 1742) ("giving, and by these Presents granting unto the said T.L. full Power to Act as aforesaid, in and about the said Premisses, as if I the said H.T. were personally present ... ratifying and hereby confirming whatsoever the said T.L. shall do, or cause to be done, in and about the Premisses, as fully to all Intents and Purposes, as if the same were done by myself, and I were personally present. ..."); 2 JOHN LILLY, THE PRACTICAL CONVEYANCER 694 (1742) ("and also to do and execute all and every such other lawful Acts and Things pertaining to the Office aforesaid in as large and ample manner as I the said G. H. might, may or can do") (language in a deputation of a bishop's register).

91 *Letters of Attorney*: THE YOUNG CLERK'S VADE MECUM OR COMPLEAT LAW-TUTOR 48 (1771) [hereinafter VADE MECUM] ("as he my said Attorney shall think fit"); 1 THE ATTORNEY'S COMPLEAT POCKET-BOOK 187 (5th ed., 1764) (2 vols.) [hereinafter POCKET-BOOK] ("as my said Attorney shall think fit") & 175 ("in such Manner as my said Attorney shall think fit"); COVERT, *supra* note 76, at 145 ("which ... shall to my said Attorney seem fit to be done"); ANONYMOUS, THE LAWYER'S LIBRARY: A NEW BOOK OF INSTRUMENTS 102 (2d., 1710) [hereinafter NEW BOOK] ("which my said Attorney shall think meet"); *id.* at 104 ("as he shall think fit"). *See also* Howard v. Baillie, 2 H. Bl. at 625, 126 Eng. Rep. at 741 ("as ... shall be thought adviseable [*sic*] and proper") & 2 H. Bl. at 626, 126 Eng. Rep. at 742 ("as ... shall seem meet").

Articles of agreement: 2 EDWARD WOOD, A COMPLEAT BODY OF CONVEYANCING, IN THEORY AND PRACTICE 117 (3rd ed., 1770) ("in Case the same shall be thought necessary and proper to make such Conveyance").

Royal charter: *A Copy of His Majesty's Royal Charter for Incorporating the Governors and Guardians of the Hospital for the Relief of Poor Lying-In-Women In Dublin* 8 (1756), *available at Eighteenth Century Collections Online* (Gale Cengage Learning) (organizers empowered to select "all such inferior Officers and Servants as shall be thought necessary or useful for the Purposes of the said Corporation").

Royal order: Mitchell v. Rodney (H.L. 1783) 2 Bro. PC 423, 424, 1 Eng. Rep. 1039, 1040 (quoting order to the effect that designee was to act "if you and he shall judge it necessary and proper").

Parliamentary statute: 8 Geo. iii. c.16, art. XIX (1768) ("as he shall think proper").

American colonial statutes: LAWS OF MARYLAND ENACTED ... 1732 at 26 (1733), ("unless upon such an Emergency as may be judged Necessary and Proper by the

language, the agent's subjective judgment controlled his actions,[92] in all probability subject to a good-faith standard.[93] Commissions to colonial governors included some clauses of this type, such as the standard provision conveying to the governor "full power and authority to order and appoint ... harbours, bays, havens ... and other places for the convenience and security of shipping ... as by you ... shall be thought fit and necessary."[94] The Continental Congress sometimes considered or issued directions in Formula Two.[95]

Formula Three was similar to the provision in the statutes of St. John's College.[96] It was objective in nature, but phrased its requirements in the disjunctive, so that the power-holder acted within authority if he met any of two or more standards. Thus, an instrument might grant

Field Officers"); PUBLIC LAWS OF THE STATE OF SOUTH CAROLINA 122 (1722) (1790 compilation) (as road commissioners "shall see necessary"); *id.* at 270 (1769) (empowering courts to make orders "as to them shall seem necessary and proper").; *id.*, Appendix 24 ("as by their discretion shall be thought necessary and convenient") (1552 Parliamentary statute adopted in South Carolina).

American postindependence statutes: NORTHWEST ORDINANCE, §7 (1787) ("the governor shall appoint such magistrates and other civil officers in each county or township, as he shall find necessary"); LAWS OF THE STATE OF NEW YORK 107 (1788) (empowering justices to make rules "as to them shall appear necessary and proper") & *id.* at 183 (authorizing municipal officials to adopt a by-law "if they shall deem it necessary and proper").

Other documents: 1 WILLIAM NEWNAM, THE COMPLETE CONVEYANCER 154 (1786) (grant of annuity: "as shall be thought proper and necessary"); 3 WOOD, *op. cit.*, at 286 (grant of an annuity: "as shall be thought proper and necessary"); *MacKreth v. Fox* (H.L. 1791) 4 Bro. P.C. 258, 267, 2 Eng. Rep. 175, 181 (private trust deed: "as they or he should think necessary and proper").

92 *Cf.* GERARD MAYNES, CONSUETUDO, VEL, LEX MERCATORIA: OR, THE ANCIENT LAW-MERCHANT 80 (3rd ed., 1686):

> ... when Merchants by their Letters or Commissions use these or the like words, *Let all things be done as shall be thought most expedient or convenient*, that the said Commissions or Directions are to be left to the interpretation of the Arbitrators when any question ariseth. ..."

93 *See generally* Natelson, *supra* note 10 (summarizing fiduciary duties in the eighteenth century).

94 STOKES, *supra* note 79, at 163. For other eighteenth-century gubernatorial commissions, see 2 ROYAL INSTRUCTIONS TO BRITISH COLONIAL GOVERNORS 1670–1776, 816–35 (Leonard Woods Labaree, ed., 1935) [hereinafter ROYAL INSTRUCTIONS].

95 *E.g.*, 10 J. CONT. CONG. 55 (Jan. 15, 1778) (empowering the Board of War "to limit the prices to be given for the said wheat and flour, and to give such orders and directions to the commissioners as they shall think proper or necessary"); 18 *id.* at 1172 (adding to the diplomatic instructions of Francis Dana the following: "And, in general, you shall pursue all such measures as shall appear to you conducive to the interests of the United States.").

96 *Supra* page 69.

authority to do things that were "necessary or proper,"[97] "necessary or expedient,"[98] or "necessary or convenient."[99] Acts of Parliament conferring powers on agents frequently adopted Formula Three.[100] Depending on how liberal the adjectives employed were, a Formula Three clause might grant only incidental powers or somewhat more.

Formula Four required the power-holder to meet a single standard, which might be expressed in one word. This word might be "proper" or "expedient,"[101] but much more commonly was "necessary" or its synonym, "needful."[102] Thus, royal governors received power "to constitute and appoint Judges ... Commissioners ... Justices of the Peace and other *necessary* Officers."[103] The Articles of Confederation granted the Committee of the States authority "to appoint such other committees and civil officers as may be *necessary* for managing the general affairs of the United States."[104] The commission by which the Confederation Congress empowered George Washington to negotiate agreements for the exchange of prisoners empowered him "in general to do and perform

97 *E.g.*, An Act for Dividing and Inclosing Several Common Fields and Grounds within the Manor of Fillingham, in the County of Lincoln 4, *available at Eighteenth Century Collections Online* (Gale Cengage Learning) (1759) (granting commissioners necessary or proper powers).

98 Covert, *supra* note 76, at 157 (letter of attorney).

99 New Book, *supra* note 91, at 178 (trust document); *id.* at 92 (whatsoever ... shall be needful, necessary or convenient to be done).

100 *E.g.*, Charles Nalson Cole, A Collection of Laws 434 (1761) (reproducing a statute granting commissioners of works necessary or proper powers); An Act for Dividing and Inclosing Several Common Fields and Grounds within the Manor of Fillingham, in the County of Lincoln 4 (1759) (granting commissioners necessary or proper powers); An Act for Dividing and Inclosing the Open and Common Field, Common Meadows, Common Pastures, Common Grounds, and Commonable Lands, with the Hamlet and Liberties of Princethorp in the Township and Parish of Stretton upon Dunsmore, in the County of Warwick 20 (1762) (granting convenient or necessary powers). All these sources are available at *Eighteenth Century Collections Online* (Gale Cengage Learning).

101 The Compleat Clark [*sic*] and Scrivener's Guide 152 (1655) [hereinafter Compleat Clark] ("expedient").

102 2 Lilly, *supra* note 90, at 692 ("to do, execute and perform all and every other Act and Thing necessary") (language appeared in a deputation of bailiffship); 9 Covert, *supra* note 76, at 135 (to do and execute all and every Matter and Thing necessary to be done) (letter of attorney), 136 (and generally to do and perform all other Matters necessary) (letter of attorney), 3 Wood, *supra* note 91, at 224 ("necessary or needful" in a "Deputation or Appointment of a Steward and Receiver of Rents"); Compleat Clark, *supra* note 101, at 478 (letter of substitution conveying like power and authority to do all acts and things, to be needfull [*sic*] to be done).

103 Stokes, *supra* note 79, at 158.

104 Arts. Confed. art. IX.

every matter and thing which shall in any wise be *necessary* for the final and perfect accomplishment thereof."[105]

A common variation of Formula Four expressed a single standard with a pair of synonymous words or phrases,[106] attached either conjunctively or disjunctively. By far, the most frequent synonyms were "needful" and "necessary,"[107] although "requisite" sometimes appeared.[108] Giles Jacob's 1750 manual on conveyancing included a form with the words "to do, execute and accomplish all and whatsoever shall be *needful and necessary* to be done in or about the Premises."[109]

When a provision used the word "necessary" or "needful" – or, of course, "incidental"[110] – as the single standard, the provision communicated the grant of incidental powers, but no more or less.

One might reasonably ask why, if incidental powers tacitly accompanied a grant, a drafter would include a Formula Four clause. The answer was that not everyone reading a legal document would be knowledgeable about the law. As Coke explained, such language was to "declare and express to laymen which [*sic*] have no knowledge of the law, what the law requires in such cases."[111] This, even though *expressio eorum quae tacite insunt nihil operatur*[112] (the expression of those things that are

[105] 23 J. CONT. CONG. 581 (Sep. 16, 1782). The document also gave him the express power to appoint "such and so many commissioners as he shall judge necessary." *Id.* at 582.

[106] *E.g.*, 2 LILLY, *supra* note 90, at 696 ("all other Matters and Things that are most beneficial for the said B.F. *or* for his Profit and Advantage") (emphasis added) (the language appeared in a bond with an annexed letter of attorney).

[107] *E.g.*, 1 POCKET-BOOK, at *supra* note 91, at 190 ("needful and necessary"); VADE MECUM, *supra* note 91, at 46 (same); WOOD, *supra* note 91, at 429 (same); EDWARD COCKER, *The Young Clerk's Tutor Enlarged* 38 (12th ed. 1728)(necessary and needful); NEW BOOK, at *supra* note 91, 126 (needful or necessary).

[108] *E.g.*, 1 POCKET-BOOK, *supra* note 91, at 189 ("requisite and necessary") & 190 ("needful and requisite"); VADE MECUM, *supra* note 91, at 45 ("requisite and needful") & 55 (requisite and necessary); COVERT, *supra* note 76, at 152 ("requisite and necessary"); COMPLEAT CLARK, *supra* note 101, at 473 (same); NEW PRECEDENTS IN CONVEYANCING, *supra* note 90, at 319 ("requisite or necessary"); NEW BOOK, *supra* note 91, at 91 (needful or requisite); 1 LAWS OF THE STATE OF DELAWARE, 24 Geo. ii (1751) c.140 (1797) ("necessary and requisite").

[109] GILES JACOB, THE ACCOMPLISH'D CONVEYANCER 73 (2d ed., 1750) (emphasis added).

[110] 10 J.CONT. CONG. 222 (Mar. 4, 1778) ("other matters incidental thereto").

[111] Boroughe's Case (K.B. 1596) 4 Co. Rep. 72b, 73b, 76 Eng. Rep. 1043, 1044–45 (reporter's commentary) ("and yet, as Littleton saith, it is well done to put in such clauses to declare and express to laymen which have no knowledge of the law, what the law requires in such cases"). *See also* Shelley's Case (C.P. 1581) 1 Co. Rep. 93b, 104b, 76 Eng. Rep. 206, 235 (expressing similar sentiments).

[112] Boroughe's Case, 4 Co. Rep. at 72b, 76 Eng. Rep. at 1044 (reporter's commentary). *See, e.g.* Case of Mines (Exch. 1568) 1 Pl. Com. 310, 317, 75 Eng. Rep. 472, 483

silently inherent has no legal effect); still, *abundans cautela non nocet* – "overflowing caution does no harm."

The Constitution contains a Formula Four provision: The Enclave Clause, which empowers Congress to create federal enclaves, with state consent, "for the Erection of Forts, Magazines, Arsenals, dock-Yards, *and other needful Buildings*.[113]

Formula Five clauses required the agent to meet two separate standards, phrased conjunctively. Typical was the following language from an eighteenth-century letter-of-attorney form:

> ... and also to do, execute and perform all other Things whatsoever, which are *necessary and proper*, in and about the executing of these Presents, according to the Tenor and true Intention thereof.[114]

Also, orders from the House of Lords directing lower courts to take action routinely imposed "necessary and proper" standards.[115]

(stating that the King had incidental power to dig gold and silver ore he owned and the clause of licence is but matter of curtesy, and serves only to give notice to the possessor of the soil, and is not of necessity to be had); The King v. Mayor of Durham (K.B. 1757) 1 Keny. 512, 523, 96 Eng. Rep. 1074, 1078 (reporting counsel as agreeing that corporations have an incidental power of making by-laws and where a charter gives a general power, it is superfluous).

113 U.S. CONST. art. I, §8, cl. 17 (emphasis added). Arguably, the Property Clause also is in this category, *id.* art. IV, §3, cl. 2 ("The Congress shall have Power to dispose of and make all needful Rules and Regulations respecting the Territory or other Property belonging to the United States") because it is technically superfluous: Congress clearly has power to manage any property it retains under its enumerated powers.

114 1 NICHOLAS COVERT, THE SCRIVENER'S GUIDE 158 (1740) (2 vols.) (a later edition of COVERT) (language appearing in a letter of attorney). *See also* GILBERT HORSEMAN, PRECEDENTS IN CONVEYANCING 243 (1744) (letter of attorney stating "and for that Purpose for me, and in my Name, and as my Act and Deed to make, seal, deliver and execute any Lease ... as shall be necessary and proper in that Behalf"); JOB MILL, THE PRESENT PRACTICE OF CONVEYANCING 238 (1745) (bargain and sale deed empowering trustee, "as shall be needful, necessary and proper"); 2 NEWNAM, *supra* note 90, at 219 (letter of attorney empowering agent "to make ... any ... instruments ... as shall be necessary and proper").

115 *See e.g. John Earl of Buckingham v. Drury* (H.L. 1762) 3 Bro. P.C. 492, 505, 1 Eng. Rep. 1454, 1462 ("and that the said court do give all necessary and proper directions for carrying this judgment into execution"); *West v. Erisey* (H.L. 1727) 1 Bro. P.C. 225, 233, 1 Eng. Rep. 530, 536 ("[A]nd the Court of Exchequer was to give all necessary and proper directions for the making [of] this judgment effectual."); Pelham v. Gregory (H.L. 1760), 3 Bro. PC 204, 219, 1 Eng. Rep. 1271, 1280 ("And it was further ORDERED, that the said court should give all necessary and proper directions for carrying this judgment into execution."); Attorney-General v. Wall (H.L. 1760), 4 Bro. PC 665, 680, 2 Eng. Rep. 452, 461–62. ("ORDERED, that the said Court of Chancery should give all necessary and proper directions for carrying this judgment into execution").

The effect of this kind of "necessary and proper" (or "proper and necessary")[116] language was to inform the reader both of the grant of implied power and that its exercise should meet standards of propriety. However, not all Formula Five clauses used these two adjectives. While departures from the standard of necessity (or needfulness) were rare,[117] substitutes for proper were frequent. Colonial governors were given power to establish courts "with all *reasonable* and necessary powers ... belonging thereto."[118] They also could acquire "ordinance, ammunition, and all sorts of arms *fit* and necessary."[119] Another common replacement for "proper" was "expedient."[120]

As in Formula Four, the term "necessary" in Formula Five was explanatory and without independent force. Whether "proper" was also explanatory or served as an affirmative limitation on power would depend on the meaning of the word in its context.

3. The Meaning of "Proper" and Its Effect on Formulas Three, Four and Five

The meaning of "proper" seems not to have been defined in reported cases, so we can do no more than deduce it. As noted earlier, the word was a translation of *opportuna*, which usually meant *suitable* or *fit*. Its direct linguistic forebear was the Latin *proprius*,[121] related closely to property[122] (*proprietas*).[123] Variants of *proprius* had been used in Roman law to mean "unique to" or "peculiar to" – that is, not common with

But see Rous v. Barker (H.L. 1725) 4 Bro. PC 660, 665, 2 Eng. Rep. 449, 452 ("it was ORDERED and ADJUDGED, that the decree complained of should be reversed; and that the Court of Exchequer should award a commission, directed to such persons *as they should think proper*") (emphasis added).

116 *E.g.*, N.Y. LAWS, 1784 c. 1, art. IV (giving Clerk of the Masters and Wardens of the Port of New York various powers to collect tonnage duty and adding the power "to do and perform all other Acts, proper and necessary for securing and collecting the said duty").

117 For an exception, see COVERT, *supra* note 76, at 190 ("meet and expedient").

118 STOKES, *supra* note 79, at 157 (emphasis added).

119 *Id.* at 159 (emphasis added).

120 *E.g.*, 3 WOOD, *supra* note 91, at 426 ("expedient and necessary").

121 LEWIS & SHORT, *supra* note 77, at 1472 ("not common with others, one's own, special, particular, proper" – in opposition to *communis*).

122 Indeed, the neuter substantive, *proprium*, can mean property. *id.*, at 1472.

123 Educated people in the founding generation were grounded thoroughly in Latin and would have internalized these connections. *See generally* CARL J. RICHARD, THE FOUNDERS AND THE CLASSICS: GREECE, ROME, AND THE AMERICAN ENLIGHTENMENT (1994). On the Latinate English of the framers, see GARRY WILLS, INVENTING AMERICA: JEFFERSON'S DECLARATION OF INDEPENDENCE 93 (1979);

other things,[124] a meaning reflected in the English expression "proper name."[125]

By the eighteenth century, the English "proper" had become more flexible than the Latin *proprius*. Samuel Johnson's Dictionary contained ten entries for the word, four representing plausible meanings in the legal context.[126] These included two overlapping entries partaking of the original restrictive denotation,[127] one signifying "suitable"[128] and one stating "exact; accurate; just."[129]

As explained in the next chapter, the Committee of Detail that prepared the Necessary and Proper Clause at the Constitutional Convention deliberately added the word "proper" to an earlier draft of the Clause. So it was considered to serve a purpose separate from that of "necessary." At the least, one can say that an action by an agent that violated then-prevailing fiduciary norms would have been considered "improper." As noted above, those norms included remaining within the scope of authority (i.e., complying with the original sense of *proprius* or proper),[130] proceeding in good faith, maintaining undivided loyalty

FORREST MCDONALD, NOVUS ORDO SECLORUM: THE INTELLECTUAL ORIGINS OF THE CONSTITUTION xi (1985).

124 The Institutes of Justinian often used *proprius* in this way: *J. Inst.* 1.14.1 (*Sed et servus proprius testamento cum libertate recte tutor dari potest*). *See also id.* at I. 2.12. pr; I. 1.2.pr; I.2.1.27.

125 *Id.* at: I. 2.13.1 (stating that one can be disinherited "*non adiecto proprio nomine* – without using his proper name).

Cf. 1 THE RECORDS OF THE FEDERAL CONVENTION OF 1787, at 153 (Max Farrand, ed., rev. ed., 1937) [hereinafter FARRAND] (describing speech by John Dickinson: He compared the proposed national system to the solar system, in which the states were the planets, and ought to be left to move freely in their proper orbits); *id.* at 153–54 (quoting James Wilson: Within their proper orbits they must still be suffered to act for subordinate purposes).

126 The other six were:

2. Noting an individual. ...
4. Natural; original ...
7. Not figurative ...
8. It seems in *Shakespeare* to signify, mere; pure.
9. [*Propre*, Fr.] Elegant; pretty ...
10. Tall; lusty; handsome with bulk ...

SAMUEL JOHNSON, A DICTIONARY OF THE ENGLISH LANGUAGE (unpaginated) (1786).

127 *Id.* (1. Peculiar; not belonging to more; not common. ... 3. One's own. It is joined with any of the possessives: as, my proper, their proper).

128 *Id.* This is the fifth entry: 5. Fit; accommodated; adapted; suitable; qualified.

129 *Id.* (6. Exact; accurate; just).

130 *See* Gary Lawson & Patricia B. Granger, *The "Proper" Scope of Federal Power: A Jurisdictional Interpretation of the Sweeping Clause*, 43 DUKE L. J. 267 (1994).

to the principal, accounting to the principal, and proceeding with due care.

Thus, a Formula Four clause empowering the agent to act in a "proper" manner would signal that the agent was bound by fiduciary responsibilities. This would include the obligation to remain within the scope of express and incidental authority. A Formula Three clause granting "necessary *or* proper" authority might seem more liberal because it is more disjunctive in form, but it really was not more liberal. The word "necessary" signaled the grant only of powers truly incidental (included even when unmentioned), and the alternative word "proper" still bound an agent to fiduciary limits, including the limits of express and incidental authority. A Formula Five clause empowering an agent to act in a "necessary and proper" manner was more restrictive yet: It affirmed that the agent had incidental powers, but only to the extent exercised in conformance with the full panoply of fiduciary duties. Consider the following scenario:

> Peter, a principal, is in the shipping business. [Peter] directs his agent, Ascot, to manage the business and perform all other actions in that regard that are "necessary and proper." It is "necessary"[131] for Ascot to purchase insurance, so Ascot has incidental power to do so. There are three established (customary) insurance providers: Baker, Charley, and Dogg. But Baker is also a shipper, and is in fierce competition with Peter. Charley's proffered insurance contract is much less favorable to Peter than the others.[132] Under the incidental powers doctrine, agent Ascot could select any of these insurers. But because of Ascot's fiduciary duties of loyalty and care, only the selection of Dogg would be *proper.*

C. The Baillie Cases: An Illustration of the Eighteenth-Century Incidental Powers Doctrine

During the 1790s, litigation arose in England that illustrated the extent, and limitations, of the incidental powers doctrine. James Baillie died leaving a large estate, offset by large debts. His will named his wife, Colin, as executrix. The litigation gave rise to two reported cases in the Court of King's Bench, then headed by Chief Justice Lord Kenyon.[133]

[131] *See supra* notes 64–66 and accompanying text.

[132] Presumably the disparity had to be greater than in Moore v. Mourgue (K.B. 1776) 2 Cowp. 479, 98 Eng. Rep. 1197 (upholding the agent's selection of insurer).

[133] On Lord Kenyon, see Douglas Hay, *Kenyon, Lloyd, first Baron Kenyon (1732–1802), judge*, in THE OXFORD DICTIONARY OF NATIONAL BIOGRAPHY (2004–09).

The two cases were *Gardner v. Baillie*,[134] decided in 1795, and *Howard v. Baillie*,[135] decided the following year. The cases will be discussed together.

Mrs. Baillie gave a letter of attorney to two people, one of whom was her accountant, Edmund Thornton, so the two could assist her in administering her husband's estate. This letter of attorney was a lengthy, sprawling document that read much like a badly drafted eighteenth-century British statute. It contained a number of express-power discretion clauses and further-powers clauses drafted in different ways. One further-powers clause gave Thornton and his fellow agent authority to do whatever Mrs. Baillie could have done "if personally present" (a Formula One clause). Two others granted the agents authority to act as "shall be thought advisable and proper" and "shall seem meet" (Formula Two clauses). Still another empowered the agents to undertake actions "as shall be necessary or proper" (Formula Three).[136]

Acting under the letter of attorney, Thornton entered into agreements with creditors to obtain extensions of time for payment. In exchange for their forbearance, he accepted on Mrs. Baillie's behalf bills of exchange drawn by the creditors not just on her *as executrix*, but on her *personally*. Some creditors were not paid in a timely manner, and they sued Mrs. Baillie, as drawee under the bills, in the Court of Common Pleas and in King's Bench.

The letter of attorney had authorized Thornton to collect assets and pay estate debts. Mrs. Baillie argued that the portion of the letter devoted to debt-paying had not created authority extensive enough to permit Thornton to bind her personally. Given the broad scope of the letter, this argument seems specious at first glance. However, the portion of the letter directly and exclusively addressing payment of debts was drafted in Formula Three, which was more restrictive than the letter's Formula One and Formula Two provisions. It provided, "and also for me and in my name ... as executrix ... and agreeable to the due order and course of law, to pay ... debts ... payable by [James Baillie] ... which ... may become due and payable by me as executrix ... and to take such ... discharges ... *as shall be necessary or proper* ..."[137] Accordingly, in

[134] (K.B. 1795) 6 T.R. 591, 101 Eng. Rep. 720

[135] (K.B. 1796) 2 H. Bl. 618, 126 Eng. Rep. 737.

[136] The power is reproduced in *Howard* at 2 H. Bl. at 624–26, 126 Eng. Rep. at 740–42. It is not always clear which clauses are of the express-power discretion type and which of the further-powers type, but for purposes of these cases, it makes no difference.

[137] 2 H. Bl. at 26, 126 Eng. Rep. at 741 (emphasis added).

1795, King's Bench concluded that Thornton had exceeded his authority, and dismissed a creditor's claim. Following the lead of King's Bench, Common Pleas did the same in the cases before it.

The following year, another creditor's claim came before King's Bench, and this time Lord Kenyon issued a decision for the creditor. While the court conceded that the language of the letter of attorney was not broad enough *expressly* to authorize Thornton to commit Mrs. Baillie's assets, it found that Thornton had implied, incidental authority to do so.

The normal rule, Lord Kenyon observed, was that delegated powers were strictly construed. But the intent behind this letter of attorney was to give Thornton authority to handle the estate, and honoring that intent required that he be able to perform acts incidental to the task. Lord Kenyon conceded that "the words construed very strictly" might not include the actions Thorton had taken, but added, "I am of opinion that both the particular provisions and the general words ought to receive the most liberal construction, which construction should, as far as possible, place the attornies [*sic*] where the executrix intended to place them ..."[138] The court's conclusion that committing Mrs. Baillie's personal assets was within Thornton's authority was based on a blend of necessity (Thornton had to do it) and custom (Mrs. Baillie could have foreseen that he would). On the latter point, Lord Kenyon asserted that Mrs. Baillie could have expected that Thornton would seek extensions of time for payment and that creditors would ask for personal guarantees to protect them against possible waste of the estate during the delay. If asked at the time she entrusted the estate to Thornton and his associate (Lord Kenyon said), she certainly would not have hesitated in granting her agents the necessary power and discretion to handle the business.

It is not clear why King's Bench found for the creditor in 1796 after finding against another creditor the year before. Possibly the creditors' lawyers had failed to raise the implied authority argument in the earlier case. Or perhaps – as Henry Blackstone,[139] who reported the latter case, speculated – the court was influenced by evidence that Mrs. Baillie had known what Thornton was doing and had approved of it.

The *Baillie* cases are the clearest judicial statement of the incidental powers doctrine from around the time of the American founding. When read together, the two decisions support the view that incidental powers

[138] *Howard*, 2 H.Bl. at 620, 126 Eng. Rep. at 738.
[139] William Blackstone's nephew.

represented those nonexpress powers the parties presumptively intended to grant – of the kind the principal, if asked, would have approved in advance. Thus, incidental authority was that authority required to expand the scope defined by strict interpretation to that defined by intent-based (Chief Justice Marshall called it "fair"[140]) interpretation. The value of the cases is circumscribed by the fact that they were decided shortly *after* the Constitution was adopted, so their precise holdings could not have been within the contemplation of the ratifiers or a reasonable observer. On the other hand, their holding fit well with settled law[141] and, unlike many postratification expositions of constitutional meaning, was not the product of self-interested and unconstrained constitutional reinterpretation.[142]

[140] MARSHALL, DEFENSE *supra* note 66, at 92 & 167.

[141] Hill v. Grange (K.B. 1556) 1 Pl. Rep. 164, 168, 75 Eng. Rep. 253, 260 (reporting as argued and admitted that land is not incident to a messuage, because it is not intended to be granted with it).

[142] *See* Robert G. Natelson, *The Founders' Hermeneutic: The Real Original Understanding of Original Intent*, 68 OHIO ST. L.J. 1239, 1289–90 (2007) (discussing the risks in the use of postratification evidence).

5

The Framing and Adoption of the Necessary and Proper Clause

Robert G. Natelson

I. DRAFTING THE NECESSARY AND PROPER CLAUSE AT THE CONSTITUTIONAL CONVENTION

A. *Original Intent vs. Original Understanding vs. Original Meaning*

Under the founders' rules of interpretation, deducing the force of the Constitution requires that one read the text as it was understood by the ratifiers ("original understanding").[1] When a coherent original understanding is not recoverable – due to lack of evidence or contradictory evidence – the interpreter must seek the meaning of the document that a reasonably well-informed hypothetical ratifier would have ascribed to it ("original meaning" or "original public meaning"). The intent of the delegates at the drafting convention ("original intent") has no direct legal force, but often provides evidence of the understanding or meaning at the time of ratification.

In the case of the Necessary and Proper Clause, the convention record is particularly useful for deducing the understanding and meaning at the ratification because the delegates who, directly or indirectly, were most responsible for shaping the Clause all served as leading ratification figures as well. Those delegates were Charles Pinckney of South

[1] The founders' rules are discussed at length in Robert G. Natelson, *The Founders' Hermeneutic: The Real Original Understanding of Original Intent*, 68 OHIO ST. L.J. 1239 (2007). The following discussion follows those rules because the document was debated and ratified with the expectation that the document would be interpreted according to previously and well-established rules of construction.. Before that article appeared, most modern originalist scholars had committed themselves to giving primacy to original public meaning.

Carolina and John Dickinson of Delaware and the five members of the drafting committee: John Rutledge of South Carolina, Edmund Randolph of Virginia, James Wilson of Pennsylvania, Oliver Ellsworth of Connecticut, and Nathaniel Gorham of Massachusetts. All except Gorham later assumed major roles in representing the Constitution to the ratifying public, and all except Dickinson were delegates in their state ratifying conventions.

B. The Legal Knowledge of the Framers

Most, if not all, of the framers would have been at least somewhat familiar with legal uses of the phrase "necessary and proper" and its variants. As noted in the last chapter, legal knowledge was common among the general public during the founding era – and the convention delegates were a particularly learned group. All were men of affairs, public and private, and a clear majority were, or had been, practicing lawyers. Seven of the fifty-five, including Rutledge and Dickinson, had attended London's Inns of Court.[2]

The committee that drafted the Necessary and Proper Clause was particularly laden with legal talent. Only Gorham was not a lawyer, and he would have become familiar with legal terminology, if not from his mercantile activities, then from his extensive public service, including the presidency of Congress. Randolph[3] reputedly had enjoyed the busiest private practice in Virginia.[4] He had taken over Thomas Jefferson's clients, represented George Washington in his business affairs, and had served as attorney general of Virginia for ten years. As president, Washington would select Randolph to be the first attorney general of the United States.

After his stint at the Middle Temple, Rutledge[5] became one of the top practitioners in Charleston, and then served as state chancellor,

2 Charles Pinckney had been admitted to the Middle Temple by correspondence, but did not attend. The other five who did were John Blair, William Houston, Jared Ingersoll, William Livingston, and Charles Cotesworth Pinckney. *See generally* E. ALFRED JONES, AMERICAN MEMBERS OF THE INNS OF COURT (1924).

3 On Randolph, see JOHN J. REARDON, EDMUND RANDOLPH: A BIOGRAPHY 15 (1974).

4 "Enjoyed" is a bit of a stretch, because Randolph worked himself into a frazzle. *id.* at 70–78.

5 For Rutledge's career, see JAMES HAW, JOHN AND EDWARD RUTLEDGE OF SOUTH CAROLINA (1997). There is no reliable full-length biography devoted exclusively to John Rutledge.

governor, and the primary drafter of the South Carolina 1776 constitution. Washington would place him on the Supreme Court and unsuccessfully nominate him for chief justice. Wilson was a former law clerk of Dickinson, a leading Pennsylvania practitioner, and another future Supreme Court justice.[6] Ellsworth[7] had enjoyed an extremely large law practice[8] and had served on the Connecticut governor's council, which was also the state's highest court. At the time of the convention, he was a judge of the state superior court. He was destined to become the U.S. Supreme Court's third chief justice.

Not only had these men had extensive exposure to both private and public law, but like other members of their generation, they tended to think of government responsibilities in terms of agency and other fiduciary relationships.[9]

C. *The Constitutional Convention's Committee of Detail*

Under the Articles of Confederation, the states, acting as sovereign governments, had granted Congress only sharply circumscribed powers. The Articles specified that all powers not *expressly* granted were reserved to the states.[10] This provision precluded congressional exercise of incidental authority. Most of the delegates at the Philadelphia gathering were determined to change that.

In the early weeks of the federal convention, the delegates adopted resolutions contemplating a national government of expansive, largely undefined, capacity.[11] Only a minority spoke in favor of circumscribing

[6] *See* CHARLES PAGE SMITH, JAMES WILSON: FOUNDING FATHER 1742–1798 (1956).

[7] For Ellsworth, see WILLIAM GARROT BROWN, THE LIFE OF OLIVER ELLSWORTH (1905).

[8] *Id.* at 31. On Ellsworth's practice, see *id.* at 30–33.

[9] Robert G. Natelson, *The Constitution and the Public Trust*, 52 BUFF. L. REV. 1977 (2004).

[10] ART. CONFED. art. II ("Each state retains its sovereignty, freedom, and independence, and every power, jurisdiction, and right, which is not by this Confederation *expressly* delegated to the United States, in Congress assembled.") (emphasis added).

[11] *See, e.g.*, 1 THE RECORDS OF THE FEDERAL CONVENTION OF 1787, at 131–32 (Max Farrand, ed., rev. ed., 1937) (hereinafter FARRAND):

> Resolved that the Legislature of the United States ought to possess the legislative Rights vested in Congress by the Confederation; and moreover to legislate in all Cases for the general Interests of the Union, and also in those Cases to which the States are separately incompetent, or in which the Harmony of the United States may be interrupted by the Exercise of individual Legislation.

federal competence to a precise enumeration.[12] One of the minority was Pinckney, whose outline of a constitution listed specific powers and excluded incidental authority.[13] Another was Dickinson, who crafted an outline for a constitution[14] that enumerated congressional powers and added that "the Legislature of the United States ought to be authorized *to pass Acts for enforcing* an Observance of the Laws of Nations and an Obedience to their own Laws – for raising a Revenue by levying Duties ... for the Regulation of Trade and Commerce."[15]

On July 23, 1787, Elbridge Gerry of Massachusetts moved to establish a Committee of Detail to organize into a draft constitution the resolutions previously agreed to.[16] The convention approved his motion without dissent[17] and voted to set the number of committee members at five.[18] The following day, the convention elected the membership.[19] The convention later provided the committee with copies of its prior resolutions and a copy of the Pinckney Plan.[20] The Dickinson Plan has not been found among the committee records, but in view of Dickinson's interest in the subject, he likely had provided its members with a copy, which his prestige and legal reputation would have motivated them to read.[21]

[12] Robert G. Natelson, *The Constitutional Contributions of John Dickinson*, 108 PENN. STATE L. REV. 415, 472–73 (2003) (describing the progress of the convention from undefined to enumerated powers).

[13] Pinckney's wording was, "Each State retains its Rights not expressly delegated." 2 FARRAND, *supra* note 11, at 135. Later in life, Pinckney claimed authorship of a plan that contained something very similar to the Necessary and Proper Clause, but the latter plan was almost certainly a later invention. For that plan, the reconstructed original, and discussion, see Appendix D, *The Pinckney Plan*, in 3 *id.* at 595–609.

[14] The Dickinson Plan lay undiscovered until the 1980s. James H. Hutson, *John Dickinson at the Federal Constitutional Convention*, 40 WM. & MARY Q. 256, 262–69 (1983).

[15] SUPPLEMENT TO MAX FARRAND'S RECORDS OF THE FEDERAL CONVENTION OF 1787, at 89 (James H. Hutson, ed. 1987) [hereinafter HUTSON, SUPPLEMENT] (emphasis added); *see also id.* at 86.

[16] 2 FARRAND, *supra* note 11, at 86, 95.

[17] *Id.* at 95.

[18] *Id.* at 96.

[19] *Id.* at 97.

[20] *Id.* at 129–37.

[21] For Dickinson's influence at the convention and a discussion of his plan, see Natelson, *supra* note 12, at 449–76 (2003). It used to be thought that Dickinson was absent from the convention for over a month. We now know that this was not the case. *Id.* at 426 n.59.

The Committee of Detail decided to adopt the Pinckney-Dickinson approach of enumerating legislative powers rather than stating them broadly.[22] To Randolph and Ellworth, the process must have seemed familiar: In 1781, both had served on the three-man congressional committee that proposed an enumeration of additional powers for Congress.[23]

Randolph was selected to make an initial outline, and a draft in his handwriting is still extant. The draft contains a provision designed to address potential conflicts between state and federal spheres:

> All laws of a particular state, repugnant hereto, shall be void, and in the decision thereon, which shall be vested in the supreme judiciary, all incidents without which the general principles [*sic*] cannot be satisfied shall be considered, as involved in the general principle."[24]

The language was awkward, but its core meaning was clear: (a) within the federal sphere, inconsistent state laws would be invalid; (b) the determination on whether state laws infringed the federal sphere would be a question for the courts; and (c) in making their decisions, the courts were to be guided by the doctrine of principals and incidents. This provision was simultaneously a supremacy clause, a grant of jurisdiction, and an instruction to the judiciary.

Chancellor Rutledge then undertook a revision.[25] Rutledge replaced the original wording with the phrase: "and a right to make all Laws necessary to carry the foregoing Powers into Execu –."[26] (The committee later inserted a supremacy clause in another part of the document.)[27] The word "necessary" was, of course, shorthand for the incidental powers doctrine, an understanding Randolph confirmed explicitly in his Bank Opinion four years later.[28] The clause was now a Formula Four

[22] 2 FARRAND, *supra* note 11, at 142–44. There has been some scholarly discussion of the committee's motivation.

[23] 21 J. CONT. CONG. 894–96 (Aug. 22, 1781). The committee members are listed at *id.* at 896 n.1. James Varnum was the other member.

[24] 2 FARRAND, *supra* note 11, at 144.

[25] LORD CHANCELLOR. "Allow me, as an old Equity draftsman, to make a suggestion. The subtleties of the legal mind are equal to the emergency. The thing is really quite simple – the insertion of a single word will do it."
William S. Gilbert (of Gilbert & Sullivan), *Iolanthe*, Act II.

[26] *Id.* at 144.

[27] 2 FARRAND, *supra* note 11, at 169.

[28] *Opinion of Edmund Randolph, Attorney General of the United States, to President Washington, reprinted in* LEGISLATIVE AND DOCUMENTARY HISTORY OF THE BANK OF THE UNITED STATES 89 (M. St. Clair Clarke & D.A. Hall eds., Augustus M. Kelley photo. reprint 1967) (1832) [hereinafter BANK HISTORY].

provision – that is, it memorialized the incidental powers doctrine, but did no more.

The committee later added the phrase "and proper." This tightened the scope of the clause from Formula Four to Formula Five. The record does not tell us why the committee did this. Wilson had been dallying with a provision in the New Jersey Plan that would have granted Congress authority to raise revenue, "to be applied to such foederal [*sic*] Purposes as they shall deem proper and expedient."[29] It has been argued that a clause in the New Jersey Plan suggested the word "proper," and that the committee adopted the basic approach of that clause.[30] Actually, though, the New Jersey Plan had contemplated a subjective, Formula Two approach.[31] The Committee of Detail adopted a clause in Formula Four and then switched it to one in Formula Five.

The final committee draft, extant in Wilson's hand with emendations by Rutledge, was similar to the Necessary and Proper Clause in the finished Constitution: "And to make all laws that shall be necessary and proper for carrying into execution the foregoing powers, and all other powers vested, by this Constitution, in the government of the United States, or in any department or officer thereof."[32]

D. *"And Proper"*

The fact that the Committee of Detail separately added "and proper" to the incidental powers clause strongly suggests that the committee considered "proper" to be more than merely (as some have suggested) a repetition or boilerplate companion of "necessary." As noted earlier, the law of the time would have considered breaches of fiduciary duty to be "improper," and various comments made at the convention show that the framers also often thought of "proper" in a fiduciary sense. For example, in an important study, Professor Gary Lawson and Patricia B. Granger concluded that the founders frequently used the term "proper" to refer to the obligation of each governmental branch to respect its

29 2 FARRAND, *supra* note 11, at 157 (emphasis added).

30 JOSEPH M. LYNCH, NEGOTIATING THE CONSTITUTION: THE EARLIEST DEBATES OVER ORIGINAL INTENT 20 (1999).

31 It read, "such foederal [*sic*] Purposes as they shall deem proper and expedient." 2 FARRAND, *supra* note 11, at 157. Thus, it was discretionary and did not include the term of art, "necessary."

32 *Id.* at 182.

jurisdictional boundaries[33] – the fiduciary duty to remain within powers and follow instructions. And in fact, this usage appeared often in the convention debates.[34] Moreover, a fiduciary had a duty to keep his principal informed. Amid the convention discussion of whether to retain a clause requiring Congress to publish its proceedings, the following colloquy took place between two delegates who were members of the Committee of Detail:

> Mr. Elseworth [*sic*]. As the clause is objectionable in so many shapes, it may as well be struck out altogether. The Legislature will not fail to publish their proceedings from time to time – The <people> will call for it if it should be *improperly* omitted.
>
> Mr. Wilson thought the expunging of the clause would be very *improper*. The people have a right to know what their Agents are doing or have done. ...[35]

A fiduciary representing several principals had a duty of impartiality. At the convention, several delegates denounced as "improper" obstacles to the impartiality of government officials, particularly dependence of one branch of government on another.[36] Roger Sherman "regarded the Supreme Court as *improper* to try the President, because the Judges would be appointed by him."[37] James Madison asked, "What was to be done after *improper* Verdicts in State tribunals obtained under the biased directions of a dependent Judge, or the local prejudices of an undirected jury?"[38] John Dickinson, in a subsequent letter on the convention, argued that election of the president by the legislature might

[33] *See generally* Gary Lawson & Patricia B. Granger, *The "Proper" Scope of Federal Power: A Jurisdictional Interpretation of the Sweeping Clause*, 43 DUKE L. J. 267 (1994).

[34] *See, e.g.*, 1 FARRAND, *supra* note 11, at 65–66 (comments by James Wilson); *id.* at 139 ("There wd. in truth however be no improper mixture of these distinct powers in the present case."); *id.* at 140 ("He thought too a junction of the Judiciary to it, involved an improper mixture of powers.").

[35] 2 *id.*, at 260 (emphasis added).

[36] The founders' value of independence is explored in Robert G. Natelson, *A Reminder: The Constitutional Values of Sympathy and Independence*, 91 KY L. J. 353 (2003).

[37] 2 FARRAND, *supra* note 11, at 551 (emphasis added).

[38] *Id.* at 124 (emphasis added). *See also id.* at 44 ("improper dependence in the Judges"); 250 ("It was as improper as to allow them to fix their own wages, or their own privileges. It was a power also, which might be made subservient to the views of one faction agst. another."); & 551 ("The President under these circumstances was made improperly dependent.").

have resulted in "an improper Dependence and Connection."[39] Elbridge Gerry thought it "improper" for the vice-president to preside in the Senate because his necessary intimacy with the president could result in legislative dependence on the president.[40]

Agents had to avoid conflicts of interest. Hamilton thought it "highly improper" for the state legislatures to pay federal officials because of the potential rivalry between state and federal governments.[41] Similar conflict-of-interest concerns induced Pierce Butler of South Carolina to argue that new immigrants serving in the Senate would be "improper agent[s]" for the people.[42] George Mason argued that "the Senate did not represent the people, but the States in their political character. It was *improper* therefore that it should tax the people."[43]

On August 20, 1787, delegates offered amendments to the draft constitution produced by the Committee of Detail. Butler prepared a motion to remove "proper," but he never introduced it. One explanatory hypothesis is that Butler decided not to jeopardize what his state already had won at the convention.[44] More likely, however, is that someone pointed out to Butler that the effect of the word "proper" was to *confine* rather than expand the scope of congressional authority – and Butler was an advocate of limiting the federal government to enumerated powers.[45]

E. Approval by the Federal Convention

Also on August 20,

> Mr. Madison and Mr. Pinkney moved to insert between "laws" and "necessary" "and establish all offices" it [*sic*] appearing to them liable to cavil that the latter was not included in the former.

[39] HUTSON, SUPPLEMENT, *supra* note 15, at 301 (John Dickinson to George Logan, Jan. 16, 1802). *See also* 1 FARRAND, *supra* note 11, at 59 ("Mr. Mason was of [the] opinion that it would be highly improper to draw the Senate out of the first branch [because of difficulties filling vacancies and] besides which it would make the Members too dependent on the first branch.").

[40] 2 *id.* at 536–37.

[41] 1 *id.* at 378–79.

[42] *Id.* at 236.

[43] 2 *id.* at 273 (emphasis added).

[44] LYNCH, *supra* note 30, at 20.

[45] *See* 1 FARRAND, *supra* note 11, at 53 (speech by Butler), *id.* at 168 (opposing congressional veto of state laws), 2 *id.* at 17 (discussing comments by Butler, which questioned the grant of power to Congress "to legislate in all cases to which the separate States are incompetent").

> Mr. Govr. Morris, Mr. Wilson, Mr Rutlidge and Mr. Elseworth [all members of the Committee of Detail] urged that the amendment could not be necessary.

The Madison-Pinckney motion was defeated by a vote of nine states to two. The convention then approved the Necessary and Proper Clause unanimously.[46] Thus, as the convention neared its end, most delegates were satisfied that the Clause was sufficient to accomplish its purposes.

Three delegates disagreed. On September 10, just a week before adjournment, Randolph announced that he would not sign the Constitution. Although his Virginia Plan had contemplated a consolidated government and he had helped draft the Necessary and Proper Clause, he apparently had undergone a conversion of some kind. One of his many "objections to the System" was the "general clause concerning necessary and proper laws."[47]

Randolph continued to recognize the Necessary and Proper Clause as an expression of the incidental power doctrine. But he seems to have avoided signing the Constitution for two reasons. One was to protect himself politically in his home state, where his foe, arch-Antifederalist Patrick Henry, was lying in wait. His other goal was more statesmanlike: He sought to force the friends of the Constitution to agree to amendments that would assure that the incidental powers doctrine was not pushed too far. In his letter a month later to the speaker of the Virginia House of Delegates,[48] Randolph made the latter point explicit:

> [I]t is better to amend, while we have the constitution in our power ... In drawing a line between the powers of congress and individual States; and in defining the former, so as to leave no clashing of jurisdictions nor dangerous disputes; and to prevent the one from being swallowed up by the other, under cover of general words, and implication.[49]

The two other convention dissenters were George Mason of Virginia and Elbridge Gerry of Massachusetts. Among Mason's objections was the claim that the Necessary and Proper Clause was a subjective Formula Two provision.[50] Mason's confusion on that point may have been understandable. He was not a lawyer, and his introduction to grants of official

46 1 *id.* at 345.

47 *Id.* at 563.

48 *Letter from Edmund Randolph to the Speaker of the Virginia House of Delegates* (Oct. 10, 1787), in 3 FARRAND, *supra* note 11, at 123–27.

49 *Id.* at 127.

50 *See Mason's Objections to the Constitution of Government Formed by the Convention*, *reprinted in* 13 THE DOCUMENTARY HISTORY OF THE RATIFICATION OF

powers may have come during his service in the House of Burgesses when that body was struggling against royal governors operating under commissions that contained a fair amount of discretionary language.[51] Gerry interposed a number of objections, but added that he "could however ... get over all these, if the rights of the Citizens were not rendered insecure ... by the general power of the Legislature to make what laws they may please to call necessary and proper."[52] Like Mason, Gerry was a nonlawyer who had begun his legislative service in conflict with royal governors.

On the other hand, the dissents of Randolph, Mason, and Gerry should not obscure the fact that there were thirty-nine other delegates present, and none raised objections to the Necessary and Proper Clause.

F. *Some Observations from the Federal Convention Records*

Except for the dissents of Mason and Gerry, the convention records strongly corroborate the view of the Necessary and Proper Clause that one could deduce from contemporaneous legal usage of similar provisions: The word "necessary" was inserted into the proposed Constitution to communicate that Congress would enjoy incidental powers. The separate insertion of the word "proper" strongly suggests it had a meaning separate from necessary, and almost certainly a restrictive one. Pierce Butler's consideration of a motion to delete "proper" also suggests the word had independent meaning to him as well, and his decision to abandon his motion fits well with his known states-rights views.

Finally, the manner in which the delegates employed the word "proper" strongly suggested that federal laws, even if "necessary," would not be proper if they violated Congress's fiduciary responsibilities.

THE CONSTITUTION 350 (John P. Kaminski & Gaspare J. Saladino eds., 1981) [hereinafter DOCUMENTARY HISTORY] ("the Congress may grant monopolies in trade and commerce, constitute new crimes, inflict unusual and severe punishments, and extend their powers ... as far as *they shall think proper*").

[51] To be precise, however, the "Formula Two"-type discretionary language in royal commissions usually defined the scope of express powers rather than general clauses added to previous enumerations. Terms reciting the latter usually, although not always, used the objective language of Formulas Four and Five. *See generally* ANTHONY STOKES, A VIEW OF THE CONSTITUTION OF THE BRITISH COLONIES, 150–64 (1783) (reproducing the form of a royal commission). *But see* ROYAL INSTRUCTIONS TO BRITISH COLONIAL GOVERNORS 1670–1776, at 629 (Leonard Woods Labaree ed., 1935) (a nonstandard form with the words "or such others as you shall think most proper").

[52] 2 FARRAND, *supra* note 11, at 632–33.

II. THE RATIFICATION AND BEYOND

Ultimately, the meaning of the Constitution was the understanding of the ratifiers.[53] This section examines the ratification debates, and the Bill of Rights that emerged from those debates, to determine whether that understanding was the same as or differed from the meaning deduced thus far from contemporaneous legal sources and the proceedings at the Federal Convention.

A. *The Antifederalist Attack*

Once the Constitution became public, Antifederalists made the Necessary and Proper Clause a highly contentious issue. Comments such as the foregoing by Patrick Henry, their leading spokesman at the Virginia ratifying convention, show that they feared the prospect of a central government with implied powers. For many, these fears were aggravated by acceptance of the Gerry-Mason view that the Clause gave Congress unreviewable discretion as to what measures were "necessary and proper."

As elaborated during the weeks following the national convention, the principal Antifederalist case consisted of five points:

> First: The Constitution will grant Congress the power to provide for the common defense and general welfare, if not by the Preamble,[54] then by the Taxation Clause,[55]
> Second: The Necessary and Proper Clause will grant Congress power to pass all laws that Congress shall deem necessary and proper for the common defense and general welfare,[56]
> Third: here will be no effective judicial review of such laws,[57]

[53] *Supra* Part I-A.

[54] *Letter from Massachusetts Gentleman to his Friend*, N.Y.J., Nov. 23, 1787, *reprinted in* 19 The Documentary History of the Ratification of the Constitution, at 293–94 (John P. Kaminski, Gaspare J. Saladino, Richard Leffler & Charles H. Schoenleber eds., 2003) ("A Customer").

[55] U.S. Const. art. I, § 8, cl. 1 ("The Congress shall have Power To lay and collect Taxes, Duties, Imposts and Excises, to pay the Debts and provide for the common Defence and general Welfare of the United States; but all Duties, Imposts and Excises shall be uniform throughout the United States.").

[56] *See, e.g.*, 2 Farrand, *supra* note 11, at 640 (comments by Mason); *An Old Whig II*, Philadelphia Indep. Gazetteer, Oct. 17, 1787, *reprinted in* 13 Documentary History, *supra* note 50, at 402.

[57] *An Old Whig II*, Philadelphia Indep. Gazetteer, Oct. 17, 1787, *reprinted in* 13 Documentary History, at 402 ("Who shall judge for the legislature what is necessary and proper? Who shall set themselves above the sovereign?"). The lack of judicial review was implied in many other Antifederalist treatments of the Necessary

Fourth: As a result, Congress will be able to legislate at its discretion;[58] and

Fifth: Congress will then be able to emasculate or abolish the state legislatures,[59] abolish state taxes,[60] destroy state governments,[61] render itself perpetual or hereditary,[62] impose a draft,[63] abolish the rights of the people,[64] create a king,[65] and do other nefarious things.[66]

and Proper Clause. *See, e.g.*, *A Federal Republican, A Review of the Constitution Proposed by the Late Convention Held at Philadelphia* (Nov. 28, 1787), *reprinted in* 14 The Documentary History of the Ratification of the Constitution, 269–70 (John P. Kaminski & Gaspare J. Saladino eds., 1983).

58 *See, e.g.*, *Brutus V*, N. Y. J., Dec. 13, 1787, *reprinted in* 14 Documentary History, *supra* note 57, at 423 ("This amounts to a power to make laws at discretion: No terms can be found more indefinite than these, and it is obvious, that the legislature alone must judge what laws are proper and necessary for the purpose.").

59 *Brutus I*, N.Y. J., Oct. 18, 1787, *reprinted in* 13 Documentary History, *supra* note 50, at 416.

60 *An Old Whig VI*, Philadelphia Indep. Gazetteer, Nov. 24, 1787, *reprinted in* 14 Documentary History, *supra* note 57, at 216–17; *The Address and Reasons of Dissent of the Minority of the Convention of the State of Pennsylvania to Their Constituents*, Pennsylvania Packet, Dec. 18, 1787, *reprinted in* 15 The Documentary History of the Ratification of the Constitution, 22 (John P. Kaminski & Gaspare J. Saladino eds., 1984); *A Farmer*, Philadelphia Freeman's J., Apr. 16, 23, 1788, *reprinted in* 17 The Documentary History of the Ratification of the Constitution, 142 (John P. Kaminski & Gaspare J. Saladino eds., 1995); 2 The Debate in the Several State Conventions on the Adoption of the Federal Constitution, 339 (Jonathan Elliot, 2nd ed., 1891) [hereinafter Elliot's Debates] (John Williams, at the New York ratifying convention).

61 *George Lee Turberville to James Madison* (Dec. 11, 1787), *reprinted in* 14 Documentary History, *supra* note 57, at 407.

62 *A Customer*, N. Y. J., Nov. 23, 1787, *reprinted in* 19 Documentary History, *supra* note 54, at 296.

63 *Brutus VIII*, N. Y. J., Jan. 10, 1788, *reprinted in* 15 The Documentary History of the Ratification of the Constitution, 336 (John P. Kaminski & Gaspare J. Saladino eds., 1984).

64 3 Elliot's Debates, *supra* note 60, at 218 (James Monroe, at the Virginia ratifying convention, fearing abolition of trial by jury and freedom of the press); *id.* at 442 (George Mason, making the same argument at the same convention).

65 *Id.* at 455 (John Tyler, at the Virginia ratifying convention).

66 *See* George Mason, *Objections to the Constitution of Government Formed by the Convention*, *reprinted in* 13 Documentary History, *supra* note 50, at 348–51 (claiming federal judiciary would destroy state judiciaries, among other things); 3 Elliot's Debates, at *supra* note 60, 56 (Patrick Henry, fearing suspension of state laws); *Agrippa X*, Mass. Gazette (Jan. 1, 1788), *reprinted in* 5 The Documentary History of the Ratification of the Constitution, 576 (John P. Kaminski & Gaspare J. Saladino eds., 1998) (predicting that the federal government could seize control of all civil cases); *Brutus V*, N. Y. J., Dec. 13, 1787, *reprinted in* 14 Documentary History, *supra* note 57, at 424–25 (claiming that the Taxation Clause and Necessary and Proper Clause could result in taxes on cider and just about everything else); *Brutus VI*, N. Y. J., Dec. 27, 1787, *reprinted in* 15 Documentary

To hammer it all home, Antifederalists labeled the Necessary and Proper Clause the "Sweeping Clause"[67] – or sometimes the "Omnipotent Clause."[68]

There were a few variations on these themes. Some Antifederalists suggested that the drafters did not intend such unlimited power, but that had chosen language that invited abuse.[69] Patrick Henry advanced the novel contention that a plenary interpretation of congressional powers "was warranted ... by the addition of the word department, at the end of the clause, and that they could make any laws which they might think necessary to execute the powers of any department or officer of the government."[70] But for the most part, Antifederalists merely repeated the themes listed above.

Of course, one considering the document in legal context can see that, other than the discretion imported by the word "necessary," the Antifederalist position had little basis. A preamble granted no power; it was an expression of purpose only.[71] The "general Welfare" language of the taxation clause was not a grant, but only a qualification of the immediately preceding grant.[72] And while the incidental powers doctrine granted considerable discretion, that discretion certainly was not unreviewable.

HISTORY, *supra* note 63, at 113–14 (explaining Mason's objections); Robert Whitehill, *Address at the Pennsylvania Convention* (Nov. 30, 1787), *reprinted in* 2 THE DOCUMENTARY HISTORY OF THE RATIFICATION OF THE CONSTITUTION, 426 & 428 (Merrill Jensen ed., 1976) (suggesting that Congress could abolish the states' role in federal elections).

[67] 3 ELLIOT'S DEBATES, *supra* note 60, at 150 (Patrick Henry, at the Virginia ratifying convention).

[68] *The Federal Republican VI*, MASS. CENTINEL, Feb. 2, 1788, *reprinted in* 5 DOCUMENTARY HISTORY, *supra* note 66, at 846.

[69] *Brutus I*, N. Y. J., Oct. 18, 1787, *reprinted in* 13 DOCUMENTARY HISTORY, *supra* note 50, at 416 ("It is not meant, by stating this case, to insinuate that the Constitution would warrant a law of this kind!") & *Brutus XII*, N. Y. J., Feb. 14, 1787, *reprinted in* 16 THE DOCUMENTARY HISTORY OF THE RATIFICATION OF THE CONSTITUTION, 120 (John P. Kaminski & Gaspare J. Saladino eds., 1986) (responding to Alexander Hamilton's *Federalist* No. 31).

[70] 3 ELLIOT'S DEBATES, *supra* note 60, at 439 (speaking at the Virginia ratifying convention).

[71] 4 MATTHEW BACON, A NEW ABRIDGMENT OF THE LAW, 645 (5th ed., 1786).

[72] Robert G. Natelson, *The General Welfare Clause and the Public Trust: An Essay in Original Understanding*, 52 U. KAN. L. REV. 1 (2003). Antifederalists sometimes obliquely conceded this. *See, e.g.*, *Brutus I*, N. Y. J., Oct. 18, 1787, *reprinted in* 13 DOCUMENTARY HISTORY, *supra* note 50, at 414 (conceding it only as to form, not substance).

B. *The Federalist Defense*

It took several months for friends of the Constitution to react to the Antifederalist assault on the Necessary and Proper Clause. There was little by way of rejoinder before November 26, 1787, when William Cranch wrote to John Quincy Adams that if Congress had not been given authority to make laws necessary and proper to execute the other powers, "the powers would be of no service."[73] When the Federalists finally responded, they did so by presenting their version of what the Necessary and Proper Clause meant. Their case included nontechnical expositions of the incidental powers doctrine, as limited by agents' fiduciary duties. Federalists also enumerated certain exclusive state powers to illustrate the limits of implication, and they eventually agreed to a Bill of Rights, including the Ninth and Tenth Amendments, to define those limits further. Because the ratifiers ultimately relied on Federalist representations of meaning, those representations are powerful indicators of original understanding.

The following discussion is divided into four portions. The first tells the story of how the Constitution's advocates presented the Clause in general. The second focuses on the presentation of "proper." The third discusses their specific representations as to matters that would be outside the scope of federal power, and addresses briefly the effect of the Bill of Rights. The fourth addresses a recent claim that the Clause, at least as limited by the Tenth Amendment, prohibited Congress from adopting laws not *expressly* authorized by a strict construction of enumerated powers.

1. Federalist Representations of the General Meaning of the Clause

The first major clash over the Necessary and Proper Clause occurred at the Pennsylvania ratifying convention, held from November 20 through December 15, 1787. There, leading Federalists secured approval of the Constitution by pointing out that statutes authorized by the Clause could serve only the powers expressly enumerated. James Wilson argued:

> The gentleman in opposition strongly insists that the general clause at the end of the eighth section gives to Congress a power of legislating generally; but I cannot conceive by what means he will render the words susceptible of that expansion. Can the [Clause] be capable of giving them

[73] *William Cranch to John Quincy Adams*, Nov. 26, 1787, *reprinted in* 14 Documentary History, *supra* note 57, at 224, 226.

> general legislative power? ... On the contrary, I trust it is meant that they shall have the power of carrying into effect the laws which they shall make under the powers vested in them by this Constitution.[74]

On another occasion, Wilson added that the Necessary and Proper Clause does not "in any degree, go beyond the particular enumeration.... It is saying no more than that the powers we have already particularly given, shall be effectually carried into execution."[75] His ally Thomas McKean echoed the point.[76]

Moreover, Wilson emphasized that congressional discretion was subject to judicial review:

> If a law should be made inconsistent with those powers vested by this instrument in Congress, the judges, as a consequence of their independence, and the particular powers of government being defined, will declare such law to be null and void; for the power of the Constitution predominates.[77]

On January 2, 1787, an anonymous Massachusetts essayist ("A.B."), responding to the influential Antifederalist essays of "Brutus,"[78] wrote that the powers pursuant to which Congress must act were confined to "objects particularly stated and clearly defined by the [C]onstitution."[79] To underscore his point, "A.B." enumerated powers that the federal government would *not* have – that would remain in the states.[80] These included "jurisdiction over murther [*sic*], adultery, theft, robbery, burglary, lying, perjury, defamation," as well as land titles and possession of men's "houses, wives, children and many other objects."[81]

Pennsylvania ultimately ratified the Constitution, becoming the second state to do so, after Delaware. New Jersey and Georgia followed in quick succession. Both of their conventions were unanimous. With the Connecticut convention about to meet, Oliver Ellsworth wrote a series of articles under the name of "A Landholder." In his essay published on December 3, 1787, he strongly implied that the Necessary and

[74] 2 ELLIOT'S DEBATES, *supra* note 60, at 448–49.
[75] *Id.* at 468.
[76] *Id.* at 537.
[77] *Id.* at 489.
[78] On the disputed authorship of the "Brutus" essays, see 13 DOCUMENTARY HISTORY, *supra* note 50, at 411 (editor's note) (listing possible authors of the "Brutus" essays).
[79] *A.B.*, HAMPSHIRE GAZETTE, Jan. 2, 1788, *reprinted in* 5 DOCUMENTARY HISTORY, *supra* note 57, at 596–97.
[80] *Id.* at 599.
[81] *Id.*

Proper Clause was merely a rule of construction – a guard against those who might misrepresent the Constitution to destroy the central authority: "[Congress]," he wrote, "must have authority to enact any laws for executing their own powers or those powers will be evaded by the artful and unjust, and the dishonest trader will defraud the public of its revenue."[82]

On December 18, in *Federalist* No. 23, Alexander Hamilton addressed how the Clause tied laws to specific enumerated powers:

> If the circumstances of our country are such as to demand ... a confederate instead of a sole, government, the essential point which will remain to be adjusted will be to discriminate the OBJECTS ... which shall appertain to the different provinces or departments of power; allowing to each the most ample authority for fulfilling the objects committed to its charge. Shall the Union be constituted the guardian of the common safety? Are fleets and armies and revenues necessary to this purpose? The government of the Union must be empowered to pass all laws, and to make all regulations which have relation to them. The same must be the case in respect to commerce, and to every other matter to which its jurisdiction is permitted to extend.[83]

Ellsworth's Connecticut ratified in January 1788, but by that time, the writings of "Brutus" were beginning to affect debate in other states. On January 3, Hamilton published *Federalist* No. 33 in response. Hamilton rendered explicit what Ellsworth had implied: The Necessary and Proper Clause gave Congress no power. It was a rule of construction. Hamilton's defense also suggests that the word "and" was conjunctive rather than disjunctive – that a law must be necessary AND proper:

> [The Necessary and Proper Clause and Supremacy Clauses] are only declaratory of a truth which would have resulted by necessary and unavoidable implication from the very act of constituting a federal government, and vesting it with certain specified powers.
>
> What is a power, but the ability or faculty of doing a thing? What is the ability to do a thing, but the power of employing the *means* necessary to its execution?[84] What is a LEGISLATIVE power, but a power of making

[82] 14 DOCUMENTARY HISTORY, *supra* note 57, at 338 (Dec. 3, 1787).

[83] ALEXANDER HAMILTON, JAMES MADISON & JOHN JAY, THE FEDERALIST NO. 23, at 114 (George W. Carey & James McClellan eds., 2001) (Alexander Hamilton) [hereinafter THE FEDERALIST].

[84] This means-end argument sometimes was expressed by the maxim: "*Qui dat finem, dat media ad finem necessaria*" [who gives the end, gives the means necessary for the

> LAWS? What are the *means* to execute a LEGISLATIVE power but LAWS? ... What are the proper means of executing such a power, but *necessary* and *proper* laws?
>
> ... If there is any thing exceptionable, it must be sought for in the specific powers upon which this general declaration is predicated. The declaration itself, though it may be chargeable with tautology or redundancy, is at least perfectly harmless.
>
> But SUSPICION may ask, Why then was it introduced? The answer is, that it could only have been done for greater caution,[85] and to guard against all cavilling refinements in those who might hereafter feel a disposition to curtail and evade the legitimate authorities of the Union. The Convention probably foresaw ... that the danger which most threatens our political welfare is that the State governments will finally sap the foundations of the Union; and might therefore think it necessary, in so cardinal a point, to leave nothing to construction. ...[86]

On January 25, 1788, Madison added another *Federalist* essay in which he affirmed that the Clause gave no additional authority to Congress, and further explained the consequences that might have ensued if it had been omitted:

> Had the [C]onstitution been silent on this head, there can be no doubt that all the particular powers requisite as means of executing the general powers would have resulted to the government, by unavoidable implication. No axiom is more clearly established in law, or in reason, than that wherever the end is required, the means are authorized; wherever a general power to do a thing is given, every particular power necessary for doing it is included. Had this last method, therefore, been pursued by the

end]. *See, e.g.*, the sarcastic reference in Timoleon, N. Y. J., Nov. 1, 1787, *reprinted in* 13 DOCUMENTARY HISTORY, *supra* note 50, at 534, 535 ("Timoleon"). The maxim appears in Algernon Sidney, DISCOURSES CONCERNING GOVERNMENT 529 (Thomas G. West ed., 1996), but I have been unable to locate prior judicial use of it. Sidney cited Grotius for it, but Grotius said something very different, for he was speaking of the duty of a parent to support a child:

> *Quia dat formam, dat quae ad formam sunt necessaria, dictum est Aristotelis: quare qui causa est ut homo existat, is quantum in se est, et quantum necesse est, prospicere ei debet de his quae ad vitam humanam, id est naturalem ac socialem, nam ad eam natus est homo, sunt necessaria.*

Hugonis Grotii, DE JURE BELLI ET PACIS 356 (1853) (1625).

85 This is an oblique reference to the legal maxim, *Abundans cautela non nocet*. It literally means "Overflowing caution doesn't hurt," but can be translated more melodiously as "An abundance of caution does no harm."

86 THE FEDERALIST NO. 33, *supra* note 83, at 158–59 (Alexander Hamilton).

> convention [i.e., leaving out the Clause] ... the real inconveniency would be incurred of not removing a pretext which may be seized on critical occasions for drawing into question the essential powers of the union.[87]

As Wilson had done, Madison then affirmed that congressional usurpation could be curbed by judicial review.[88]

On January 31, 1788, Alexander Contee Hanson, a member of Congress from Maryland writing under the name "Aristides," published a pamphlet that surveyed the Constitution from a Federalist point of view. Hanson wrote of the Clause, "I take the construction of these words to be precisely the same, as if the clause had ... said, 'No act of Congress shall be valid, unless it have relation to the foregoing powers, and be necessary and proper for carrying them into execution.'"[89] Hanson then reinforced the argument of Wilson and Madison that federal laws would be subject to judicial review.[90] On the other hand, Hanson was one of the very few Federalists who did not think the Clause was surplusage: "Without this general clause, it were easy to suppose cases, wherein a particular clause might be incompetent to its own purpose."[91] However, he offered no examples. Hanson concluded by offering, as "A.B." had previously, an enumeration of subjects that would remain in state control and beyond federal interference.[92]

On February 6, the Massachusetts convention became the sixth to ratify, doing so narrowly and demanding amendments.[93] The first of these was "[t]hat ... all powers not expressly delegated by the aforesaid Constitution are reserved to the several states, to be by them exercised."[94]

87 THE FEDERALIST NO. 44, *supra* note 83, at 234–35.

88 *Id.* at 235.

89 Alexander Contee Hanson as "Aristides," *Remarks on the Proposed Plan of a Federal Government* (Jan. 31, 1788), *reprinted in* 15 DOCUMENTARY HISTORY, *supra* note 60, at 531. Hanson's work apparently was well received. Letter from Contee Hanson to Tench Coxe (Mar. 27, 1788), *reprinted in* 5 DOCUMENTARY HISTORY, *supra* note 66, at 520–21 (referring to the "avidity, with which I am informed my humble essay has been bought up.").

90 *Id.* at 531.

91 *Id.* at 532.

92 *Id.* at 545 ("[T]he regulations of property, the regulations of the penal law, the protection of the weak, the promotion of useful arts").

93 The vote was 187–168. 13 DOCUMENTARY HISTORY, *supra* note 50, at xli. Federalist delegate Dr. Charles Jarvis of Boston justified ratification with amendments by reference to the incidental agency powers doctrine. 2 ELLIOT'S DEBATES, *supra* note 60, at 151 ("It is a maxim, I believe, universally admitted, that, in every instance, the manner in which every power is to be exerted, must be in its nature discretionary with that body to which this power is delegated.").

94 2 *id.* at 177.

Edmund Randolph, who, as we have seen, also sought amendments, was not happy with the Massachusetts language, characterizing it as "among the rocks on which the old confederation has split"[95] – because its reservation of authority not "expressly" granted would eliminate Congress's incidental authority. Massachusetts' ratification came before that state's chief justice, Caleb Cushing, was able to deliver a speech asserting that the Necessary and Proper Clause was "no more than was necessarily implied in the powers themselves. For if [Congress] could not make laws that were necessary and proper to carry [t]hem into [execution], the powers themselves would be totally dead & Useless."[96] Although an undelivered speech could not have been persuasive, it offers further insight into the representations that all Federalists (with the partial exception of Hanson) were advancing.

After the Bay State convention, Federalists found progress harder. The New Hampshire convention adjourned without having ratified,[97] and Rhode Island voters rejected the Constitution in a referendum.[98] On March 12, with North Carolina about to elect its delegates,[99] one of that state's leading citizens, James Iredell (a future Supreme Court justice, then writing as "Marcus") addressed the subject of the Necessary and Proper Clause:

> These [enumerated] powers would be useless, except acts of Legislation could be exercised upon them ... If Congress, under pretence of exercising the power delegated to them, should, in fact, by the exercise of any other power, usurp upon the rights of the different Legislatures, or of any private citizens, the people will be exactly in the same situation as if there had been an express provision against such power in particular, and yet they had presumed to exercise it. It would be an act of tyranny....[100]

Iredell confronted the Antifederalist argument that the new government might seize control of the criminal law. On the contrary, he responded, "Congress can exercise no other power of this kind, except in the enacting of penalties to enforce their actions of Legislation in the

[95] Reardon, *supra* note 3, at 132.

[96] William Cushing, *Undelivered speech*, Feb. 4, 1788, *reprinted in* 6 The Documentary History of the Ratification of the Constitution, 143 (John P. Kaminski & Gaspare J. Saladino eds., 2000).

[97] 13 Documentary History, *supra* note 50, at xli–ii.

[98] The vote was overwhelming: 2,711 to 239. 13 *id.* at xli.

[99] The election was held March 28 and 29. 13 *id.* at xli.

[100] *Marcus IV*, Norfolk and Portsmouth J., Mar. 12, 1788, *reprinted in* 16 Documentary History, *supra* note 69, at 379–80.

cases where express authority is delegated to them, and if they could not enforce such acts by the enacting of penalties, those powers would be altogether useless ..."[101] Iredell thereby reinforced two points the Federalists already had made repeatedly: (1) Congress could not legislate for any purpose other than those enumerated, and (2) the Necessary and Proper Clause added no substantive authority, because Congress's enumerated powers already carried incidental powers with them. At the North Carolina ratifying convention, one of the two delegates named MacLaine (whether Archibald or William is not clear) reinforced them further.[102]

Iredell made a potent contribution to that convention. One of his strategies was to show the link between the Constitution's enumeration of powers and a private power of attorney:

> [The Constitution] is a declaration of particular powers by the people to their representatives, for particular purposes. It may be considered as a great power of attorney, under which no power can be exercised but what is expressly [*sic*] given."[103]

But despite the efforts of Iredell, MacLaine, and other Federalists, the North Carolina convention adjourned without having ratified.[104]

In April, Maryland became the seventh state to ratify.[105] In May, South Carolina became the eighth (although it offered amendments).[106] Nine states were needed for the Constitution to be effective, and with opposition so strong in North Carolina, New Hampshire, and Rhode Island, it looked like the fate of the Constitution would be decided in New York and Virginia. The contest in both states was extremely close.[107] It was in Virginia that the climactic battle was fought.[108]

[101] *Id.* at 381.

[102] 4 ELLIOT'S DEBATES, *supra* note 60, at 141.

[103] *Id.* at 148. *See also id.* at 166 (repeating same argument); *Conciliator*, INDEPENDENT GAZETTEER, Jan. 15, 1788, *reprinted in* 2 DOCUMENTARY HISTORY, *supra* note 66, at microfilm supp. 1485–95 (analogizing the Constitution's grant of powers to grant of powers to a ship captain and discussing the inherent limits in such a grant and the uselessness of itemizing specific limitations).

[104] 13 DOCUMENTARY HISTORY, *supra* note 50, at xlii (reported by the editor).

[105] *Id.* at xli (ratification by 63–11 margin as reported by the editor).

[106] *Id.* at xlii (ratification by 149–73 as reported by the editor).

[107] Both states ultimately ratified: New York by a margin of 30–27 and Virginia by 89–79. Both states proposed amendments. *Id.* (reported by the editor).

[108] In New York, the convention defeated a motion by John Lansing "[t]at no power shall be exercised by Congress, but such as is expressly given by this Constitution; and all others, not expressly given, shall be reserved to the respective states, to be by them exercised." 2 ELLIOT'S DEBATES, *supra* note 60, at 406.

On February 28, 1788, the *Gazette* of Petersburg, Virginia, published an essay by "An Impartial Citizen." The author attacked George Mason's broad construction of the Necessary and Proper Clause with an explicit statement of the incidental powers doctrine:

> Now, I insist that Mr. Mason's construction on this clause is absolutely puerile, and by no means warranted by the words, which are chosen with peculiar propriety. When a power is vested anywhere, from the nature of things it must be understood to be attended by such other incidental powers as are necessary to give it efficacy; for to say, that a power is given, without the power of enforcing it, is a solecism in language.[109]

On April 2, another Federalist ("A Native of Virginia") wrote to affirm that the Clause granted no powers beyond those enumerated, but was needed only to ensure that the federal laws were not "nugatory."[110] A week later, still another Virginia Federalist ("Cassius") further emphasized that the Clause merely gave Congress capacity to effectuate its express powers.[111]

The Virginia convention met on June 2.[112] It soon erupted into oratorical fireworks. Patrick Henry's assaults on the Constitution were heavily punctuated with barrages against the Necessary and Proper Clause. Again and again, Henry slammed home the Antifederalist line: that, working in tandem with the Preamble and General Welfare Clause, the Necessary and Proper Clause would give Congress unfettered power to erect an absolute tyranny in America!

Henry was an orator equal to any four men. Fortunately for the Constitution, he faced – without eloquent assistance on his own side – not four, but five highly talented opponents.[113] They were Edmund

[109] *An Impartial Citizen V*, PETERSBURG VA. GAZETTE, Feb. 28 1788, *reprinted in* 8 THE DOCUMENTARY HISTORY OF THE RATIFICATION OF THE CONSTITUTION, 431 (John P. Kaminski & Gaspare J. Saladino eds., 1988).

[110] "A Native of Virginia," *Observations upon the proposed plan of Federal Government with an attempt to answer some of the principal objections that have been made to it*, VA. GAZETTE, April 2, 1788, *reprinted in* 9 THE DOCUMENTARY HISTORY OF THE RATIFICATION OF THE CONSTITUTION, 675 (John P. Kaminski & Gaspare J. Saladino eds., 1990).

[111] *Cassius II, To Richard Henry Lee, Esq.*, VA. INDEP. CHRON., Apr. 9, 1788, *reprinted in* 9 DOCUMENTARY HISTORY, *supra* note 110, at 714 ("Congress can make no laws, except such, as are, essentially, necessary to carry into execution the particular powers, given to them by the constitution").

[112] 13 DOCUMENTARY HISTORY, *supra* note 50, at xlii (reported by the editor).

[113] For a contemporary reaction to Henry's brilliant battle against very talented Federalists, see William Nelson, Jr. to William Short, July 12, 1788, *reprinted in* 10 THE DOCUMENTARY HISTORY OF THE RATIFICATION OF THE CONSTITUTION, 1701–02 (John P. Kaminski & Gaspare J. Saladino eds., 1993).

Pendleton, George Nicholas, James Madison, John Marshall[114] – and Governor Edmund Randolph.[115] For Randolph was aligned once again with the friends of the Constitution. To be sure, he continued to express doubts and assert his wish for amendments.[116] Nonetheless, he argued that when all was said and done, the Constitution had to be ratified. On June 10, he opened his defense of the Necessary and Proper Clause with the standard Federalist position:

> This formidable clause does not in the least increase the powers of Congress. It is only inserted for greater caution, and to prevent the possibility of encroaching upon the powers of Congress. No sophistry will be permitted to be used to explain away any of those powers; nor can they possibly assume any other power, but what is contained in the Constitution, without absolute usurpation.[117]

Randolph's argument fit well with a comment on a related topic the previous day by pro-Constitution delegate Henry Lee of Westmoreland County: "[I]f a man delegated certain powers to an agent, it would be an insult upon common sense to suppose that the agent could legally transact any business for his principal which was not contained in the commission whereby the powers were delegated."[118]

Later on June 10, George Nicholas – lawyer, former state legislator, former colonel in the Continental Army,[119] and Randolph's brother-in-law[120] – rose to speak:

[114] Marshall did not address the Necessary and Proper Clause directly, but gave a lengthy speech in which he stressed the role of government officials as the people's agents. 3 ELLIOT'S DEBATES, *supra* note 60, at 225, 227 & 233.

[115] Pendleton was of the former generation, REARDON, *supra* note 3, at 31, but the others were all tightly knit. George Nicholas was the brother of Randolph's wife. *Id.* at 125. Madison and Randolph had a long-time political alliance, *id.* at 43 and passim, and Madison was the godfather to Randolph's third child. *Id.* at 75. When Randolph left law practice to become governor, he handed over his clients to Marshall. *Id.* at 88. Nicholas and his brother, Wilson Cary Nicholas (also a delegate at the Virginia convention), had worked closely with Madison before, notably in obtaining passage of the Virginia Statute for Religious Freedom.

[116] 3 ELLIOT'S DEBATES, *supra* note 60, at 25 ("As with me the only question has ever been between previous and subsequent amendments").

[117] *Id.* 206. To be sure, Randolph had alluded earlier to the issue of delegated powers. *Id.* at 70–71.

[118] *Id.* at 186. Lee was arguing that a bill of rights was unnecessary because the powers delegated to the federal government did not extend to suppressing citizen rights.

[119] Brief biographical facts are at http://www.anb.org.weblib.lib.umt.edu:8080/articles/02/02-00246.html?a=1&g=m&n=Nicholas%2C%20George&ia=-at&ib=-bib&d=10&ss=0&q=1.

[120] REARDON, *supra* note 3, at 125.

> The gentleman [Henry] has adverted to what he calls the sweeping clause, & c., and represents it as replete with great dangers. ... The committee will perceive that the Constitution had enumerated all the powers which the general government should have, but did not say how they were to be exercised. It therefore, in this clause, tells how they shall be exercised. Does this give any new power? I say not. ... This clause only enables them to carry into execution the powers given to them, but gives them no additional power.[121]

Then it was Madison's turn. In response to a renewed offensive from Henry, Madison, who had earlier in the convention made clear his own adherence to the agency theory of government,[122] now resorted to the doctrine of incidental powers:

> [W]hat new terrors can arise from this particular clause? It is only a superfluity. If that latitude of construction which he [Henry] contends for were to take place with respect to the sweeping clause, there would be room for those horrors. But it gives no supplementary power. It only enables them to execute the delegated powers. If the delegation of their powers be safe, no possible inconvenience can arise from this clause. It is at most but explanatory. For when any power is given, its delegation necessarily involves authority to make laws to execute it.[123]

Reinforcing Madison was the Old Dominion's most respected lawyer, Chancellor Edmund Pendleton, another devotee of the agency theory of government:[124]

> I understand that clause as not going a single step beyond the delegated powers. What can it act upon? Some power given by this Constitution. If they should be about to pass a law in consequence of this clause, they must pursue some of the delegated powers, but can by no means depart from them, or arrogate any new powers; for the plain language of the clause is, to give them power to pass laws in order to give effect to the delegated powers.[125]

In the words of the reporter, "Mr. GEORGE NICHOLAS, in reply to the gentlemen opposed to the clause under debate, went over the same grounds, and developed the same principles, which Mr. Pendleton and

[121] 3 ELLIOT'S DEBATES, *supra* note 60, at 245–46 (emphasis in original).
[122] *Id.* at 306 ("The members of the one government, as well as of the other, are the agents of, and subordinate to, the people").
[123] *Id.* 438 (emphasis added).
[124] *Id.* at 298 & 550.
[125] *Id.* at 441.

Mr. Madison had done."[126] Nicholas then examined the remedies for congressional usurpation: "[W]ho is to determine the extent of such powers? I say, the same power which, in all well-regulated communities, determines the extent of legislative powers. If they exceed these powers, the judiciary will declare it void, or else the people will have a right to declare it void."[127]

Meanwhile, when Antifederalists argued that the new federal government might use the treaty power to make land cessions that damaged the Southern states, Randolph responded with the standard Whig doctrine that such a breach of the trust duty of impartiality would be *ultra vires*. "There is a prohibition naturally resulting from the nature of things, it being contradictory and repugnant to reason, and the law of nature and nations, to yield the most valuable right of a community, for the exclusive benefit of one particular part of it."[128]

I have reproduced these quotations (and could have produced much more) to demonstrate the clarity with which the Federalists asserted that the Necessary and Proper Clause had no substantive effect, but was merely a recital of the incidental powers doctrine. It is true that near the end of the convention, Governor Randolph could not resist muddying the issue with one of his characteristic turns. While still supporting the Constitution, he now told the convention that perhaps both sides had erred:

> [T]he construction which had been put on this clause by the advocates of the Constitution was too narrow, and that the construction put upon it by the other party was extravagant ... The former contend that it gives no supplementary power, but only enables them to make laws to execute the delegated powers – or, in other words, that it only involves the powers incidental to those expressly delegated. By incidental powers they mean those which are necessary for the principal thing. ...[But a] constitution differs from a law; for a law only embraces one thing, but a constitution embraces a number of things, and is to have a more liberal construction. ... On this principle, what should be said of the clause under consideration? ... If incidental powers be those only which are necessary for the principal thing, the clause would be superfluous.[129]

[126] *Id.* at 442.

[127] *Id.* at 443.

[128] *Id.* at 362. *See also id.* at 504–05 (Randolph and Madison) & 501 (Madison, pointing out that not even the king of England could dismember the empire by treaty).

[129] *Id.* at 463–64.

After digressing to other subjects, Randolph returned to the Clause later in his speech:

> My objection is, that the clause is ambiguous, and that that ambiguity may injure the states. My fear is, that it will, by gradual accessions, gather to a dangerous length.[130]

As far as I have been able to determine, Randolph was the only Federalist who ever argued that the "sweeping clause" was ambiguous. But Randolph was playing a deep game. He seems to have had several goals in mind: (1) to ensure that Virginia ratified, (2) to ensure that she proposed amendments, including one declaring that ungranted powers would remain with the states, (3) to ensure that this "reservation" amendment preserved the federal government's incidental authority – i.e., that it did not limit the central government to powers "expressly" granted, and (4) to preserve his own popularity.

It worked. Governor Randolph achieved all four.[131]

2. The Federalist Representations as to the Meaning of "Proper"

The view that legislation, to be "proper," should comply with fiduciary obligations[132] receives some support from the ratification record. In Number 33 of *The Federalist*, Hamilton implied that a law that exceeded the federal government's jurisdiction would be improper and added that "the propriety of a law, in a constitutional light, must always be determined by the nature of the powers upon which it is founded."[133] Given that the "nature" of governmental powers was thought to be fiduciary, the standard of "propriety" had to be defined by fiduciary rules.

The "Impartial Citizen," another Federalist, wrote:

> In this case, the laws which Congress can make ... must not only be necessary, but proper – So that if those powers cannot be executed without

130 *Id.* at 470.

131 Virginia ratified on June 25, 1788, by a margin of 89–79. 13 DOCUMENTARY HISTORY, *supra* note 50, at xlii (reported by editor). She proposed twenty amendments, but the Virginia predecessor of the Tenth Amendment, unlike the Massachusetts version, reserved powers not granted, rather than powers not "expressly" granted. 3 ELLIOT'S DEBATES, *supra* note 60, at 659.

132 *Supra* Part I-D. See also the previous chapter.

133 THE FEDERALIST NO. 33, 5 DOCUMENTARY HISTORY, *supra* note 83, at 160 (Alexander Hamilton). Thus, the determination is not based primarily on questions of, for example, social convenience, but on the kind of powers granted (here, agency powers).

> the aid of a law, granting commercial monopolies, inflicting unusual punishments, creating new crimes, or commanding any unconstitutional act; yet, as such a law would be manifestly not proper, it would not be warranted by this clause, without absolutely departing from the usual acceptation of words.[134]

All of the items on the Impartial Citizen's list of improper laws were violations of fiduciary duty. A government granting a commercial monopoly bestowed a favor on one group to the exclusion of others, which was widely considered a breach of the duty of impartiality.[135] Inflicting unusual punishments breached both the duty of impartiality and the duty of loyalty, for an agent must not oppress his principals. Laws creating new crimes or commanding unconstitutional acts violated the agent's obligation to remain within the scope of authority.

Requiring laws to accord with fiduciary duty also was consistent with Federalist representations that the Necessary and Proper Clause was without substantive force. It was standard Whig theory that any measure by which a government violated its fiduciary obligations was inherently void.[136] So just as the word "necessary" merely informed the reader of incidental powers that Congress would have enjoyed even without the Clause, the word "proper" reminded the reader of limitations that would have existed without it.

3. Federalist Enumerations and Agreement to Amendments

During the ratification process, the line between laws "proper" or "improper" was sharpened by specific Federalist representations as to what powers would be reserved exclusively to the states. In the first six months of 1788, many promoters of the Constitution – especially prominent lawyers – issued representations of this kind. The authors of short lists included Hamilton, Madison, Wilson, Pendleton, Iredell, John Marshall,

[134] *An Impartial Citizen V*, PETERSBURG VA. GAZETTE, Feb. 28 1788, *reprinted in* 8 THE DOCUMENTARY HISTORY OF THE RATIFICATION OF THE CONSTITUTION, 431 (John P. Kaminski & Gaspare J. Saladino eds., 1988).

[135] Natelson, *supra* note 9, at 1157–58.

[136] *See, e.g.*, RICHARD PRICE, OBSERVATIONS ON THE NATURE OF CIVIL LIBERTY, THE PRINCIPLES OF GOVERNMENT, AND THE JUSTICE AND POLICY OF THE WAR WITH AMERICA 15 (5th ed., 1776), *available at* http://www.constitution.org/price/price_3.htm; ("[P]arliaments) possess no power beyond the limits of the trust for the execution of which they were formed. If they contradict this trust, they betray their constituents and dissolve themselves."). John Dickinson expressed similar sentiments, Natelson, *supra* note 12, at 437. So did James Madison in his *Memorial and Remonstrance against Religious Assessments* (1785), and so did many others.

and several anonymous essayists.[137] More elaborate and complete lists came from the pens of other Federalist writers, anonymous[138] and otherwise. A pseudonymous Federalist ("A.B.") began the process[139] and Alexander Contee Hanson ("Aristides")[140] continued it. Other enumerators included Nathaniel Peaslee Sargeant, a justice (and, shortly thereafter, chief justice) of the Massachusetts Supreme Judicial Court;[141] Alexander White, a distinguished Virginia lawyer;[142] and businessman Tench Coxe.[143] All of these enumerations were remarkably consistent, with much overlap but relatively little dispute among Federalist writers about which powers were reserved to the states.[144] In capsule form, the Federalist representations were that, outside the capital district, national authority would not include training the militia or appointing militia officers, nor control over local government, real property, personal property outside of commerce, domestic or family affairs, crimes *malum in se* (except treason, piracy, and counterfeiting), state court systems, the law of torts or contracts (except in suits between citizens of different states), religion, education, services for the poor and unfortunate, agriculture, or other business enterprises.[145] This list reassured the wavering public that incidental powers would not be construed too broadly, and that the Constitution sanctioned only laws that were truly "proper" to congressional agents' sphere of authority.

[137] For detailed citations and who said what, see Robert G. Natelson, *The Enumerated Powers of States*, 3 Nev. L.J. 469, 476–88 (2003).

[138] A.B., Hampshire Gazette, Jan. 2, 1788, *reprinted in* 5 Documentary History, *supra* note 66, at 599; Anonymous, Mass. Gazette, Jan. 8, 1788, *reprinted in* 5 Documentary History, *supra* note 66, at 651–52. Both clearly were intended to be relied on. The former was in specific response to the claims of the Antifederalist essayist "Brutus" that the Constitution imposed insufficient limits on the federal government. The latter was reprinted in two other papers. In the Massachusetts Centinel, the piece was published under the headline, "READ THIS! READ THIS!" Anonymous, Mass. Gazette, Jan. 8, 1788, *reprinted in* 5 Documentary History, *supra* note 66, at 652.

[139] A.B., Hampshire Gazette, Jan. 2, 1788, *reprinted in* 5 Documentary History, *supra* note 66, at 599.

[140] "Aristides," *Remarks on the proposed plan of a Federal Government* (1788), *reprinted in* 1 Founders' Constitution 462 (Philip B. Kurland & Ralph eds., 1987).

[141] Nathaniel Peaslee Sargeant to Joseph Badger, 1788, *reprinted in* 8 Documentary History, *supra* note 134, at 568.

[142] The relevant (first) portion of White's essay (with explanatory annotations) is found at Alexander White, *Essay*, Va. Gazette, Feb. 22, 1788, *reprinted in* 8 Documentary History, *supra* note 134, at 401–08.

[143] Tench Coxe, *A Freeman III*, Pa. Gazette, Feb. 6, 1788, *reprinted in* 5 Documentary History, *supra* note 66, at 49.

[144] Natelson, *supra* note 137.

[145] *Id.* at 481–88. In addition, see *Roger Sherman to Unknown Recipient*, Dec. 8, 1787, in Hutson, Supplement, *supra* note 15, at 288 (stating that state courts will have

In the end, seven of the thirteen states (representing a clear majority of the American people) proposed amendments when ratifying.[146] The outgrowth of these proposals was the Bill of Rights. The Ninth and Tenth Amendments[147] preserved the incidental agency doctrine, but assured that it would not be applied with too much latitude. When the First Congress met in 1789 and James Madison introduced his proposed amendments, much of his case centered on the need to limit the scope of implication under the Necessary and Proper Clause.[148]

4. Was the Necessary and Proper Clause Limited to Means Within Expressly Enumerated Powers?

A distinguished commentator, Professor Kurt T. Lash,[149] has argued that Federalist representations during the ratification debates, coupled with the Tenth Amendment,[150] created an understanding that the Necessary

exclusive jurisdiction over "all causes between citizens of the same State, except where they claim lands under grants of different states").

146 Amendments were proposed by Massachusetts, South Carolina, New Hampshire, Virginia, New York, North Carolina, and Rhode Island. 13 DOCUMENTARY HISTORY, *supra* note 50, at xli – xlii.

An extant letter from Madison to Hamilton offers a glimpse into the bartering process. James Madison to Alexander Hamilton, Jun. 22, 1788, *reprinted in* 10 DOCUMENTARY HISTORY, *supra* note 113, at 1665 (discussing the plan of the Federalists to concede recommendatory amendments so as to secure ratification in Virginia).

147 U.S. CONST. amend. IX ("The enumeration in the Constitution, of certain rights, shall not be construed to deny or disparage others retained by the people."); *id.*, amend. X ("The powers not delegated to the United States by the Constitution, nor prohibited by it to the States, are reserved to the States respectively, or to the people.").

148 2 ANNALS CONG., at 455–56 (stating that Congress may, in absence of a bill of rights, abuse the Necessary and Proper Clause by adopting measures neither necessary nor proper). James Monroe (the future president) had made a similar argument. James Monroe, *Some Observations on the Constitution* (May 25, 1788), *reprinted in* 9 DOCUMENTARY HISTORY, *supra* note 110, at 859. To prevent Congress from concluding that abolishing the right of trial by jury, freedom of conscience, or freedom of the press was within its implied powers, Monroe favored enumerating those rights. *Id.*

The version of the *Annals* employed in this chapter is that of Gales & Seaton (1834), reproduced on the Library of Congress's *American Memory* Web site, http://memory.loc.gov/ammem/amlaw/lwac.html.

149 Kurt T. Lash, *The Original Meaning of an Omission: The Tenth Amendment, Popular Sovereignty, and 'Expressly' Delegated Power*, 83 NOTRE DAME L. REV. 1889 (2008). Professor Lash cites what is apparently a different edition of the *Annals of Congress* than that employed here, with different pagination. It is available at the subscription Web site, Hein Online.

150 U.S. CONST. amend X ("The powers not delegated to the United States by the Constitution, nor prohibited by it to the States, are reserved to the States respectively, or to the people.").

and Proper Clause authorized only laws within Congress's express powers. Professor Lash acknowledges that the Clause as produced by the federal convention had a wider scope, but maintains that the ratification process and the Tenth Amendment narrowed that scope. He contends that the Tenth Amendment should be read as if it reserved to the states and people all powers not "expressly" delegated. He cites comments by several Federalists who represented (or were transcribed as representing) that the new government would be limited to powers expressly granted,[151] and notes the common law rule that delegated powers were to be strictly construed.

Yet Professor Lash does not claim the Necessary and Proper Clause is merely an express-power discretion clause.[152] He explains that several of those who assured the ratifying public that the Constitution conferred only express powers conceded that it granted implied powers as well. However, these were only implied powers "necessarily incident to the express grant of authority"[153] or that "could be clearly comprehended within *any* accurate definition of the general power."[154]

Some of the ratification-era sources Professor Lash collects were previously neglected in the scholarly literature. They tend to confirm how restricted federal powers were represented to be. However, the view that a document conveying only express powers also conveys implied powers does not accord with the usual understanding of "express." Perhaps the speakers were using the word in accordance with the alternative eighteenth-century meaning of "clear" or "apparent."[155] Perhaps they were

[151] *E.g.*, 2 ELLIOT'S DEBATES, *supra* note 60, at 259 (quoting Charles Pinckney in the South Carolina legislature). *See also id.* at 286 & 315 (quoting Charles Cotesworth Pinckney in the same venue; 4 *id.* at 140–41 (quoting Archibald MacLaine at the North Carolina ratifying convention), 142 (quoting Samuel Johnston at the same convention), & 148–49 (quoting James Iredell at the same convention) & 2 *id.* at 362 (quoting Alexander Hamilton at the New York ratifying convention). Hamilton's statement is arguably ambiguous, since he was speaking of "federal" governments in general and the new government was considered only partly federal. THE FEDERALIST NO. 39, *supra* note 83, at 199.

[152] *See* the previous chapter for the distinction between express-power discretion clauses and further-powers clauses.

[153] *Lash*, *supra* note 149, at 1895.

[154] 1 ANNALS OF CONGRESS 790 (Aug. 18, 1789) (comments of Rep. Thomas Tudor Tucker of South Carolina) (emphasis added). Tucker, a physician, had been neither a framer nor a ratifier, and apparently had opposed the Constitution.

[155] *E.g.*, NATHAN BAILEY, A UNIVERSAL ETYMOLOGICAL ENGLISH DICTIONARY (unpaginated) (1783) (including "clear," "plain," and "manifest" as definitions of "express"); THOMAS SHERIDAN, A COMPLETE DICTIONARY OF THE ENGLISH LANGUAGE (unpaginated) (1789).

treating the Necessary and Proper Clause as an express power rather than as recital. In any event, the scope of the implied powers they admitted to be in the Constitution – "necessarily incident" and "comprehended within any accurate definition" (including, presumably, an intent-based definition) – was identical to the scope of the common-law incidental powers doctrine under the Necessary and Proper Clause.

The ratifying conventions of Massachusetts, South Carolina, and New Hampshire recommended federalism amendments limiting the new government to powers expressly delegated.[156] But most state conventions considering such amendments rejected them. Pennsylvania and Maryland refused to recommend those amendments (or any others).[157] Virginia offered a proto-Tenth Amendment, but omitted "expressly" because Federalists explained that it would re-create the limits that had plagued the Articles of Confederation.[158] Although James Iredell had told the North Carolina convention that the new government would enjoy only express powers, the amendments he presented did not include "expressly"[159] – nor did the federalism amendment North Carolina finally proposed.[160] The New York convention rejected Melancton Smith's motion for an amendment limiting Congress to powers "expressly given,"[161] adopting instead the phrase "clearly delegated."[162] Thus, New York accepted the view that the federal government would have implied powers: The convention rejected a word (expressly) that could

[156] *E.g.* 2 ELLIOT'S DEBATES *supra* note 60, at 177 (reproducing the amendment suggested by Massachusetts: "That it be explicitly declared, that all powers not expressly delegated by the aforesaid Constitution are reserved to the several states, to be by them exercised.").

[157] *Id.* at 547–56; *see particularly id.* at 555. Lash *supra* note 149, at 1917 erroneously states that Maryland proposed an "expressly" amendment.

[158] *E.g.*, 3 ELLIOT'S DEBATES *supra* note 60, at 442 (quoting George Mason, arguing for such a provision at the Virginia ratifying convention). However Virginia's proposed amendment did not include the word. *Id.* at 659 ("That each state in the Union shall respectively retain every power, jurisdiction, and right, which is not by this Constitution delegated to the Congress of the United States, or to the departments of the federal government."). Randolph lamented the predicament of the Confederation Congress – holding express authority over war and peace, but without incidental power to issue passports. *Id.* at 28–29. Later, Randolph suggested language that, he said, would limit Congress to express delegations, 3 *id.* at 576, but his suggestion was not adopted.

[159] 4 *id.* at 248–49.

[160] *Ratification of the Constitution by the State of North Carolina; November 21, 1789, available at* http://avalon.law.yale.edu/18th_century/ratnc.asp.

[161] 2 ELLIOT'S DEBATES *supra* note 60, at 406.

[162] *Ratification of the Constitution by the State of New York; July 26, 1788, available at* http://avalon.law.yale.edu/18th_century/ratny.asp.

be interpreted to exclude implied powers and substituted its alternative meaning – "clearly." The Rhode Island convention recommended the same formula as New York.[163]

In drafting the Tenth Amendment, the First Congress elected to follow the majority of states. In floor comments, Representatives James Madison and Roger Sherman (both of whom had been framers and ratifiers) pointed out the difficulties with limiting the federal government to express powers. Sherman specifically pointed to the law of incidental powers, citing, perhaps from Blackstone, the incidents of corporations.[164]

As for the common-law maxim that delegations of power were strictly construed, the doctrine of incidental authority seems to have qualified it greatly. Nor was there a consensus that powers were construed strictly if conveyed by the people, as later suggested by St. George Tucker.[165] In fact, founders such as Edmund Randolph and James Madison argued that constitutions should be construed liberally.[166]

III. CONFIRMATION IN THE DEBATES OVER THE FIRST BANK OF THE UNITED STATES

The first great debate over the Necessary and Proper Clause after ratification of the Constitution occurred in 1791. The subject was the

[163] *Ratification of the Constitution by the State of Rhode Island; May 29, 1790, available at* http://avalon.law.yale.edu/18th_century/ratri.asp.

[164] 1 ANNALS OF CONGRESS 790 (Aug. 18, 1789). The version of the Annals employed in this chapter is that of Gales & Seaton (1834), reproduced on the Library of Congress's *American Memory* Web site, http://memory.loc.gov/ammem/amlaw/lwac.html. The edition by Professor Lash, although by the same editors and indicating the same date, employs different pagination. It is available at the subscription Web site, Hein Online.
The passage in Blackstone is at 1 WILLIAM BLACKSTONE, COMMENTARIES ON THE LAWS OF ENGLAND 463–63 (1765–69).

[165] Tucker cited Vattel's *Law of Nations* for the proposition that derogations of sovereignty must be strictly construed, EMER DE VATTEL, THE LAW OF NATIONS 86, 436 & 439–40 (Bela Kapossy & Richard Whatmore eds., 2008) (1758), then applied that proposition to state-federal relations. ST. GEORGE TUCKER, A VIEW OF THE CONSTITUTION OF THE UNITED STATES 345–46 (Clyde N. Wilson ed., 1999) (1803); *cf.* Lash *supra* note 149, at 1908–09 & 1941–42. However, postratification evidence such as this (*compare id.* at 1926–50) is of limited value in reconstructing the original understanding. Natelson, *supra* note 1, at 1289–90; *infra* note 293 and accompanying text. The addition to the Tenth Amendment of the phrase "or to the people," also mentioned by Professor Lash as an indication of a commitment to popular sovereignty, acknowledged that states differed as to which powers the people had granted to state government or retained.

[166] 3 ELLIOT'S DEBATES, *supra* note 60, at 463 ("A constitution differs from a law; for a law only embraces one thing, but a constitution embraces a number of things, and is

constitutionality of the federal government granting a corporate charter to a Bank of the United States.

As a rule, statements made and events occurring in Congress in 1791 are not strongly probative of original understanding or original meaning. By that time, the Constitution had been in effect for two years. All thirteen states had ratified the Constitution; the Bill of Rights had been sent by Congress to the states and was very near approval; and the political alignments that had characterized the ratification and the first session of the First Congress had changed radically.[167] No additional states had joined Virginia and New York in applying for a new federal convention. The Constitution was pretty much a *fait accompli*, and politicians could make claims of constitutional meaning without much chance of them affecting the viability of the union. Furthermore, "legislators have very different incentives and operate under very different institutional restraints than do constitutional drafters or ratifiers."[168]

In this debate, however, most of the disputants on both sides agreed on the principles underlying the Clause, so their agreement tends to confirm the evidence from before and during the ratification era. The differences between the disputants were primarily on how to apply those principles in a close case.

The ultimate decision to authorize a bank charter sometimes is cited as one of those momentous events whereby the advocates of a broad and salutary construction of the Necessary and Proper Clause won out over the proponents of cramped and niggardly construction. This por trayal is encouraged, perhaps, by popular historians' unfortunate focus on the formal opinions on the subject given to President Washington by Secretary of State Thomas Jefferson and Secretary of the Treasury

to have a more liberal construction"); *cf.* 2 FARRAND *supra* note 11, at 137 (quoting Randolph's initial draft for the Committee of Detail: "To insert essential principles only, lest the operations of government should be clogged by rendering those provisions permanent and unalterable, which ought to be accomodated [*sic*] to times and events").

See also 3 ELLIOT'S DEBATES, *supra* note 60, at 530 (quoting James Madison as interpreting the Constitution according to a "fair and liberal interpretation"). For a preratification case construing a state constitution according to its intent rather than strictly, see *Commonwealth v. Caton*, 8 Va. (4 Call) 5 (1782).

167 CHARLES C. THATCH, JR., THE CREATION OF THE PRESIDENCY, 1775–1789: A STUDY IN CONSTITUTIONAL HISTORY 125–26, 150) (1923) (reprint, Liberty Fund, Indianapolis, 2007) (discussing why the first congressional session only should be considered part of the constitution-making process).

168 Steven G. Calabresi & Gary Lawson, *The Unitary Executive, Jurisdiction Stripping, and the* Hamdan *Opinions: A Textualist Response to Justice Scalia*, 107 COLUM. L. REV. 1002, 1045 (2007).

Alexander Hamilton – two gentlemen who represented perhaps the most extreme views possible in American political life. Hamilton's opinion is subject to further discounting, because we know that at that point in his career he was scheming to remold the Constitution into the consolidated system he had favored but that the framers and ratifiers had resoundingly rejected.[169] Far more representative views were expressed in the Bank Opinion by Attorney General Edmund Randolph and by representatives of both sides of the debate in Congress. While they show some differences, particularly in how to apply the Necessary and Proper Clause, they also show wide areas of agreement.

The first area of agreement among both sides of the debate was that the Necessary and Proper Clause was an expression of the incidental powers doctrine. Randolph put it this way:

> [W]e come to the last inquiry, which has been already anticipated, whether [the bank bill] be sanctified by the power to make all laws, which shall be necessary and proper for carrying into execution the powers vested by the Constitution. To be necessary is to be incidental, or, in other words, may be denominated the natural means of executing a power.[170]

The second point of agreement was that an incidental power had to be tied to one or more express powers.[171] The third point of agreement was that the Necessary and Proper Clause gave Congress no power not inherent in the other enumerated powers.[172] Bank opponent James Madison stated,

[169] Hamilton was, on the founding generation's political spectrum, an extreme consolidationist – hostile to the concept of limited government, and perhaps to republicanism. At the federal convention, he had proposed a plan for an unlimited national authority. 1 FARRAND, *supra* note 11, at 291–93. Of the finished Constitution, he admitted: "No man's ideas were more remote from the plan than his own were known to be." 2 *id.* at 645–46. His private papers show that around the time the federal convention adjourned, he had determined on a campaign to undermine the constitutional limitations on the federal government. Alexander Hamilton, *Conjectures About the Constitution, reprinted in* 13 DOCUMENTARY HISTORY, *supra* note 50, at 278.

Marshall can be accused of no bad faith, but his opinion in *McCulloch* was composed more than 30 years after his role in the ratification, after long and vicious battles against the same people who opposed the bank.

[170] *Opinion of Edmund Randolph, Attorney General of the United States, to President Washington*, in BANK HISTORY, *supra* note 89, at 89.

[171] *E.g.*, 2 ANNALS CONG., at 1992, 1994 (quoting Rep. William Branch Giles); *id.* at 1972–73 (quoting Rep. Elias Boudinot).

See also Alexander Hamilton, *Opinion on the Constitutionality of the National Bank*, in BANK HISTORY, *supra* note 18, at 99, 103 ("[T]he doctrine [that Congress may charter a corporation] is stated with this express qualification, that the right to erect corporations does only extend to cases and objects within the sphere of the specified powers of the Government."). (emphasis in original).

[172] *E.g.*, 2 ANNALS CONG., at 1959 (quoting Rep. Fisher Ames, a supporter of the bank).

"The clause is in fact merely declaratory of what would have resulted by unavoidable implication, as the appropriate, and, as it were, technical means of exercising those powers."[173] Bank supporter Fisher Ames agreed.[174]

The fourth point of agreement was implicit rather than express. It was over the issue of when a power qualified as "incidental." In their debate over whether chartering a bank was incidental to powers expressly enumerated, the disputants seemed to agree an incident had to be less "worthy" than its principal.[175] They also agreed that an incidental power had to be customary or necessary to the exercise of the principal power – although some seem to have disagreed as to the extent of necessity required.[176] Thus, bank advocates argued that chartering a national bank was incidental to several of the federal government's

[173] *Id.* at 1947. *See also id.* at 1982 (quoting Rep. Michael Jennifer Stone as claiming a consensus "that Congress ought not to exercise, by implication, powers not granted by the Constitution").

Randolph was unsure of the effect of the word "proper," but was certain that it did not grant any power:

> The phrase, "and proper," if it has any meaning, does not enlarge the powers of Congress, but rather restricts them. For no power is to be assumed under the general clause [i.e., the Necessary and Proper Clause], but such as is not only necessary but proper, or perhaps expedient also.
>
> But as the friends to the bill ought not to claim any advantage from this clause [i.e., the Necessary and Proper Clause], so ought not the enemies to it, to quote the clause as having a restrictive effect. Both ought to consider it as among the surplusage which as often proceeds from inattention as caution.

Edmund Randolph, *Opinion of Edmund Randolph*, in BANK HISTORY, *supra* note 18, at 89. Perhaps a hint of resentment against the Committee of Detail for adding "proper" to his initial draft?

[174] 2 ANNALS CONG., at 1959 (quoting statement by Rep. Fisher Ames). *See also id.* at 1955 (quoting Rep. Fisher Ames as comparing government to a corporation and its incidents).

[175] *Id.* at 950 (quoting Rep. James Madison that incorporation was not an incidental power because it was "a distinct, an independent and substantive prerogative"). *Cf. id.* at 1991 (quoting Rep. William Branch Giles as stating that the probank argument assumed that "the incidental authority is paramount to the principal, for the right of creating the ability to lend [i.e., through the proposed bank], is greater than that of borrowing," and adding "the right to borrow, if there be a connexion [*sic*] at all, would be incidental to the right to grant charters of incorporation, than the reverse").

On the probank side, see *id.* at 1964 (quoting Rep. Theodore Sedgwick as arguing that incorporation was a subordinate power).

[176] For the argument that necessity had to be absolute, see *id.* at 1993 (quoting William Branch Giles: "I have been taught to conceive that the true exposition of a necessary mean to produce a given end was that mean without which the end could not be produced."); Thomas Jefferson, *Opinion of Thomas Jefferson, Secretary of State*, in BANK HISTORY, *supra* note 18, at 92–93. At least one proponent, Rep. Fisher Ames of Massachusetts, claimed a national bank met that test. 2 ANNALS CONG., at 1956–57 (quoting Rep. Fisher Ames).

express powers because it was customary for governments to execute those powers in that manner.[177] Bank opponents retorted that chartering a financial institution for such purposes did not rise to the level of custom.[178] Advocates also contended that power to incorporate a bank was incidental to the federal government's express powers because it was necessary to their exercise.[179] Opponents argued a lack of necessity.[180]

Thirty-three years later, Virginia judge Spencer Roane, son-in-law of Patrick Henry, pseudonymously attacked Chief Justice John Marshall's construction of the Necessary and Proper Clause in *McCulloch v. Maryland*.[181] One of Roane's central arguments was that the Clause, correctly understood, was merely a rule of construction that added no power to the federal store.[182] John Marshall – who must himself be accounted a leading founder, for he had been a principal Federalist spokesman at the Virginia ratifying convention – pseudonymously responded with newspaper articles in defense of McCulloch. He did not find much to agree

But see id. at 1961–62 (quoting Rep. Theodore Sedgwick as arguing for a "greatest possible degree of public utility" standard for "known and usual means"); *id.* at 1998–99 (quoting Rep. Elbridge Gerry as arguing for what was essentially a reasonable necessity standard).

[177] *Id.* at 1959 (quoting Rep. Fisher Ames: "He then considered the power to borrow money. He said it was natural to understand that authority as it was actually exercised in Europe; which is to borrow of the bank."); *id.* at 2007 (quoting Rep. John Vining for the view that the power of incorporation was customary in governments similarly circumstanced); *id.* at 1961 (quoting Rep. Theodore Sedgwick: "[W]herever a power is delegated for express purposes, all the known and usual means for the attainment of the objects expressed are conceded also"); *id.* at 1962 ("known and usual means"); *id.* at 1974 (Rep. Elias Boudinot, referring to "the common and usual necessary means"). Hamilton also made this point. Alexander Hamilton, *Opinion on the Constitutionality of the National Bank*, in BANK HISTORY, *supra* note 18, at 111–12.

A precedent tending to prove custom was the Bank of England. FORREST MCDONALD, NOVUS ORDO SECLORUM: THE INTELLECTUAL ORIGINS OF THE CONSTITUTION 117–18 (1985).

[178] 2 ANNALS CONG. at 1969 (quoting Rep. James Jackson as distinguishing the U.S. bank proposal from foreign banks); *id.* at 1985 (quoting Rep. Michael Jennifer Stone as expressing similar sentiments).

[179] *Id.* at 1958 (quoting Rep. Fisher Ames as saying the business of a national bank could be done "badly" without incorporation, but that incorporation was indispensable for doing it "well, safely, and extensively"); *id.* at 1975 (quoting Rep. Elias Boudinot: "He had not heard any argument by which it was proved that [in absence of a bank] either individuals, private banks, or foreigners could with safety and propriety be depended on as the efficient and necessary means for so important a purpose"); *id.* at 1998–2001 (quoting Rep. Elbridge Gerry).

[180] *Id.* at 2009 (quoting Rep. James Madison). The parties disagreed over the degree of necessity required.

[181] 17 U.S. (4 Wheat.) 316 (1819).

[182] JOHN MARSHALL'S DEFENSE OF MCCULLOCH V. MARYLAND 115, 117, 124–25 (Gerald Gunther ed., 1969).

with Roane about. But he did concur wholeheartedly with Roane's argument that the Necessary and Proper Clause had no independent legal effect – that it simply memorialized the preexisting doctrine that incidental powers followed principal ones.[183]

IV. CONCLUSION

The Necessary and Proper Clause served to inform the reader that, by the Constitution, the American people had granted Congress implied authority incidental to that granted expressly. The doctrine of principal and incidents was a product of the common law, and was well understood at the American founding. The word "necessary" was used as a term of art to signify incidence.

Incidental powers were those that, while not within a strict construction of express powers, were intended in the grant. To be incidental, a power had to be lesser in importance to the principal power. Intent to include it could be deduced by the fact that it was a customary way of exercising the principal power. If not customary, it still could be incidental if indispensable to the exercise of the principal power or if its absence would greatly impair the exercise of the principal.

To be "proper," a law had to be, at the least, in compliance with the fiduciary duties expected of all public officials. Thus, to be proper, the law had to be within constitutional authority, reasonably impartial, adopted in good faith, and with due care – that is, with some reasonable, factual basis.

The Bill of Rights did not alter the meaning of the Necessary and Proper Clause, but the Ninth and Tenth Amendments did serve as a reminder of the limited scope of Congress's incidental authority.

[183] *Id.*, at 97, 176, 186.

The editor of this exchange, the late Harvard University professor Gerald Gunther, remarked, "Clearly these essays give cause to be more guarded in invoking *McCulloch* to support views of congressional power now thought necessary." *Id.* at 20. This understanding of the Necessary and Proper Clause as a pure rule of construction was confirmed by Justice Joseph Story, Marshall's right-hand man on the Court:

> The plain import of the clause is, that [C]ongress shall have all the incidental and instrumental powers, necessary and proper to carry into execution all the express powers. It neither enlarges any power specifically granted; nor is it a grant of any new power to [C]ongress. But it is merely a declaration for the removal of all uncertainty, that the means of carrying into execution those, otherwise granted, are included in the grant.

3 JOSEPH STORY, COMMENTARIES ON THE CONSTITUTION OF THE UNITED STATES § 1238 (1833) (*available at* http://www.constitution.org/js/js_324.htm).

6

Necessity, Propriety, and Reasonableness

Gary Lawson and Guy I. Seidman

As the previous two chapters have illustrated, reasonable eighteenth-century American drafters and readers would have considered, and actual drafters and readers did consider, private agency law, including norms of fiduciary duty and the doctrine of principals and incidents, as part of the background that helped define a legal phrase such as "necessary and proper for carrying into Execution." The Constitution, of course, is a "public law" rather than "private law" document; it was a charter for government, not the appointment of a factor or guardian. As it happens, however, that public-law character strengthens rather than weakens the evidence mustered by Professor Natelson in favor of understanding the Necessary and Proper Clause through the lenses of agency law and fiduciary duty. In addition to background principles of private law that help explain the Necessary and Proper Clause, there were background principles of public law that would have been known to an informed eighteenth-century observer that shed important light on the clause's origins. Those principles are a remarkably elegant fit with the agency law and fiduciary origins of the Necessary and Proper Clause.

To fill in this piece of the story, we move from agency law to administrative law. By the eighteenth century, English law had developed a bedrock principle of public administration that today is known as the *principle of reasonableness*. While the doctrine's label was not developed until well after the eighteenth century, and its contours were not clearly elaborated until the twentieth century, the broad outlines of the principle of reasonableness were firmly in place when the American Constitution was drafted, read, and ratified. Those principles required delegated power to be exercised with impartiality, efficacy, proportionality, and regard for people's rights – much as one would expect from an extension of private agency law into the public realm. The language of the Necessary and Proper Clause neatly encapsulates the essential elements of the principle of reasonableness, as we will illustrate through study of the principle's foundations and the Constitution's terms and structure.

I. THE ORIGINS OF THE PRINCIPLE OF REASONABLENESS

All of the powers vested by the Constitution are delegations from the ultimate source of positive law, which the Constitution identifies as "We the People".[1] Many of these grants of power unavoidably confer discretion on the empowered government officials. It was well understood in eighteenth-century British administrative law that delegations from Parliament of discretionary governmental authority carried the implied prescription that exercises of such authority conform to fundamental norms of justice. Modern law describes this obligation of government agents as a requirement of reasonableness. We accept that description with some hesitation. The term "reasonableness" has a chameleonic character in the law. It appears in many contexts – private and public, civil and criminal – and takes on many guises. We do not in this book suggest that there is, or was in the eighteenth century, a general concept of reasonableness in the law that has, or had, a specific application to the duties of public officials under the U.S. Constitution. Rather, we seek to describe a singular set of norms that apply in one narrow context, without attempting to relate those norms to broader themes in the law. One could just as well, and perhaps even more accurately, describe the doctrine that forms the basis for this Chapter as the "principle of public faithfulness"[2] or "the principle of official responsibility" or "the principle of fiduciary public agency." History, however, has chosen to call it the "principle of reasonableness," and with the understanding that one

1 U.S. CONST. Preamble ("We the People of the United States ... do ordain and establish this Constitution for the United States of America"). For a truly elegant exploration of the Preamble and the role of "We the People" in constitutional creation, see AKHIL REED AMAR, AMERICA'S CONSTITUTION: A BIOGRAPHY ch. 1 (2005).

2 We are indebted to Elizabeth Nowicki for suggesting that faithfulness might be a better description of the underlying norm than is reasonableness. Indeed, Professor Nowicki's account of the "good faith" obligations of corporate directors bears directly on the fiduciary obligations of government officials. *See* Elizabeth A. Nowicki, *A Director's Good Faith*, 55 BUFF. L. REV. 457 (2007).

should not try to import general notions of reasonableness into the doctrine but should instead simply accept the doctrine for what it purports to be, we accede to history and use the umbrella term "reasonableness" to describe the obligations of government officials that were part of the background of public law in eighteenth-century America.[3]

This principle regarding the exercise of delegated power is typically traced to *Rooke's Case*, which was decided in 1598.[4] A statute from the reign of Henry VIII in 1531 gave to sewer commissioners the power to determine needed repairs to water-control measures "as case shall require, after your wisdoms and discretions" and the power to assess landowners for the costs of maintenance and repairs of such projects as the commissioners "shall deem most convenient to be ordained."[5] It is difficult to imagine a statute whose terms grant broader discretion to an executive agent. The Commissioners of Sewers under this statute[6] had assessed on one landowner, Carter, who owned seven acres of land adjoining the Thames, the full costs of a repair to a bank on the river, even though "divers other Persons had Lands to the Quantity of 800 Acres within the same level, and subject to Drowning, if the said bank be not repaired. ..."[7]

The court, through Sir Edward Coke, upheld the assessed landowner's challenge to the assessment. An adequate ground for the decision might well have been language in the 1427 predecessor to the statute making clear that "no tenants of land or tenements ... shall in any way be spared in this,"[8] but the court added, in now-classic language:

> [N]otwithstanding the Words of the commission give Authority to the commissioners to do according to their Discretions, yet their Proceedings

3 Implicit in this study is an account of the transportation – and transformation – of British law into the United States in the eighteenth century. For an exploration of related ideas, see MARY SARAH BILDER, THE TRANSATLANTIC CONSTITUTION: COLONIAL LEGAL CULTURE AND THE EMPIRE (2004). We hope to provide such an account in future work. For now, it is enough to focus on the limited extent to which English principles of administration apparently influenced the construction of one specific clause of the Constitution.

4 5 Co. Rep. 99b (1598). On *Rooke's Case* as the foundational authority for the principle of reasonableness, see WILLIAM WADE AND CHRISTOPHER FORSYTH, ADMINISTRATIVE LAW 293–94 (10th ed, 2009).

5 23 Hen. 8, c. V, § 3, cls. 2–3 (1531), 4 Stat. at Large 223, 224 (1763).

6 The statute of 1531 expired by its own terms after twenty years, but it was continued indefinitely in 1549. *See* 3 & 4 Edw. 6, c. 8 (1549), 5 Stat. at Large 341 (1763).

7 5 Co. Rep. at 99b.

8 6 Hen. 6, c. V, 3 (1427), Stat. at Large 108, 110. The vitality of this statute was specifically confirmed in the 1531 enactment, *see* 23 Hen. 8, c. V, § 6,4 Stat. at Large 227 (1763), and the court in *Rooke's Case* invoked it. *See* 5 Co. Rep. at 99b.

> ought to be limited and bound with the Rule of Reason and law. For Discretion is a Science or Understanding to discern between Falsity and Truth, between Wrong and Right, between Shadows and Substance, between Equity and colourable Glosses and Pretences, and not to do according to their Wills and private Affections; for as one faith, *Talis discretio discretionem confundit.*[9]

Even though the statutory grant of discretion was exceedingly broad, and perhaps even textually unlimited, the delegation of authority was understood to carry the implicit requirement that exercises of such authority be reasonable.

The same principle was reflected a decade later in *Keighley's Case*, decided in 1609.[10] The case held that a landowner who was obliged by prescription to keep a wall in good repair was not liable for damages or solely liable for the subsequent repairs if the wall failed to hold back water through no fault of the landowner, such as a "sudden and unusual increase of water." In such a case, the court ruled, the Commissioners of Sewers "ought to tax all such persons who hold any [affected] lands or tenements ... according to the quantity of their land. ..."[11] For our purposes, the crucial aspect of the case concerned the underlying statutory authority of the Commissioners of Sewers. A statute empowered the commissioners "to make and ordain statutes, ordinances, &c. after the laws and customs of Romney-Marsh in the county of Kent, or otherwise, after your own wisdoms and discretions."[12] Of the final clause in this statute, which bore striking similarity to the statute at issue in *Rooke's Case*, the reported decision of the court said:

> Lastly, it was resolved, that these words in the said Act, *sc.* "according to your wisdoms and discretions," are to be intended and interpreted according to law and justice, for every Judge or commissioner ought to have *duos sales, viz. salem sapientae, ne sit insipidus, & salem conscientiae ne sit diabolus* [two talents, that is to say, the talent of wisdom, so as not to be foolish (or tasteless), and the talent of conscience, so as not to be a devil]. Also discretion, as it is well described, is *scire per legem quid sit justum* [to know through the law what is just]. ...[13]

9 *Id.*
10 10 Co. Rep. 139a.
11 *Id.*
12 23 H. 8. c.V.
13 10 Co. Rep. at 140a. We are grateful to Robert Natelson for providing the translations from Latin. He notes that "*salem*" (literally "salt") could also mean "acuteness," "good taste," or "sharpness" but believes that "talent" is the most natural-sounding translation in this context.

Coke, the author of *Rooke's Case* and the reporter of *Keighley's Case*, added: "And therewith agrees the description of discretion in *Rook's case*, in the Fifth Part of my Reports."[14] It was thus a basic principle of early administrative law that authority delegated to sewer commissioners had to be exercised non-arbitrarily, or reasonably, whether or not that requirement was expressly spelled out in the authorizing statutes.

By the middle of the seventeenth century, it was clear that this principle requiring statutory discretion to be exercised reasonably applied generally to all delegated power and was not confined to sewer commissioners. In *Estwick v. City of London* in 1647, the court stated that "wheresoever a commissioner *or other person* had power given to do a thing at his discretion, it is to be understood of sound discretion, and according to law, and that this court has power to redress things otherwise done by them."[15] The principle was emphasized repeatedly throughout the seventeenth century,[16] as in *R. v. Commissioners of Fens*, in which the court granted a certiorari against the commissioners on the allegation "that they had proceeded unreasonably," for "this court may judge wither they have pursued their powers."[17]

The principle of reasonableness in the exercise of delegated authority was powerfully restated near the time of the American framing in 1773 in *Leader v. Moxon*.[18] A statute gave paving commissioners power to pave and repair streets "in such a manner as the commissioners shall think fit." The commissioners thought fit to order part of a street to be raised so high that it obstructed the plaintiff's doors and windows, and the court awarded damages to the homeowner. "The commissioners," wrote the court, "had grossly exceeded their Powers, which must have a reasonable construction. Their Discretion is not arbitrary, but must be limited by Reason and Law."[19] As the court explained,

> the Act could never intend that any of the Householders should pay a Rate of 1*s*. 6*d*. in the Pound in order to have their Houses buried under Ground, and their Windows and Doors obstructed. ... [H]ad Parliament intended to demolish or render useless some houses for the Benefit or Ornament of

[14] *Id.*
[15] *Quoted in* WADE & FORSYTH, *supra* note 4, at 294.
[16] *See* STANELY DE SMITH ET AL., JUDICIAL REVIEW OF ADMINISTRATIVE ACTION 297–98 (5th ed. 1995).
[17] 2 Keb. 43, 84 Eng. Rep. 28 (1666).
[18] 2 W. Bl. 924 (1781).
[19] *Id.* at 925–26.

> the rest, it would have given express Powers for the Purpose, and given an Equivalent for the loss that Individuals might have sustained thereby.[20]

In England today, the basic principle derived from *Rooke's Case* "has lost nothing of its accuracy in over 400 years"[21]; the principle of reasonableness remains one of the bedrocks of English administrative law. As a twentieth-century British court explained:

> A person in whom is vested a discretion must exercise his discretion upon reasonable grounds. A discretion does not empower a man to do what he likes merely because he is minded to do so – he must, in the exercise of his discretion do not what he likes but what he ought. In other words, he must, by the use of his reason, ascertain and follow the course which reason directs. He must act reasonably.[22]

II. THE PRINCIPLE OF REASONABLENESS IN CONSTITUTIONAL CONTEXT

In England before the founding, delegated power effectively meant executive power, and the principle of reasonableness was accordingly a principle governing executive implementation of parliamentary delegations. For most of this time, judicial power was understood to be an aspect of executive power rather than a distinct form of governmental authority; the separation of judicial from executive power is a relatively recent development in governmental theory.[23] The principle of reasonableness has thus been conceptualized as an assumption – albeit perhaps a fictitious one – about the intentions of the enacting Parliament when delegating implementational executive or judicial authority.[24]

The principle of reasonableness in the exercise of delegated discretionary power is a common-law principle that the eighteenth-century American colonists would have found very congenial given its antimonarchical and rights-protective character. But in ascertaining the relevance of the principle to American constitutionalism, and in particular to the Necessary and Proper Clause, we must answer two questions: (1) Are

[20] *Id.* at 926.

[21] WADE & FORSYTH, *supra* note 4, at 293.

[22] Roberts v. Hopwood [1925] AC 578, 613.

[23] *See* MARTIN H. REDISH, THE CONSTITUTION AS POLITICAL STRUCTURE 103–05 (1995) (discussing pre-American conceptions of separated powers that did not include judicial power as a distinct element).

[24] WADE & FORSYTH, *supra* note 4, at 291–92.

there textual and structural reasons to think that the principle was actually constitutionalized in the Necessary and Proper Clause and, if so, (2) What is the content of the principle of reasonableness in that particular constitutional context? We answer those questions from the perspective of a hypothetical reasonable observer of the Constitution of 1788; our argument accordingly is founded more on structural inference than on direct historical evidence.[25]

We start with the first question: whether the principle of reasonableness can actually be located in the Necessary and Proper Clause. To explore whether and how the principle of reasonableness informs the Necessary and Proper Clause, it is necessary to explore a related riddle about the constitutional text: Why does Article I, section 8, clause 18, which grants authority to Congress to implement federal powers, contain the phrase "necessary and proper for carrying into Execution" while no such phrase appears anywhere in Article II or Article III, which empower, respectively, the president and the federal courts? The Constitution gives the president the "executive Power" and the federal courts the "judicial Power," but it nowhere says that the president and the courts may take those steps (but only those steps) necessary and proper for carrying their powers into execution. Before asking how the principle of reasonableness informs the Necessary and Proper Clause, it is helpful first to show how that principle applies to and constrains the president and the federal courts.

A. *Executive and Judicial Power*

One of the great controversies in American constitutional law concerns the significance of the so-called "Vesting Clauses" that begin each of the

[25] For an extended explication of this interpretative methodology, see Gary Lawson and Guy Seidman, *Originalism as a Legal Enterprise*, 23 Const. Commentary 47 (2006). Under this methodological approach, the actual subjective intentions of concrete historical figures can be relevant evidence of constitutional meaning, but they do not determine constitutional meaning. Our methodology thus differs in important respects from that employed by Professor Natelson in Chapters 4 and 5 – which perhaps makes the substantive convergence between those chapters and this study all the more striking. As a consequence of our methodology, we do not focus on the extent to which actual persons expressly employed the kind of reasoning that we find implicit in the legal background of the late eighteenth century. We might be more inclined to adopt such a focus if the "principle of reasonableness" was a well-articulated doctrine rather than, as we think it was, an abstract idea about (for want of a better phrase) necessary and proper official conduct whose contours were not clearly understood or clearly observable.

first three articles of the Constitution. Article I's first sentence says that "[a]ll legislative Powers herein granted shall be vested in a Congress of the United States," Article II begins by declaring that "[t]he executive Power shall be vested in a President of the United States of America," and Article III opens with the statement that "[t]he judicial Power of the United States, shall be vested in one supreme Court, and in such inferior Courts as the Congress may from time to time ordain and establish." Each Article then contains, among many other provisions, extensive enumerations regarding the respective departments.[26] Article I sets out, primarily through section 8, the bulk of the "legislative Powers herein granted" to Congress in the Constitution. Article II, in sections 2 and 3, contains a list of powers and duties of the president, such as the power to grant pardons and reprieves and the duty to take care that the laws be faithfully executed. Article III enumerates nine classes of disputes for which the federal courts have jurisdiction and specifies in which of those cases the Supreme Court will have original or appellate jurisdiction.

Scholars have long contested, and will no doubt continue to contest, whether the powers of the president and the federal courts stem from the opening Vesting Clauses or whether those clauses, like the Article I Vesting Clause, merely designate the person or institution that will exercise powers elsewhere granted in the Constitution. In prior work, we have vigorously defended the former proposition – generally described by modern scholars as "the Vesting Clause thesis" – on textual and structural grounds.[27] First, the language of the Article II and III Vesting Clauses – "[t]he executive Power shall be vested" and "[t]he judicial Power shall be vested" – strongly supports a power-grant reading. As one of us has said elsewhere: "It is very hard to read a clause that speaks of vesting power in a particular actor as doing anything other than vesting power in a particular actor."[28] Second, as Professor Steven Calabresi has discussed at

[26] The various Articles also contain limitations on powers, organizational provisions, and occasionally grants of power to actors who are not the principal subjects of the Articles. Article I, for example, grants to the president the presentment and veto power, *see* U.S. Const. art. I, § 7, cls. 2–3; Article II gives the Senate power to approve appointments and treaties and Congress the power to permit inferior officers to be appointed without senatorial confirmation, *see id.* art. II, § 2, cl.. 2; and Article III gives Congress power to declare the punishment for treason, *see id.* art. III, § 3, cl. 2.

[27] *See* Gary Lawson and Guy Seidman, *The Jeffersonian Treaty Clause*, 2006 U. Ill. L. Rev. 1, 22–43.

[28] Gary Lawson and Christopher D. Moore, *The Executive Power of Constitutional Interpretation*, 81 Iowa L. Rev. 1267, 1281 (1996).

some length, the dictionary meanings of the verbs "vest" and "extend" – from the eighteenth century onward – strongly indicate that the Article II and III Vesting Clauses grant power, while subsequent provisions in each Article clarify, qualify, and describe the spheres of application of that power. As Professor Calabresi has noted, "The verb 'vest' (derived from the word vestment with its connotations of royal and ecclesiastical authority and clothing) seems to refer in this context to placing authority in the control of the supreme and inferior courts [or the president]. Put another way, it 'clothes' them with the authority to act."[29] Third, the uses in the Constitution of the word "vest" in provisions other than the Vesting Clauses strongly support the power-grant reading of the Article II and III Vesting Clauses. The Necessary and Proper Clause, of course, gives Congress power to pass laws "necessary and proper for carrying into Execution the foregoing Powers and all other Powers *vested* by this Constitution in the Government of the United States, or in any Department or Officer thereof." There is no way to read this provision as anything but a reference to powers actually granted by the Constitution to various federal actors or institutions.[30] Similarly, the Appointments

[29] Steven G. Calabresi, *The Vesting Clauses as Power Grants*, 88 Nw. U.L. Rev. 1377, 1380–81 (1994).

[30] There is some ambiguity about exactly who those actors and institutions in whom power is vested might be. It is clear enough in what circumstances the Constitution vests authority in an "Officer" of the United States: The vice-president is given power to preside over the Senate and to cast tie-breaking votes in that body, U.S. Const. art. I, § 3, cl. 4; the chief justice is given power to preside over presidential impeachments, *id.* art. I, § 3, cl. 6; and department heads and courts of law may receive authority from Congress to appoint inferior officers, *id.* art. II, § 2, cl. 2. It is less clear what the Necessary and Proper Clause means by a "Department." Does that refer to congressionally created executive departments, such as the Department of State or the Department of War? This seems unlikely, because nowhere does the Constitution grant any power directly to a department so defined (though the Appointments Clause permits heads of such departments to appoint inferior officers if Congress so directs). The better view is that the word "Department" in this context means one of the three primary units of government in whom the Constitution itself vests considerable powers: the Congress, the president, and the federal judiciary. That is in fact the standard usage of the word "department" in the founding era, see Steven G. Calabresi and Kevin H. Rhodes, *The Structural Constitution: Unitary Executive, Plural Judiciary*, 105 Harv. L. Rev. 1153, 1156 n.6 (1992), though certainly not the exclusive usage (as the Appointments Clause demonstrates). The most problematic portion of the Sweeping Clause is the reference to powers vested in "the Government of the United States." There are no powers vested by the Constitution in "the Government of the United States" as a unitary entity; all power grants are addressed to specific institutions or actors. The best reading of that phrase is thus something like "other principal institutions of the Government of the United States," which would cover the

Clause provides that "Congress may by Law *vest* the Appointment of such inferior Officers, as they think proper, in the President alone, in the Courts of Law, or in the Heads of Departments." This clearly describes a circumstance in which Congress grants power to the named actors. It is conceivable, of course, that the Article II and III Vesting Clauses use the word "vest" in a manner entirely different from the usages in other constitutional provisions and from established dictionary meanings, but that seems unlikely.

Other scholars have argued with equal vigor (though we obviously think not with equal persuasiveness) that all of the constitutional powers of the president and the federal courts stem from enumerations other than the Vesting Clauses.[31] As it happens, the strongest arguments for this position come from none other than Professor Natelson, who finds the power-grant reading of the Vesting Clauses inconsistent with eighteenth-century drafting practices in other power-granting instruments.[32] He sees the president's law enforcement powers stemming by implication from the obligation to take care that the laws be faithfully executed, he sees various foreign affairs powers stemming by implication from the express grants of presidential foreign affairs powers, and he believes that the Supreme Court gets the power to act from Article III, section 2, clause 2, which specifies its original and appellate jurisdiction, while the lower courts get their power to act from Congress when they are created.

For purposes of this chapter, it does not matter which of those positions is correct, as long as one acknowledges that the Constitution *somewhere* gives the president executive power and *somewhere* gives the federal courts (or at least the Supreme Court) judicial power. If someone believes that the Constitution *nowhere* grants these powers to the president and the courts, so that all law-executing and case-deciding

individual houses of Congress, which are neither "Department[s]" nor "Officer[s]," but which are granted significant powers in Article I, sections 2–4 that it makes sense for Congress to be able to effectuate by statute.

31 *See, e.g.*, Curtis A. Bradley and Martin S. Flaherty, *Executive Power Essentialism and Foreign Affairs*, 102 MICH. L. REV. 545 (2004); A. Michael Froomkin, *The Imperial President's New Vestments*, 88 NW. U.L. REV. 1346 (1994); Lawrence Lessig and Cass R. Sunstein, *The President and the Administration*, 94 COLUM. L. REV. 1 (1994). For our response to these arguments, see Lawson and Seidman, *supra* note 27, at 27–40.

32 Robert G. Natelson, *The Original Meaning of the Constitution's "Executive Vesting Clause" – Evidence from Eighteenth-Century Drafting Practice*, 31 WHITTIER L. REV. 1 (2010).

authority stems from congressional statutes, then we would need to convince that person that they are wrong. We obviously believe that these powers come from the Vesting Clauses, and that lower federal courts thus automatically gain constitutional power from the Article III Vesting Clause once created, but for purposes of this chapter, it is fine if the reader thinks that such powers flow from other constitutional sources.

For those who accept the Vesting Clause thesis, Article III vests the federal courts with "judicial Power." For those who think that the relevant power grant is Article III, section 2, clause 2, Article III grants to the Supreme Court original or appellate "Jurisdiction" over certain cases. The precise contours of either the "judicial Power" or "Jurisdiction" as it would have been understood by a reasonable eighteenth-century observer are far from clear, if only because of the then-recent vintage of the very concept of judicial power as a distinct form of governmental authority. But in its most basic sense, the judicial power (using the term generically to include jurisdictional power rather than as a textual reference to the Article III Vesting Clause) is the power to decide cases, along with subsidiary powers that are ancillary to that principal function, such as the power to identify and interpret applicable law. This idea that the judicial power is, quintessentially, the power to decide cases is so basic that it is almost impossible to find direct authority for it; it is not the sort of proposition that people have ever found it necessary to state.[33] There is, to be sure, a substantial literature addressing what kinds of ancillary powers might accompany the case-deciding power,[34] but that debate need not concern us here. Those discussions all presuppose the (obvious) proposition that the case-deciding power is the essence of judicial power, and whatever the precise content of that judicial power turns out to be, the Constitution vests that power in – that is, delegates it to – validly appointed federal judicial officials.

While there is ample room for dispute about what ancillary powers accompany the power to decide cases, there is at least one power

[33] Accordingly, efforts to find traditional source material on the original meaning of the judicial power have generally turned up very little. *See* Gary Lawson, *Controlling Precedent: Congressional Regulation of Judicial Decision-Making*, 18 CONST. COMMENTARY 191, 203 (2001).

[34] For explorations of what other powers might be ancillary to the courts' case-deciding function, see Amy Coney Barrett, *The Supervisory Power of the Supreme Court*, 106 COLUM. L. REV. 324, 353–66 (2006); James E. Pfander, *Jurisdiction-Stripping and the Supreme Court's Power to Supervise Inferior Tribunals*, 78 TEX. L. REV. 1433, 1500–11 (2000); Robert J. Pushaw, Jr., *The Inherent Powers of Federal Courts and the Structural Constitution*, 86 IOWA L. REV. 735, 843–66 (2001).

undeniably ancillary to the case-deciding power. In order to decide a case, a court must apply some method(s) of decision, both to find the relevant facts and to determine the applicable law. The power to decide a case necessarily carries with it the power to employ methods of reasoning to reach a decision. The judicial power, therefore, includes at least that power (and duty) to adopt decision-making methodologies. Unless there is a single methodology appropriate in all circumstances such that a writ of mandamus (or its modern equivalent) would lie if a judge used any other methodology, there is inevitably a degree of discretion involved in the selection of a method of decision-making. It is a separate question whether Congress can control or mandate those methodologies through legislation under the Necessary and Proper Clause.[35] But at the very least, in the absence of any such statutes, the courts can and must act on their own. The Article III source of judicial power, be it the Vesting Clause or the Original Jurisdiction Clause, implicitly grants to federal courts discretionary authority to structure their process of judicial decision-making.

Similarly, whatever constitutional source of power gives the president the power of law execution also confers on the president the ancillary power to select means for carrying out that function. Just as courts exercising judicial power must select some methodology for deciding cases, presidents exercising executive power must select techniques for carrying out that task, which means that a grant of the law-executing executive power carries with it the implied ancillary power to choose means to accomplish executive ends. Specifically, in order to execute the laws, presidents must be able to interpret and apply the laws, investigate potential violations, and prosecute where appropriate. And just as there is a range of permissible judicial methodologies, there is a range of permissible executive means to employ in execution of the laws.

Nothing in *any* of the possible sources of presidential and judicial power, whether they are the Vesting Clauses or other provisions such as the Take Care Clause or the Original Jurisdiction Clause, place explicit textual limitations on the manner in which executive and judicial actors should carry out their functions. There is nothing in Article II or Article III, however those articles are read to grant power, which expressly requires implementing actions to be "necessary and proper for carrying into Execution" the basic powers of the president and the federal courts.

35 One of us says no. *See* Lawson, *supra* note 33.

Does this mean that the president and the federal courts are constitutionally unlimited in their choice of ancillary means for carrying out their tasks?

The answer is no, but that answer is found, not in the specific text of Articles II and III, but in the background principles of administrative law that lie behind them. We can now consider how the principle of reasonableness informs the constitutional delegation of judicial power. One must keep in mind that whatever powers the Constitution grants to executive or judicial officials are a delegation from "We the People," the supreme positive lawmaking authority. Suppose that a federal judge exercises his or her delegated power to decide a case by consulting an Ouija board. The judge's decision could certainly be reversed on appeal. The judge could certainly be impeached and removed by Congress. But more profoundly, the judge has violated the Constitution. There is nothing in Article III that expressly says that judges must decide cases rationally or sensibly, but given the eighteenth-century background norms regarding delegated governmental power, there would be no need for such a specification. Courts are delegated the judicial power, which includes as a necessary element the discretionary power to choose a decision-making methodology. It would simply be taken as given by a founding-era reasonable observer that the delegation to the courts, although seemingly without any internal textual limit, carries the implicit requirement that the power be exercised reasonably. There is substantial room within that grant of power for different methodologies, and even substantial room for error that does not rise to a constitutional violation, but at some point a judgment falls so far off the map that it simply ceases to be an exercise of the judicial power. Put another way: Not everything done by a judge, even in the guise of deciding a case, is an exercise of judicial power (or jurisdiction) within the meaning of Article III. The limits may be broad, but there are limits.

The principle of reasonableness applies to the constitutional delegation of executive power in the same way and for the same reasons that it applies to the constitutional delegation of the judicial power. Could the president, exercising discretion in the selection of forms and means of law enforcement, apprehend a suspect holed up in Concord by leveling the entire town? Could the president, exercising discretion in the forms and means of legal interpretation, interpret laws by consulting an astrologer (or perhaps consulting his wife who in turn consulted an astrologer)? Could the president in 1790, prior to ratification of the Fourth Amendment, exercise discretionary investigative powers by indiscriminately searching an entire region? We think that all of these measures would be not merely ill-advised, but unconstitutional. Article II grants the president discretion in law execution, but that discretion is bounded. Put another way: Not everything done by the president, even in the guise of executing the laws, is an exercise of executive power within the meaning of Article II. The limits may be broad, but there are limits.

The delegated powers to execute the laws and to decide cases are both implementational, rather than ends-setting, powers. Accordingly, they necessarily carry with them the principle of reasonableness in the exercise of discretionary delegated powers. That principle did not need to be expressly stated in the Constitution because it is part of the very nature of delegations of implementational powers, such as (if we are right about the Vesting Clause thesis) the grants of the "executive Power" and the "judicial Power," as understood in eighteenth-century administrative law.

B. Whither Congress?

There are several important structural differences between Article I of the Constitution and Articles II and III. Perhaps the most obvious difference is that there can be no dispute that the Article I Vesting Clause is a designation of office rather than a grant of power. Article I's Vesting Clause grants to Congress "[a]ll legislative Powers *herein granted*." Congress is thus granted only a subset of the potential universe of legislative powers – namely, that subset of powers granted elsewhere in the Constitution. Under the Vesting Clause thesis, for the president and the courts, it is enough to identify a governmental power as executive or judicial in order to bring it within the Article II or Article III Vesting Clause. For Congress, one must find authorization for the exercise of a legislative power in some specific constitutional provision beyond the Article I Vesting Clause; it is not enough simply to identify a power as legislative in character. Thus, even if one takes the view that the Constitution generally uses the language of vesting power to describe power grants, the Article I Vesting Clause, unlike the Article II and Article III Vesting Clauses, is not itself a grant of power but rather a designation of where otherwise-granted legislative powers must be lodged.

Another difference, a bit subtler than the first, is that Congress's Article I powers are primarily about the setting of governmental ends rather than the implementation of those ends. Executive and judicial power is principally implementational, involving the enforcement and adjudication of norms generated by the legislative power. Of course, there is a "lawmaking" component to both the executive and judicial powers: For example, the president can (and must) govern occupied territory during wartime,[36] and federal courts may have some authority to fashion substantive rules of decision in the absence of legislative specification.[37] But the paradigmatic exercises of executive and judicial power focus on the implementation – the carrying into execution, if you will – of legislatively determined (or constitutionally determined) policies, while the paradigmatic exercise of legislative power is the establishment of a binding norm.

There is, however, an implementational aspect to the legislative powers conferred on Congress by the Constitution. That aspect, of course, is the Necessary and Proper Clause, which grants Congress power "[t]o make all Laws which shall be necessary and proper for carrying into Execution the foregoing Powers, and all other Powers vested by this Constitution in the Government of the United States, or in any Department or Officer thereof." The implementational executive and judicial powers of the president and federal courts are implicitly constrained by the principle of reasonableness. The implementational legislative powers of Congress are explicitly constrained by the requirement that laws for carrying federal powers into execution must be "necessary and proper" for that purpose. What is the relationship between this explicit textual limitation on congressional powers and the implicit limitation of the principle of reasonableness on executive and judicial powers?

Because the common-law principle of reasonableness was based upon an imputed intention of Parliament when it vested discretionary authority in implementing actors,[38] the principle never applied directly to Parliament (or, more precisely, to the king or queen in Parliament). It was a principle that applied only to discretionary authority delegated from Parliament, not to supreme legislative authority. Indeed, the law imposed no substantive limits, of reasonableness or otherwise, on the

36 For a description of this power and its (occasionally ignored) limits, see GARY LAWSON AND GUY SEIDMAN, THE CONSTITUTION OF EMPIRE: TERRITORIAL EXPANSION AND AMERICAN LEGAL HISTORY 151–87 (2004).

37 This is a swamp that we urgently wish to avoid. Suffice it to say that nineteenth-century federal courts frequently exercised such power under their equity jurisdiction. *See* Kristin A. Collins, *Judges Shall Neither Make Nor Import Law, Article III, Equity, and Judge-Made Law in the Federal Courts,* 60 Duke L.J. (2010) (forthcoming).

38 WADE & FORSYTH, *supra* note 4, at 291–92.

legislative supremacy of Parliament,[39] which stood above the other two governmental departments in the legal hierarchy.

The Congress under the American Constitution, of course, is not Parliament. Congress is not hierarchically superior to the executive or judicial departments. Congress, as does the president and the federal courts, exercises only constitutionally delegated power, and that power is far from limitless. If the principle of reasonableness derives solely from the existence of delegated discretionary power, then it would follow that the constitutionally delegated authority of Congress – or at a minimum the delegated authority to implement other powers – is subject to the same requirements of reasonableness as is the constitutionally delegated authority of the president and the courts. But would a careful eighteenth-century drafter or observer be satisfied with that inference? Could someone instead plausibly argue that the principle of reasonableness does not directly apply to Parliament simply because Parliament (at least in its legislative guise) exercises legislative rather than essentially implementational executive or judicial power? If that reasoning is the correct basis for refusing to extend the principle of reasonableness to Parliament, it would apply as well to Congress, in which case grants of enumerated power to Congress, including grants of power for carrying other powers into effect, would not necessarily carry with them a requirement of reasonableness in the exercise of discretion. Accordingly, it would make sense to specify a constitutional constraint on Congress's discretionary powers if and when such a constraint was desired.

The Necessary and Proper Clause is a sensible, and even obvious, place for such a constraint. That clause grants Congress discretionary implementational authority – not directly to carry out laws, but indirectly to aid other actors in the implementation of the laws. Among all of the legislative powers granted in the Constitution, it bears the closest affinity to the implementational executive and legislative powers, and is thus a prime candidate for incorporation of the principle of reasonableness. On this analysis, there are very good reasons why the Constitution would specify in the Necessary and Proper Clause that executory laws must be "necessary and proper" but would not use equivalent language in Article II or Article III. Discretionary executive and judicial powers, by their very nature, carry with them the principle of reasonableness. Perhaps that is true as well of delegated legislative power (or perhaps at

39 A.V. Dicey, Introduction to the Study of the Law of the Constitution 3–11 (8th ed. 1982).

least of delegated implementational legislative power) so that a requirement of reasonableness would exist even in the absence of the "necessary and proper" language in the Necessary and Proper Clause. No doubt those in the founding generation who thought the Necessary and Proper Clause to be unneeded surplusage would have taken this position on the principle of reasonableness. However, the self-executing application of the principle of reasonableness to Congress is open enough to question to make it prudent explicitly to specify the desired limitation.

What is the nature of that limitation? How is Congress – and by implication the president and the federal courts – constrained by the principle of reasonableness? In order to have a good account of how the principle of reasonableness informs the federal Constitution, one must have some sense of what the principle requires.

C. *Whither Reasonableness?*

While the principle of reasonableness was well established by the eighteenth century, it had neither a name nor a precise definition at that time. Today it has both. The contours of the modern requirement of reasonableness in British administrative law were classically set out in 1948 in *Associated Provincial Picture House Ltd. v. Wednesbury Corp.*:

> It is true that discretion must be exercised reasonably. Now what does that mean? Lawyers familiar with the phraseology used in relation to exercise of statutory discretion often use the word 'unreasonable' in a rather comprehensive sense. It has frequently been used and is frequently used as a general description of the things that must not be done. For instance, a person entrusted with a discretion must, so to speak, direct himself properly in law. He must call his own attention to the matters which he is bound to consider. He must exclude from his consideration matters which are irrelevant to what he has to consider. If he does not obey those rules, he may truly be said, and often is said, to be acting 'unreasonably.' Similarly, there may be something so absurd that no sensible person could ever dream that it lay within the power of the authority. Warrington LJ in *Short v. Poole Corporation* gave the example of the red-haired teacher, dismissed because she had red hair. This is unreasonable in one sense. In another, it is taking into consideration extraneous matters. It is so unreasonable that it might almost be described as being done in bad faith; and, in fact, all these things run into one another.[40]

[40] 1 KB 223, 229 (1948).

So framed, this kind of "*Wednesbury* review," as it is typically called, has much in common with so-called "arbitrary or capricious review" in America under the Administrative Procedure Act (or relevant organic statutes).[41] As explicated in the leading Supreme Court decision articulating the "arbitrary or capricious" standard:

> Normally, an agency rule would be arbitrary and capricious if the agency has relied on factors which Congress has not intended it to consider, entirely failed to consider an important aspect of the problem, offered an explanation for its decision that runs counter to the evidence before the agency, or is so implausible that it could not be ascribed to a difference in view or the product of agency expertise.[42]

Both formulations reflect a great deal of deference to the judgment of the actor under review. It is doubtful that modern law, on either side of the Atlantic, is quite as deferential in practice as these formulations suggest[43]; current-day reasonableness review of administrative action, in England under the principle of reasonableness and in America under arbitrary or capricious review, often has considerable bite.

For our purposes, however, what matters is how a reasonable *eighteenth-century* observer would have viewed limitations on delegated power. Because the principle of reasonableness was not at that time specifically articulated as a distinct doctrine, there is no canonical source from which one can draw the contours of the principle as it stood in the founding era. Nonetheless, one can glean some general outlines from the key decided cases and from subsidiary principles that seem to underlie them.

The seminal case in the development of the principle of reasonableness, *Rooke's Case*, immediately suggests one characteristic of reasoned decision-making: Exercises of discretionary authority must be impartial and fair. The fundamental error of the Commissioners of Sewers in that case was forcing one landowner to bear a burden that, in fairness and justice, should have been borne by all affected landowners, perhaps in

41 5 U.S.C. § 706(2)(A) (2006) ("The reviewing court shall ... hold unlawful and set aside agency action, findings, and conclusions found to be – (A) arbitrary, capricious, an abuse of discretion, or otherwise not in accordance with law").

42 Motor Vehicle Mftrs. Assn. of the U.S. v. State Farm Mutual Automobile Ins. Co., 463 U.S. 29 (1983).

43 On modern American law, see GARY LAWSON, FEDERAL ADMINISTRATIVE LAW 582–650 (5th ed. 2009). On modern British law, see WADE & FORSYTH, *supra* note 4, at 297–354.

proportion to their benefit from the bank. This requirement is remarkably similar to the requirement imposed on fiduciaries, such as administrators or executors, to treat all class members fairly and impartially.[44] If Carter, the landowner assessed in *Rooke's Case*, was to bear the full burden of the repair, the commission needed to articulate some good reason why he alone should be assessed. The principle of reasonableness thus incorporates an element of "equal protection" for those affected by delegated authority. Law enforcement agents or administrators must not act out of bias or favoritism, courts must adopt decision-making methodologies that treat all parties impartially, and congressional laws pursuant to the Necessary and Proper Clause must obey the same principles of fiduciary fairness.[45]

Keighley's Case also provides, albeit indirectly, some insight into the content of the principle of reasonableness. After describing the decision's interpretation of the relevant statute,[46] Coke, the reporter, added:

> And it was well observed, that every statute, ordinance and provision which is made by force of the [C]ommission[s] of [S]ewers, ought to consist upon four causes. 1. The material cause, and that is the substance. 2. The formal cause, and that is the manner, with convenient circumstance. 3. The efficient cause, and that is their authority according to their commission. 4. Thc final causc, and that is *pro bono publico, etnunquam pro privato*.[47]

Students of philosophy will recognize the reference to Aristotle's four types of causes, as set forth in *The Physics*:

> In one sense, then, (1) that out of which a thing comes to be and which persists, is called 'cause,' e.g., the bronze of the statue, the silver of the bowl, and the genera of which the bronze and the silver are species.
>
> In another sense (2) the form or the archetype, i.e., the statement of the essence, and its genera, are called 'causes' (e.g., of the octave the relation of 2:1, and generally number), and the parts in the definition.
>
> Again (3) the primary source of the change or coming to rest; e.g., the man who gave advice is a cause, the father is cause of the child, and

44 *See supra* pages 59–60.

45 The application to the federal government of something like the equal protection principles of the Fourteenth Amendment may thus have a textual grounding – through the Necessary and Proper Clause rather than (as modern law would have it) through the Due Process Clause of the Fifth Amendment.

46 *See supra* pages 123–24.

47 10 Col Rep. 140a.

> generally what makes of what is made and what causes change of what is changed.
>
> Again (4) in the sense of end or 'that for the sake of which' a thing is done, e.g., health is the cause of walking about ('Why is he walking about?' We say, 'To be healthy', and, having said that, we think we have assigned the cause.)[48]

It is, we suppose, possible that an early seventeenth-century British court might actually have analyzed the powers of a sewer commission concerning prescriptive repair obligations by reference to the Aristotelian distinction among material, formal, efficient, and final causes. It is also possible, however, that the interjection of Aristotle into the law of sewer commissions was solely the result of some idiosyncratic reporting by Lord Coke rather than an accounting of the actual decision-making process in the case. Accordingly, it would surely be a mistake to take too seriously the notion that British administrative law required sewer commissioners to structure their actions around the ideas of material, formal, efficient, and final causation.

But even if this Aristotelian interjection was purely Coke's invention, it suggests two important things about the principle of reasonableness. First, the notion that the "final cause" of agency action should be the public good and not any particular private good reinforces the idea of impartiality reflected in *Rooke's Case.* Second, and more significantly, the reference to causation might lead us to think about how various notions of causation, Aristotelian or otherwise, might inform legal analysis of discretion. Let us take the "final cause" of any particular agency action as a given. Presumably, the agency ought to aim to achieve that final cause, which is by hypothesis the fundamental reason for its action. One obvious aspect of rationality in this context would involve selecting means for achieving those ends that are reasonably calculated actually to achieve them. That is, a dimension of reasonableness in the exercise of delegated power is the *efficacy* of the chosen implementing means. Consideration of cause and effect, in the ordinary-language senses of those terms, is a basic feature of rational decision-making. That does not mean that governmental agents fail their obligations of legality whenever they select means that are less than perfect, or even necessarily suboptimal. But it does mean that there must be some at least minimal causal connection between the chosen means and the desired ends. The dictum,

[48] Introduction to Aristotle 128–29 (Richard McKeon, ed. 1973).

whether it be the court's or Coke's, from *Keighley's Case* highlights this causal dimension of reasonableness. In turn, that dimension of reasonableness largely tracks the requirement of a duty of care for fiduciaries under agency law. Private fiduciaries generally must take account of the likelihood that their actions will achieve their prescribed goals, and public actors have a similar obligation to select efficacious means.

Leader v. Moxon from the eighteenth century suggests two further components of the principle of reasonableness. The agency in that case paved and repaired a street. There is no indication in the court's opinion that the agency's chosen means of repair were not causally efficacious; for all that we can tell from the opinion, the road was in fine shape when the agency was finished with it. The problem was that the plaintiff's house was not in fine shape: The road was raised so high that it obstructed access to the house. The agency's action may well have been *efficacious*, but it was not *measured* or *proportionate.* One does not burn down a village to kill a fox – or, perhaps more to the point, one does not ordinarily fix a road by destroying a house when less destructive alternatives are available.

Modern Continental lawyers have raised this notion of proportionality to the level of high principle, refining it and using it to require a relatively precise fit between means and ends that approximates the "least restrictive alternative" analysis familiar to First Amendment lawyers.[49] English law has never recognized this "principle of proportionality" as a distinct legal requirement, though its adoption has been urged in modern times,[50] and "it has infiltrated British law" through its adoption by the European Court of Justice.[51] Strict proportionality certainly was not a part of English law in the eighteenth century, if only because the principle was developed in Germany in the nineteenth century.[52] Nonetheless, it is not difficult to see elements of proportionality (though not the fully refined Continental principle) in the traditional common-law concept of reasonableness; "the principles of reasonableness and proportionality cover a great deal of common ground."[53] It is very natural to describe a

[49] *See* DE SMITH ET AL., *supra* note 6, at 596. For general discussions of the Continental principle of proportionality, see JURGEN SCHWARZE, EUROPEAN ADMINISTRATIVE LAW 677–88 (1992); ROBERT THOMAS, LEGITIMATE EXPECTATIONS AND PROPORTIONALITY IN ADMINISTRATIVE LAW 77–85 (2000).

[50] *See id.* 86–110.

[51] WADE & FORSYTH, *supra* note 4, at 305.

[52] DE SMITH ET AL., *supra* note 6, at 593.

[53] WADE & FORSYTH, *supra* note 4, at 312.

decision as "unreasonable" if the means are grossly disproportionate to the ends, and many English decisions, including *Leader v. Moxon*, are consistent with this observation.[54]

There is an additional principle underlying *Leader v. Moxon*. The court noted that "had Parliament intended to demolish or render useless some houses for the Benefit or Ornament of the rest, it would have given express Powers for the Purpose, and given an Equivalent for the loss that Individuals might have sustained thereby." In other words, a person's house should not be destroyed for the public benefit of a better road without just compensation, and the administrative agency should have been aware of this limitation. Framed more generally, one might say that the agency should have taken account – or at least more careful account than it did – of the underlying background *rights* of persons affected by the agency's actions, such as the right to just compensation for public takings. An aspect of reasonableness in the context of public administration would, therefore, be appropriate consideration of the rights of the affected public.

The principle of reasonableness thus requires delegated power to be exercised in an impartial, efficacious, proportionate, and rights-regarding fashion. This principle is an excellent fit with fiduciary law to the extent that government officials are analogized to fiduciaries. More to the point, it is also an excellent fit with the language and structural implications of the Necessary and Proper Clause.

D. *Necessary, Proper, and Reasonable*

The language of the Sweeping Clause is an elegant vehicle for subjecting Congress's implementational legislative powers to the principle of reasonableness. The phrase "necessary and proper for carrying into Execution" is an excellent way to describe requirements of impartiality, efficacy, proportionality, and regard for rights. The word "necessary" describes the causal relationship required between the selected means and the desired ends. Without engaging here the difficult question how close that relationship must be in any particular case,[55] at a general level, necessity incorporates considerations of efficacy (do the means actually

[54] DE SMITH ET AL., *supra* note 6, at 582–83.

[55] Professor Lawson has elsewhere entered that fray. *See* Gary Lawson, *Discretion as Delegation: The "Proper" Understanding of the Nondelegation Doctrine*, 73 GEO. WASH. L. REV. 235, 242–48 (2005).

have a substantial connection to the accomplishment of the desired ends?). The term also incorporates considerations of measuredness and proportionality (do the means achieve the desired ends at an appropriate cost?). While one might think that a word like "proper" is a better fit for "proportionate" given the linguistic similarity between the two words, it is quite natural to say that a decision is not "necessary" if it is disproportionate: "Was it really necessary," one might say to the paving commissioners, "to destroy a house to fix a road"? A measure is "necessary" if it is (reasonably) efficacious and (reasonably) cost-effective. It thus may be no accident that when the modern European Court of Justice described the principle of proportionality, it said that the principle requires measures to be "appropriate and necessary in order to achieve the objectives legitimately pursued by the legislation in question."[56]

The requirement that an executory law be "proper" is an excellent way to describe norms of impartiality and regard for rights – and fiduciary duties more broadly. The dictionary meaning of "proper" in the late eighteenth century included as its most pertinent definitions "1. Peculiar; not belonging to more; not common. ... 3. One's own. ... 4. Natural; original. 5. Fit; accommodated; adapted; suitable; qualified. ... 6. Exact; accurate; just."[57] One of us has elsewhere summarized this language as suggesting a *jurisdictional* understanding of the word "proper," in which a "proper" executory law is a law that is distinctively, peculiarly, and justly one that is appropriate to the role of the enacting body.[58] Since the first and most basic duty of a fiduciary is to remain within the scope of granted authority – that is, to exercise only those powers that are peculiarly and distinctively appropriate to the fiduciary – the connection between fiduciary norms and the jurisdictional norms of the Necessary and Proper Clause is surely more than coincidental.[59]

56 THOMAS, *supra* note 49, at 79 (*quoting* R. Ministry of Agriculture, Fisheries and Food, ex parte Fedesa, 1990 E.C.R. I-4023).

57 2 SAMUEL JOHNSON, DICTIONARY OF THE ENGLISH LANGUAGE (1785). The other definitions of "proper" provided by Johnson seem wholly inapposite to the context of the Necessary and Proper Clause ("2. Noting an individual.... 7. Not figurative. 8. It seems in *Shakespeare* to signify, mere; pure. 9. Elegant; pretty").

58 Gary Lawson and Patricia B. Granger, *The "Proper" Scope of Federal Power: A Jurisdictional Interpretation of the Sweeping Clause*, 43 DUKE L.J. 267 (1993).

59 Professor Lawson has drawn numerous implications, many of them highly controversial, from this "jurisdictional" understanding of the word "proper," including implications regarding the Ninth Amendment, *id.*, at 326–30, the nondelegation doctrine, Gary Lawson, *Delegation and Original Meaning*, 88 VA. L. REV. 327 (2002), and federalism, Gary Lawson, *A Truism with Attitude: The Tenth Amendment in Constitutional Context*, 83 NOTRE DAME L. REV. 469 (2008). Needless to say,

The close connection between the Necessary and Proper Clause and fiduciary law was highlighted – whether advertently or not we cannot say – by Joseph Story in his 1836 treatise on equity jurisprudence when he wrote: "In a general sense, a trustee is bound by his implied obligation to perform all those acts, which are necessary and proper for the due execution of the trust, which he has undertaken."[60]

It thus appears that principles of public law – the principle of reasonableness – work hand in hand with principles of private law – the law of agency – to provide an integrated account of the likely intellectual origins of the Necessary and Proper Clause. There is, however, yet another branch of the law in which principles of public and private law converge in a unique way, and that is the law of corporations. Corporate charters around the time of the founding were public-law documents, emanating from the government, which empowered actors to navigate the essentially private-law world of agency and contract. If the phrase "necessary and proper" was used in corporate charters of that era in a fashion similar to the fiduciary and jurisdictional uses of the phrase just outlined, it would be more than suggestive of the likely pedigree of the phrase.

one does not need to accept these implications (though Professor Lawson would be pleased if one does) in order to accept the role of jurisdictional, fiduciary principles in the construction of the Necessary and Proper Clause.

60 2 Joseph Story, Commentaries on Equity Jurisprudence as Administered in England and America 510 (1836).

7

The Corporate Law Background of the Necessary and Proper Clause

Geoffrey P. Miller

The Necessary and Proper Clause is perplexing. Perhaps the single greatest source of congressional power, a cornerstone of the modern administrative state, a trump card authorizing federal domination over many issues of national life, a symbol, for some, of the power of governments to improve the life of their citizens – it is all these, and more. Yet its terms are anything but pellucid. What does "necessary" mean? What about "proper"? What is the relationship between these words? The Constitution itself offers little clue. The phrase emerged from the Committee of Detail without clarification.[1] The records of the Constitutional Convention provide scant evidence as to how the framers understood the clause,[2] and the ratifying debates are not illuminating. Prior to the Supreme Court's 1819 decision in *McCulloch v. Maryland*, the clause appeared to have been nearly forgotten.[3]

The odd contrast between the importance of the clause and the lack of attention given to it during the founding era suggests that its terms must already have been in common usage. "Necessary and proper" feels like a lawyer's clause – a standard provision that, despite its importance, is not usually the subject of negotiation or debate. If the clause was indeed one commonly found in legal practice, it would be understandable why so few people found it worthy of analysis or attention at the time of its drafting.

1 *See* Mark A. Graber, *Unnecessary and Unintelligible*, 12 Const. Commentary 167, 168 (1995) (Committee of Detail "gave no hint" on why it chose the language it did).

2 *See* Bernard H. Siegan, The Supreme Court's Constitution: An Inquiry into Judicial Review and Its Impact on Society 1 (1987) ("the accounts of the 1787 Constitutional Convention are silent on the meaning of the necessary and proper power").

3 McCulloch v. Maryland, 17 U.S. (4 Wheat.) 316 (1819).

In addition to explaining the curious absence of controversy during the founding era, the hypothesis that the Necessary and Proper Clause was part of the standard repertoire of attorneys at the time suggests a possible line of research: Information about the provenance and meaning of the Necessary and Proper Clause might be found in legal practice. In particular, such information might be gleaned by examining the conventions and usages of corporate law. The Constitution, after all, was itself a corporate charter – a document creating a body corporate and defining its powers. It would not be surprising, therefore, if terminology such as "necessary and proper" turned up in other, more quotidian charters. And if such terminology is indeed found there, we might be able to draw on these documents as a guide to interpreting the meaning of similar language in the Constitution.

This chapter pursues that line of inquiry by investigating the corporate law background of the Necessary and Proper Clause. I do so by analyzing corporate charters from the colonial and early federal periods: instruments establishing the colonies, statutes creating the First and Second Banks of the United States, and charters granted by Connecticut and North Carolina from the colonial period through 1819 (the date of the Supreme Court's opinion in *McCulloch*). It turns out that terms such as "necessary," "proper," and "necessary and proper" were indeed ubiquitous in corporate practice. Hundreds of such provisions are found in the charters I reviewed – often modifying grants of rulemaking powers that directly parallel the Constitution's grant of legislative authority to Congress.

The corporate law background provides information about how the Necessary and Proper Clause might have been understood at the time of its drafting. In particular, contemporary corporate practice suggests that the Necessary and Proper Clause does not create independent lawmaking competence, does not confer general legislative power, and does not grant Congress unilateral discretion to determine the scope of its authority. The corporate law background also suggests something about how to interpret the key constitutional terms: to be "necessary," there must be a reasonably close connection between constitutionally recognized ends and the means chosen to accomplish those ends; to be "proper," a law must not, without adequate justification, discriminate against or otherwise disproportionately affect the interests of particular citizens vis-à-vis others.

These conclusions should be viewed with caution. Terms such as "necessary" and "proper" were not defined in colonial or early federal charters. Corporate practice was not uniform, and although the terms appear in reasonably predictable ways, there is also plenty of variation. Despite remarkable similarities in language and function, moreover, there is no proof that the Necessary and Proper Clause was in fact taken from corporate charters. Even if the framers of the Constitution *did* borrow from corporate charters, they may not have intended that the constitutional words be interpreted in the same way (none of the attorneys who presented arguments in *McCulloch v. Maryland* relied on corporate practice). And, of course, inferences from the corporate law background of the Necessary and Proper Clause say little, if anything, about interpretations not based on original intent. These caveats notwithstanding, an understanding of the corporate law background provides perspective and adds texture to our understanding of this important provision.[4]

This chapter is structured as follows. The first part explores the parallel between the Constitution and corporate charters. Part II reports the historical data. Part III considers how corporate attorneys of the time might have understood the Necessary and Proper Clause and the grant of legislative power within which it is embedded.

I. THE CONSTITUTION AS A CORPORATE CHARTER

I start by developing the analogy between the Constitution and corporate charters of the day. The analysis here draws on work by Robert Natelson, who observed in 2004 that the language of the Necessary and Proper Clause has roots in English agency practice.[5] In this chapter I wish to explore a related but slightly different hypothesis: It is not agency principles in general but rather one specific *application* of those principles – the corporate charter – that provides the most immediate parallel and best general framework for understanding the legal background of the Necessary and Proper Clause.[6]

4 To date, commentators on constitutional law have not fully appreciated the importance of the private law background of this and other constitutional provisions. *See* Seth Barrett Tillman, *Why Our Next President May Keep His or Her Senate Seat: A Conjecture on the Constitution's Incompatibility Clause*, 4 DUKE J. CONSTITUTIONAL L. PUBLIC POLICY, 107, 117 n.26 (2009) ("private law linguistic and intellectual traditions are not widely known to those immersed in modern public and administrative law.").

5 Robert Natelson, *The Agency Origins of the Necessary and Proper Clause*, 55 CASE WESTERN RESERVE LAW REV. 243 (2004); Robert Natelson, *The Agency Law Origins of the Necessary and Proper Clause*, this volume. *Cf.* Evan J. Criddle, *Fiduciary Foundations of Administrative Law*, 54 U.C.L.A. L. R. 117, 117 (2006) (outlining an "interpretivist model of administrative law based on the concept of fiduciary obligation in private legal relations such as agency, trust, and corporation").

6 For an interesting study deriving the principle of judicial review from the corporate law background, *see* Mary Sarah Bilder, *The Corporate Origins of Judicial Review*, 116 YALE L. J. 502 (2006).

The Constitution of the United States is a corporate charter. It establishes – to quote standard legal language of the times – a "body politic and corporate."[7] It endows that body with attributes of corporations: a name, continuity of existence, succession of leadership, and the power to sue and be sued. It specifies the purposes for which the body is established – to form a more perfect union, establish justice, ensure domestic tranquility, provide for the common defense, promote the general welfare, and secure the blessings of liberty.[8] It sets forth powers of the institution and establishes limits on the exercise of those powers. It grants exclusive privileges and rights. It delegates authority to agents and specifies rules of governance. All of these functions are commonly found in corporate charters of the late eighteenth and early nineteenth centuries.

The Constitution is no less a corporate charter because it establishes a *government* body rather than a private association. The distinction we perceive today between public and private entities was not developed during the colonial and early federal periods. Corporate charters of those days were not private contracts; they were public acts, usually embodied in legislation. Many corporations established during this period were actual governmental bodies – towns given charters to operate in corporate form. Even when the institutions were privately owned, they were often conceived of as serving a public purpose. Poorhouses and orphanages received charters to perform social services for persons in need;[9] navigation companies cleared out streams;[10] canal companies cut passages for boat traffic;[11] bridge companies raised spans over rivers and streams;[12]

7 E.g., An Act to Establish the Davidson Academy, North Carolina Laws of 1785, ch. XXIX (Davidson Academy). Technically, since the United States was already in existence under the Articles of Confederation, albeit in a different form, it might be more accurate to say that the Constitution of 1787 reestablished the United States as a corporate body rather than creating it.

8 U.S. CONSTITUTION, Preamble.

9 E.g., An Act to Establish the Fayetteville Orphan Asylum, North Carolina Laws of 1813, ch. XLIV; An Act to Erect a Poor House in the County of Lincoln, North Carolina Laws of 1818, ch. CXX.

10 *See*, e.g., An Act to Incorporate the Broad River Navigation Company, and also the Inhabitants of Rutherfordton, of the County of Rutherford, and for Other Purposes, North Carolina Statutes of 1811, ch. XXXII.

11 *See*, e.g., An Act to Incorporate Two Companies for the Purpose of Cutting a Navigable Canal from Roanoak River to Nerherrin River, and Another Navigable Canal from Bennet's Creek, in this State, to Nansemond River, in the State of Virginia, North Carolina Laws of 1804, ch. XXXIV.

12 *See*, e.g., An Act to Incorporate a Company to Build a Bridge Across the Yadkin River, North Carolina Laws of 1816, ch. XXXIX.

water companies dug and maintained aqueducts;[13] road companies built and operated turnpikes[14] – all actions serving the general welfare. Schools also served public purposes; statutes incorporating academies in North Carolina were often justified on the ground that "the good education of youth has the most direct tendency to promote virtue and ensure happiness and prosperity in the community."[15] Although business corporations in the modern sense were chartered during this period without an explicit bow to public purposes, legal practice did not sharply distinguish between public and private corporations.

Indeed, there is direct evidence that the framers of the Constitution were aware of the parallel between the federal government and a corporation. Eric Enlow observes that one of the proposals to the Committee of Detail provided that "[t]he United States shall be forever considered as one body corporate and politic in law."[16] This language is taken directly from corporate charters of the era.[17] During the debates at the Convention, Madison argued that legislation in a limited government was related to that government's constitution in the same way that a "corporation's bye laws [sic] [related] to the supreme law within a State."[18] Madison was here alluding to the nearly universal practice of including in corporate charters clauses explicitly subordinating the rulemaking authority of a corporation to the laws and constitutions of the political jurisdiction within which the corporation was formed.[19]

13 E.g., An Act to Incorporate an Aqueduct Company in the City of Norwich, Connecticut Laws, October Session, 1808, ch. VIII.

14 *See*, e.g., An Act to Establish a Turnpike Road from Mattamuskeet Lake to the Main Public Road on the East side of Pungo River, North Carolina Laws of 1818, ch. LXXI I (Pungo River Turnpike Company).

15 An Act to Erect an Academy at the Town of Edenton, in the County of Chowan, North Carolina Laws of 1800, ch. XXXIX.

16 Eric Enlow, *The Corporate Conception of the State and the Origins of Limited Constitutional Government*, 6 WASH. U. J.L. & POL'Y 1, 11 (2001).

17 See note 7, *supra*.

18 Enlow, *supra* note 16, at 12 (quoting James Madison, JOURNAL OF THE FEDERAL CONVENTION 297 (E.H. Scott ed., special ed. 1898)).

19 *See*, e.g., An Act to Incorporate the Trustees of the Missionary Society of Connecticut, Connecticut Acts & Laws 602 (1802) ("provided they are not contrary to the laws of this State, or of the United States"); An Act to Incorporate the Thames Insurance Company at New London, Connecticut Laws, October Session, 1818, ch. VIII ("not being contrary to this charter, the laws of this State, or of the United States"); An Act to Incorporate Chauncy Gleaford, Elias Cowles, and their Associates, Connecticut Acts & Laws 583 (1801) ("not being contrary to this Act, to the laws of this State, or of the United States"); An Act Incorporating the Middletown Manufacturing Company, Connecticut Laws, October Session, 1810, ch. I ("not being contrary to this charter, or to the laws of the United States, or of this State"). For a discussion of these clauses as a basis of the principle of judicial review, see Bilder, *supra* note 6.

The corporate concept of the state remained salient to the early United States Supreme Court: In *Chisholm v. Georgia*,[20] Justice Iredell observed that "[t]he word 'corporations,' in its largest sense, has a more extensive meaning than people generally are aware of. Any body politic (sole or aggregate) whether its power be restricted or transcendent, is in this sense 'a corporation.'.... In this extensive sense, not only each State singly, but even the United States may without impropriety be termed 'corporations.'"[21] Justice Marshall, the author of *McCulloch*, voiced the same view in 1823: "The United States is a government, and, consequently, a body politic and corporate, capable of attaining the objects for which it was created. ... This great corporation was ordained and established by the American people.... Its powers are unquestionably limited...."[22]

There is every reason to suppose the members of the Committee of Detail who drafted the Necessary and Proper Clause, in particular, were aware of this corporate law background. Four of the five members of the committee were lawyers: Edmund Randolph served as attorney general of Virginia for ten years and would later serve as the first attorney general of the United States;[23] John Rutledge trained at London's Middle Temple and was a drafter of South Carolina's 1776 Constitution as well as a future justice of the United States Supreme Court;[24] James Wilson was a prominent Pennsylvania lawyer and future Supreme Court justice;[25] Oliver Ellsworth sat as a Connecticut judge and later became chief justice of the United States Supreme Court.[26] Each of these men was not only a prominent public lawyer but also an active practitioner involved in a wide range of legal matters, including business law issues.[27] Given all this expertise, it would not be surprising if these men, when drafting the Necessary and Proper Clause, had employed concepts that were also current in corporate law practice of the time.

II. THE DATA

I reviewed a sample of eighteenth-century and early-nineteenth-century corporate charters. These included the federal charters of the First and

[20] 2 U.S. (2 Dall.) 419 (1793).

[21] *Id.* at 447. For discussion, see Enlow, *supra* note 16, at 12–13.

[22] United States v. Maurice, 26 F. Cas. 1211 (C.C.D. Va. 1823) (Marshall, C.J.). *See* Enlow, *supra* note 16, at 15–16.

[23] Robert Natelson, *The Agency Origins of the Necessary and Proper Clause*, 55 CASE WESTERN RESERVE LAW REVIEW 243, 270 (2004).

[24] *Id.*

[25] *Id.*

[26] *Id.*

[27] *Id.*

Second Banks of the United States, the Crown charters for the American colonies, the charter of the Massachusetts Bay Company, and charters issued by two states – North Carolina and Connecticut – from the colonial period through 1819, the date of Justice Marshall's decision in *McCulloch v. Maryland*. The choice of North Carolina and Connecticut was based partly on considerations of tractability, given the enormous volume of laws that even then were being adopted by colonial and state legislatures. To reduce the possibility of bias, I selected two states that presented contrasting situations: Connecticut, a northern and industrializing state with a substantial financial sector, including banks and insurance companies; and North Carolina, a southern, agricultural state with a less developed financial sector.[28] This review identified 144 charters in Connecticut and 230 charters in North Carolina. The principal recipients of charters in North Carolina were towns, schools, and lodges, whereas Connecticut chartered substantial numbers of banks and insurance companies. This difference was not clear-cut, however: Connecticut issued charters to towns and schools, and North Carolina chartered banks and insurance companies. Other recipients of charters in one or both states included poorhouses, asylums, bible societies, library societies, missionary societies, aqueduct companies, turnpike companies, fishing companies, medical societies, canal companies, and manufacturing concerns. Overall, my investigation revealed an extraordinary incidence of clauses that, like the Constitution's Necessary and Proper Clause, serve to limit or define the discretion of persons charged with managing the corporate entities (I refer to these clauses as "scope" clauses because they modify the scope of agency).

Scope clauses appear even in early colonial charters. The 1663 Crown charter to the organizers of the colony of Carolina confers authority to bestow titles of honor "as they shall think fit"; to make laws "as often as need shall require"; to appoint judges in such manner as "shall seem most convenient"; and to do all things "necessary" to provide for food and clothing to the colonists.[29] A 1665 restatement of that charter authorizes the governor and council to make laws "as shall be necessary for the present good and welfare" and "as shall be necessary" for well government.[30]

[28] Connecticut presented the added advantage that it was the home of Oliver Ellsworth, one of the members of the Committee of Detail.

[29] Francis Newton Thorpe, Federal and State Constitutions, Colonial Charters, and Other Organic Laws of the States, Territories, and Colonies Now or Heretofore Forming the United States 2743–53 (1909).

[30] *Id.* at 2756–61.

The 1609 charter of the Virginia colony authorizes the grantees to build forts "according to their best discretion" and to erect habitations "where they shall think fit and convenient."[31] The Virginia charter of 1611–1612 authorizes the grantees to appoint officers "as they shall think fit and requisite" and to make laws "as to them from Time to Time, shall be thought requisite and meet."[32]

The Pennsylvania charter of 1681 gives William Penn and his successors the power to sell property "as they shall thinke fitt."[33] The Pennsylvania charter of liberties of 1682 similarly grants Penn and his successors the power to pass laws "that they shall think fit."[34]

The 1662 Connecticut charter authorizes the grantees to make laws "as they shall think Fit, and Convenient," to elect officers "as they shall think fit and requisite," and to import goods "that are or shall be useful or necessary for the Inhabitants."[35]

The 1669 charter of the New Plymouth Colony authorizes the grantees to take certain actions "from tyme to tyme as shall be necessary for their strength and safety."[36]

The Massachusetts Bay Company charter of 1629 authorized the grantees to appoint officers "as they shall thinke fitt and requisite" and to make laws and ordinances "as to them from tyme to tyme shalle [be] thought meete."[37]

The Rhode Island charter of 1663 authorizes the grantees to appoint officers and grant commissions "as they shall thinke fitt and requisite" and to adopt laws that "as to them shall seeme meete for the good and welfare of the sayd Company."[38]

The Maryland charter of 1632 authorizes the Baron of Baltimore and his successors to "make and constitute fit and Wholesome Ordinances," to sell lands "as they shall think convenient," and to "do all and singular other Things in the Premises, which to him or them shall seem fitting and convenient."[39]

The Georgia charter of 1732 gives the grantees the power to adopt laws as "shall seem necessary and convenient for the well ordaining and

[31] *Id.* at 3783–89.
[32] *Id.* at 3806.
[33] *Id.* at 3042.
[34] *Id.* at 3051.
[35] *Id.* at 529–36.
[36] *Id.* at 1845.
[37] *Id.* at 1846–60.
[38] *Id.* at 3215.
[39] *Id.* at 1677–86.

governing of the said corporation," to appoint officers "as shall by them be thought fit and needful," and to act "in such manner and ways and by such expenses as they shall think best."[40]

Scope terms also appear in the charters of the First and Second Banks of the United States. The First Bank's directors were empowered to establish offices "wheresoever they shall think fit," to employ such officers "as shall be necessary for executing the business of the said corporation," to deal with the corporate seal "at their pleasure," and to "ordain, establish, and put in execution, such by-laws, ordinances and regulations, as shall seem necessary and convenient for the government of the said corporation."[41]

Relevant terms for the Second Bank were similar: The directors were authorized to establish branches "wheresoever they shall think fit," to manage the corporate seal "at their pleasure," and to "put in execution, such by-laws, and ordinances, and regulations, as they shall deem necessary and convenient for the government of the said corporation."[42]

Scope terms are ubiquitous in corporate charters from North Carolina and Connecticut. The drafters of these statutes utilized an impressive vocabulary of such terms. "Necessary" and "proper" are the most common, but "expedient,"[43] "fit,"[44] "convenient,"[45] "at pleasure,"[46] and "appertaining"[47] are also observed. Less common are "beneficial,"[48]

40 *Id.* at 767–775.

41 1 Cong. ch. 10, 1 Stat. 191; 1 Cong. ch. 11, 1 Stat. 196.

42 14 Cong. ch. 44, 3 Stat. 269.

43 E.g., an Act to Incorporate the Town of Plymouth, North Carolina Laws of 1807, ch. XLVIII (town of Plymouth). North Carolina Laws of 1808, ch, LXV (town of Jamestown); An Act to Establish Pike Academy in the County of Tyrrell, North Carolina Laws of 1818, ch. XLVIII (Pike Academy); An Act to Establish an Academy on or Near the Lands of Stephen S. Snowdon, in Camden County, North Carolina Laws of 1818, ch. LV (Camden Academy).

44 E.g., An Act to Incorporate the North River and Adams Creek Canal Company, Laws of North Carolina, 1816, ch. XL; An Act Incorporating the Humpreysville Manufacturing Company, Connecticut Laws, May Session, 1810, ch. II.

45 E.g., An Act to Incorporate the American Geological Society, Connecticut Laws, May Session, 1819, ch. XXXII.

46 E.g., An Act to Incorporate the Derby Bank, Connecticut Laws, October Session, 1809, ch. 1; An Act to Incorporate the Eagle Bank, Connecticut Laws, October Session, 1811, ch. I.

47 E.g., An Act to Incorporate the Derby Fishing Company, Connecticut Acts & Laws 737 (1806).

48 E.g., An Act to Establish a Town on John Strother's Land, on the North-East Side of French Broad River, in Buncombe County, North Carolina Laws of 1802, ch. XXXIV (town of Spaightville).

"advisable,"[49] "reasonable,"[50] "meet,"[51] "conducive to,"[52] "for the benefit of,"[53] and "according to their discretion."[54] Doublets, like the Constitution's "necessary and proper," are also attested: examples are "expedient and necessary,"[55] "necessary and expedient,"[56] "necessary or expedient,"[57] "fit and expedient,"[58] "proper and necessary,"[59] "necessary and proper,"[60]

[49] E.g., An Act to Establish an Academy in the County of Buncombe, North Carolina Laws of 1801, ch. XLIII (Union Hill Academy); An Act to Incorporate the Middlesex Fishing Company, Connecticut Acts & Laws 776 (1807).

[50] E.g., An Act to Incorporate the New Haven Bank, Connecticut Acts & Laws 431 (1792); An Act to Incorporate the Bridgeport Bank, Connecticut Acts & Laws 742 (1806); An Act to Incorporate the Ocean Insurance Company of New-Haven, Connecticut Laws, October Session, 1818, Ch. VI.

[51] E.g., An Act to Erect an Academy at the Town of Edenton, in the County of Chowan, North Carolina Laws of 1800, ch. XLVII (Edenton Academy); An Act to Establish a Seminary of Learning at Spring-Hill, in the County of Lenoir, North Carolina Laws of 1802 XXXVI (Spring Hill Seminary); Connecticut Public Records, Vol. 4, p. 370 (1701) (Collegiate School).

[52] Connecticut Public Records, Vol. 4, p. 370 (1701) (Collegiate School).

[53] An Act to Incorporate the Middlesex Fishing Company, Connecticut Acts & Laws 776 (1807).

[54] An Act to Incorporate the Trustees of the Missionary Society of Connecticut, Connecticut Acts & Laws 602 (1802).

[55] An Act to Establish a Town and Inspection of Tobacco and Flour in Caswell County, North Carolina Laws of 1796, ch. XLVIII (town of Milton).

[56] An Act to Establish a Seminary of Learning in the Town of Salisbury, North Carolina Laws of 1798, ch. LIV (Salisbury Academy); An Act to Establish an Academy in the County of Duplin, North Carolina Laws of 1798, ch. XXX (Grove Academy).

[57] An Act to Amend an Act, entitled "An Act to Establish a Seminary of Learning in the Town of Fayetteville", North Carolina Laws of 1809, ch. LXXXI (Fayetteville Academy).

[58] An Act to Incorporate a Company to Build a Bridge Across the Yadkin River, North Carolina Laws of 1816, ch. XXXIX (Yadkin Toll Bridge Company).

[59] An Act to Establish a Town at the Confluence of the Yadkin and Uharee Rivers in the County of Montgomery, North Carolina Laws of 1794, ch. XCVI (town of Henderson); An Act to Establish an Academy in Mecklenberg County, North Carolina Laws of 1811, ch. XLIV (New Providence Academy); An Act to Establish an Academy in the town of Wadesborough, in Anson County, North Carolina Laws of 1802, ch. XXXV (Wadesborough Academy); An Act to Establish an Academy in Mecklenberg County, North Carolina Laws of 1811, ch. XLIV (New Providence Academy).

[60] An Act to Establish an Academy at Smithville, in the County of Brunswick, North Carolina Laws of 1798, Ch. LX; An Act to Establish an Academy in the Town of Wilmington, North Carolina Laws of 1803, ch. XXXVII (Wilmington Academy); An Act to Incorporate a Company to Improve, Clear Out and Render Navigable Tranter's Creek, North Carolina Laws of 1818, ch. LI (Tranter's Creek Navigation Company); An Act to Incorporate the Trustees of Springfield Academy, in the County of Halifax, North Carolina Laws of 1810, ch. LXII (Springfield Academy); An Act to Incorporate the Trustees of the Milton Female Academy, North Carolina Laws of 1818, ch. CIV (Milton Female Academy); An Act to Incorporate the Newbern Marine Insurance Company, North Carolina Laws of 1804 ch. XXII (Newbern Marine Insurance

"necessary and convenient,"[61] "fit and proper,"[62] "suitable and necessary,"[63] and "necessary or convenient."[64]

III. IMPLICATIONS FOR INTERPRETATION

Although the evidence presented so far establishes an unmistakable parallel between corporate charters and the Necessary and Proper Clause, the diversity of scope terms in these charters and the lack of explicit definitions interfere with the task of deriving clear meaning from the corporate law background. The words appear in a fantastic jumble, like a bed of fossilized dinosaur bones disordered by an ancient stream. Daniel Webster, in his brief to the Supreme Court in *McCulloch v. Maryland*, suggested that the justices should simply give up trying to make much sense of the relevant terms: "[t]hese words, 'necessary and proper,' ... are probably to be considered as synonymous. Necessary powers must here intend such powers as are suitable and fitted to the object; such as are best and most useful in relation to the end proposed."[65] Excellent advocate that he was, Webster here seeks to elide any differences between "necessary" and "proper," and then to equate them both with other scope terms such as "fit," "best," and "useful" – a strategy that served the interests of his client, McCulloch, who claimed that the federal government had the authority to charter the Bank of the United States notwithstanding the lack of express constitutional authority to do so, but also one that deprived the key words of much meaning.

Company); An Act Incorporating the Humpreysville Manufacturing Company, Connecticut Laws, May Session, 1810, ch. II; An Act to Incorporate the New Haven Insurance Company, Connecticut Acts & Laws 478 (1797); An Act to Incorporate the Union Insurance Company at New-London, Connecticut Acts & Laws 709 (1805); An Act to Incorporate the Ocean Insurance Company of New-Haven, Connecticut Laws, October Session, 1818, ch. VI.

61 An Act to Incorporate the Newbern Marine Insurance Company, North Carolina Laws of 1804, ch. XXII (Newbern Marine Insurance Company).

62 Connecticut Public Records, Vol. 9, p. 117 (1745) (Yale College); An Act Incorporating the Humpreysville Manufacturing Company, Connecticut Laws, May Session, 1810, ch. II.

63 An Act for Incorporating Part of the Town of Guilford, Connecticut Laws, October Session, 1815, ch. XVII.

64 An Act to Incorporate the Bridgeport Bank, Connecticut Acts & Laws 741 (1806); An Act to Incorporate the Connecticut Assylum [sic] for the Education and Instruction of DEAF and DUMB Persons, Connecticut Laws, May Session, 1816, ch. III.

65 *McCulloch v. Maryland*, 17 U.S. (4 Wheat.) 316, 324–25 (1819).

Despite Webster's skepticism, a little paleontology can uncover information pertinent to the meaning of "necessary and proper" in the Constitution:

1. There is no evidence in the corporate law background that the Necessary and Proper Clause, standing by itself, confers any authority on the Congress. Scope clauses in colonial and early federal charters never convey independent authority. They are adjectival: they modify authority otherwise granted. It is evident that the same is true of the Necessary and Proper Clause. By its own terms it grants no authority to enact legislation: that power is conferred elsewhere in Art. I, § 8, cl. 18, granting Congress power to make "laws ... for carrying into execution" the powers of the national government. The Necessary and Proper Clause of the Constitution, like scope clauses in corporate charters, is inserted as a means of modifying this basic authority.[66]

2. The corporate law background confirms what is already implied in Art. I, § 8, cl. 18: the Necessary and Proper Clause does not confer general legislative power on Congress.

This conclusion can be derived by negative implication from the many grants of legislative authority found in corporate charters of the times. Those grants are almost always general in form: The board members are granted authority, in the words of a 1798 North Carolina charter, to make laws and regulations "for the government of the Academy and preservation of religion, order, and good morals therein."[67] Or, as an 1802 North Carolina school charter put it, the trustees are authorized to make laws for the "government and regulation" of the institution and for the "government of [the students'] morals, studies, and academic exercises."[68] To like effect, an 1802 Connecticut statute incorporating the Hartford Insurance Company authorized the company to "ordain and put in execution, such By-Laws and regulations as shall be deemed necessary and convenient, for the well ordering and governing [of] said Corporation."[69] These and many other grants conferred rulemaking power in the broadest

[66] Lawson and Granger make the same observation about the lack of independent force to the Necessary and Proper Clause, although they base their conclusion on evidence other than corporate charters. See Gary Lawson and Patricia B. Granger, *The "Proper" Scope of Federal Power: A Jurisdictional Interpretation of the Sweeping Clause*, 43 Duke L.J. 267, 274 (1993).

[67] An Act to Establish the Smithville Academy, North Carolina Laws of 1798, ch. LV.

[68] An Act to Establish a Seminary of Learning at Spring-Hill, in the County of Lenoir, North Carolina Laws of 1802, ch. XXXVI.

[69] An Act to Incorporate the Hartford Insurance Company, Connecticut Acts and Laws 650 (1802).

terms, covering all matters having to do with the welfare of the institution. That the breadth of these grants is not accidental is demonstrated by the fact that such clauses were typically accompanied by qualifications requiring that any such regulations not be otherwise contrary to law.[70]

The Necessary and Proper Clause, in contrast, does not grant general legislative authority: It limits Congress's lawmaking authority to actions that are necessary and proper for carrying into execution the powers expressly granted.[71] The contrast between the general legislative power found in corporate charters and the restricted grant found in the Constitution suggests that Congress is not given any general lawmaking power.

3. The corporate law background also suggests that the Constitution does not grant Congress unilateral discretion to define whether a given action is within its legislative power.[72] Most corporate law charters of the era contained language recognizing the discretion of the corporate managers to judge for themselves whether the conditions of the scope clause are satisfied. Thus, we observe phrases such as "as to them shall seem necessary,"[73] "as to them shall seem meet,"[74] "which they may deem necessary,"[75] "as they

70 *See*, e.g., An Act to Incorporate a Company for the Purpose of Clearing Out and Rendering Navigable Newport River, North Carolina Laws of 1811, ch XXXX (Newport Navigation Company); An Act to Erect a Poor House in the County of Lincoln, North Carolina Laws of 1818, ch. CXX; An Act to Incorporate the Middletown Insurance Company, Connecticut Acts & Laws 654 (1802); An Act to Incorporate the Union Insurance Company at New-London, Connecticut Acts & Laws 709 (1805); An Act to Incorporate the Middletown Fire Insurance Company, Connecticut Laws, May Session, 1813, ch. I.

71 The Constitution makes this even clearer by stating that the Congress shall possess "all legislative powers *herein granted*." U.S. CONST., Art. I, § 1.

72 This point is also stressed by Lawson and Granger, although on grounds other than an analysis of corporate charters. See Lawson and Granger, *supra* note 66, at 276 ("the clause does not explicitly designate Congress as the sole judge of the necessity and propriety of executory laws".)

73 E.g., An Act to Incorporate the Town of Plymouth, North Carolina Laws of 1807, ch. XLVIII; An Act to Incorporate the Town of Charlotte, North Carolina Laws of 1815, ch. XLVI; An Act for the Governance of Elizabeth City, North Carolina Laws of 1816, ch. XLIII.

74 E.g., An Act to Establish an Academy at the Town of Edenton, in the County of Chowan, North Carolina Laws of 1800, ch. XLVII (Edenton Academy); An Act to Establish a Seminary of Learning at Spring Hill, in the County of Lenoir, and to Incorporate the Same, North Carolina Laws of 1802, ch. XXXVI.

75 E.g., An Act to Establish a Seminary of Learning in the County of Montgomery, at or Near the Town of Henderson, North Carolina Laws of 1797, ch. XLVII (Stokes Academy); An Act to Incorporate the Connecticut Assylum [sic] for the Education and Instruction of DEAF and DUMB Persons, Connecticut Laws, May Session, 1816, ch. III; An Act to Incorporate the American Geological Society, Connecticut Laws, May Session, 1819, ch. XXXII.

shall think proper,"[76] "as they shall judge most convenient,"[77] "as to them may seem most convenient,"[78] "as they shall deem necessary and convenient,"[79] "as shall be deemed necessary and convenient,"[80] "as they may deem proper and necessary,"[81] "in such manner as shall best appear,"[82] "when they shall think fit,"[83] "as they ... may think most beneficial,"[84] "as they judge necessary,"[85] "as to them

[76] E.g., An Act to Establish a Town at the Place Fixed Upon for the Court House in the County of Surrey, North Carolina Laws of 1789, ch. LVIII (town of Rockford); An Act to Erect an Academy at the Town of Edenton, in the County of Chowan, North Carolina Laws of 1800 ch. XLVII (Edenton Academy); An Act to Incorporate a Company for the Purpose of Rendering Navigable Great and Little Contentnea Creeks, North Carolina Laws of 1815, ch. XVI; An Act to Establish A Turnpike Road from Mattamuskeet Lake to the Main Public Road on the East Side of Pungo River, North Carolina Laws of 1818, ch. LXXI; An Act to Incorporate the New Haven Insurance Company, Connecticut Acts & Laws 479 (1797); An Act to Incorporate the Bridgeport Bank, Connecticut Acts & Laws 741 (1806); An Act to Incorporate the Middletown Fire Insurance Company, Connecticut Laws, May Session, 1813, ch. I; An Act to Incorporate the New-Haven Fire Insurance Company, Connecticut Laws, May Session, 1813, ch. XVIII; An Act to Incorporate the Ocean Insurance Company of New-Haven, Connecticut Laws, October Session, 1818, ch. VI; An Act to Incorporate the Thames Insurance Company at New London, Connecticut Laws, October Session, 1818, ch. VIII.

[77] An Act to Establish a Town at the Place Fixed Upon for the Court House in the County of Surrey, North Carolina Laws of 1789, ch. LVIII (town of Rockford).

[78] An Act to Establish a Town at the Confluence of the Yadkin and Uharee Rivers in the County of Montgomery, North Carolina Laws of 1794, ch. XCVI (town of Henderson).

[79] An Act to Establish a Town at the Confluence of the Yadkin and Uharee Rivers in the County of Montgomery, North Carolina Laws of 1794, ch. XCVI (town of Henderson); An Act to Incorporate the Trustees of the Missionary Society of Connecticut, Connecticut Acts & Laws 602 (1802); An Act to Incorporate the Derby Fishing Company, Connecticut Acts & Laws 737 (1806). The same phrase occurs in the charter of the Second Bank of the United States. 14 Cong. ch. 44, 3 Stat. 269.

[80] An Act for Incorporating a Company to clear the Channel of Connecticut River, Connecticut Acts & Laws 542 (1800).

[81] An Act to Establish a Town at the Confluence of the Yadkin and Uharee Rivers in the County of Montgomery, North Carolina Laws of 1794, ch. XCVI (town of Henderson); An Act to Establish an Academy in Mecklenberg County, North Carolina Laws of 1811, ch. XLIV (New Providence Academy).

[82] An Act to Establish the Fayetteville Library Society, North Carolina Laws of 1794, ch. XCV.

[83] An Act to Incorporate the Newbern Steam Boat Company, North Carolina Laws of 1817, ch. XCIII (Newbern Steam Boat Company) (timing of dividends).

[84] An Act to Establish a Town on John Strother's Land, on the North-East Side of French Broad River, in Buncombe County, North Carolina Laws of 1802, ch. XXXIV (town of Spaightville).

[85] An Act to Incorporate the Bridgeport Bank, Connecticut Acts & Laws 741, 743 (1806).

may appear necessary,"[86] "as they may deem expedient,"[87] and so on. Similar language is found in the charters of the First and Second Banks of the United States: The directors of the First Bank were empowered to "to ordain, establish, and put in execution, such by-laws, ordinances and regulations, *as shall seem* necessary and convenient for the government of the said corporation,"[88] while the directors of the Second Bank were authorized to "ordain, establish, and put in execution, such by-laws, and ordinances, and regulations, *as they shall deem* necessary and convenient for the government of the said corporation."[89]

In contrast with the common practice in corporate charters of recognizing the authority of the institution or its managers to determine the scope of their own authority, the Constitution is conspicuously silent on this point. The Necessary and Proper Clause does not say, as it easily could have said, that Congress shall have power to "make all Laws which *as to it shall seem* necessary and proper" to carry into execution the powers of the federal government, or which "*it shall judge* necessary

86 An Act to Establish an Academy in the County of Wilkes, North Carolina Laws of 1801, ch. XLII (Philomathia Academy); An Act to Establish an Academy in the Town of Wadesborough, in Anson County, North Carolina Laws of 1802, ch. XXXV (Wadesborough Academy); An Act to Establish an Academy at the Court-House in Caswell County, North Carolina Laws of 1802, ch. XXXVII (Caswell Academy); An Act to Establish an Academy in the County of Greene, North Carolina Laws of 1804, ch. XLIII (Greene Academy); An Act to Establish an Academy in Trenton, in the County of Jones, North Carolina Laws of 1807, ch. LXVI (Trenton Academy); An Act to Establish an Academy on Richland Swamp, in Robeson County, North Carolina Laws of 1808, ch. LXXIV (Zion Parnassus Academy); An Act for the Promotion of Learning and Scientific Knowledge in the County of Stokes, North Carolina Laws of 1809, ch. LXXX (Germantown Academy); An Act to Incorporate the Trustees of Springfield Academy, in the County of Halifax, North Carolina Laws of 1810, ch. LXII (Springfield Academy); An Act to Revive and Amend an Act to Establish an Academy in the County of Currituck, North Carolina Laws of 1810, ch. LXX (Currituck Academy); An Act to Establish a Seminary of Learning in the County of Moore, by the Name of "Euphronean Academy," North Carolina Laws of 1811, ch. XLIII (Euphronean Academy); An Act to Establish a Seminary of Learning in Robeson County, by the Name of Philadelphus Academy, North Carolina Laws of 1812, ch. CV (Philadelphus Academy); An Act to Incorporate the Town of Oxford in the County of Granville, North Carolina Laws of 1816, ch. XLV (town of Oxford); An Act to Establish Wayne Academy, North Carolina Laws of 1818, ch. CXI (Wayne Academy); An Act to Establish a Seminary of Learning in the Town of Hertford, In Perquimons County, North Carolina Laws of 1818, ch. XLVIII (Hertford Academy).

87 An Act to Incorporate the New-London Bank, Connecticut Acts & Laws 781, 783 (1807).

88 1 Stat. 192 (emphasis added).

89 3 Stat. 269 (emphasis added).

and proper," or which "*it may deem* necessary and proper." Instead, the language is simply "which *shall be* necessary and proper." Judged by the corporate law background, the omission of language conferring authority to self-determine the scope of legislative power appears unlikely to have been accidental. It implies that Congress does not have sole or unilateral authority to determine the scope of its own legislative power, and rather that some other body (i.e., the Supreme Court) can reject congressional judgment on this score.

4. Inferences about the use of the doublet "necessary and proper" can be drawn from the corporate law background. The combination of these terms in the constitutional clause poses an interpretive dilemma. If "necessary" is simply a heightened form of "proper" – that is, if everything that is necessary is, by logical implication, also proper – then there would be no reason to include the word "proper" in the clause; all the work would be done by "necessary." The problem cannot be avoided by interpreting "and" to mean "or": "necessary *or* proper" would also involve superfluity because then "necessary" would add nothing. Other things equal, it appears undesirable to interpret constitutional terms in a way that makes any of them superfluous.

Daniel Webster's approach to this problem was to see "necessary" and "proper" as synonyms.[90] Essentially, his suggestion to the Supreme Court was to view the doublet as a sort of rhetorical flourish – a phrase that sounds attractive but has little content. Webster's idea of seeing the terms as synonymous makes it irrelevant whether "and" or "or" is used, since either would convey the same information. But it fails to resolve the scandal of superfluity. If "necessary" and "proper" mean the same thing, the framers could have been content with either. Even worse, by conflating the terms Webster discounted the meaning of both. "Necessary" and "proper" seem different as a matter of ordinary speech, but if they mean the same thing in the Constitution, it appears that they can't mean much at all. This, of course, was Webster's intention, but it is not a satisfactory solution to the problem of interpretation.

In considering the implications of the corporate law background, we can begin with the fact that the clause in question is a *doublet* – a combination of two scope words. Corporate practice frequently used doublets. A close investigation reveals that the use of such terms is not randomly distributed. Doublets are uncommon or absent in ordinary grants of corporate authority – determining times for meeting or declaring a dividend,

[90] *McCulloch v. Maryland*, 17 U.S. (4 Wheat.) 316, 324–25 (1819).

acting with respect to the corporate seal, hiring employees, setting salaries and terms and conditions of employment, purchasing property and erecting buildings, appointing or electing new trustees, raising money by lotteries, paying dividends, or increasing the capital stock. But doublets *are* often observed in clauses granting legislative powers to directors, commissioners, or trustees – the very clauses most analogous to the grant of legislative authority associated with the Necessary and Proper Clause. The heavy use of doublets in grants of corporate rulemaking power suggests that the presence of a doublet in the Constitution is not accidental: The concentration of this trope in one specific type of corporate law provision seems to have meaning.

What distinguishes legislative grants from other authority-conferring clauses? A possible answer is that legislative power clauses in corporate charters, in contrast with most other grants of authority, confer very broad power both as to means and ends. When the legislators wished to impose a meaningful scope limitation on the exercise of such broad-ranging authority, therefore, they may have included a doublet so as to emphasize that the restriction being imposed was to apply comprehensively to all aspects of the decision being taken. Even if the particular terms in the doublet have no independent meaning – if, as Webster argued, "necessary" and "proper" are mere synonyms – the fact that the Committee of Detail chose to include them both could still have significance: a rhetorical flourish, perhaps, but one that conveys information all the same (consider John Hancock's signature of the Declaration of Independence!).

5. We wish, however, to find in the corporate law background more useful information about "necessary" and "proper" – information that would give these terms some degree of distinctive meaning and defend the Necessary and Proper Clause against the accusation of superfluity.

Consider first the term "necessary." This word is not defined in corporate charters, and it is clear that it was not used with a precise, definite, and generally understood meaning. But it does not follow that we should throw up our hands. While the term "necessary" displays substantial variance in application, it also manifests a reasonably discernible average meaning.

Colonial and early federal lawmakers employed a substantial but limited number of scope terms when modifying grants of agency authority. Although these terms are not precisely defined, we can line them up in some rough order of the severity of the restriction. That way, we can get a sense, if not of their *cardinal* meaning, at least of their *ordinal* meaning: their placement vis-à-vis other words on a scale of severity of restriction. If we do this, it is obvious that the term "necessary" is the most restrictive of all the terms we observe in the lexicon: more restrictive, certainly, than terms such as "at pleasure" or "according to their discretion," which recognize nearly unchecked freedom of action, but more restrictive also than terms like "expedient," "fit," "convenient," "beneficial," "reasonable," "meet," or "advisable", which appear to require only that the means undertaken have a tendency to advance the objects of the institution. Whatever "necessary" means, it clearly requires more by way of means-end connection than other scope words found in corporate charters of the day. This fact suggests that the word "necessary," although it did not have a definite meaning, at least had a central tendency that is more demanding than other terms that were readily available to the framers.

Further information on the meaning of "necessary" can be gleaned from an examination of the context in which this term is used in corporate law charters. These charters contain a number of standardized provisions that can be associated with common scope terms. For example, many charters set forth rules for *when* the managers of a corporation must undertake certain actions such as setting a meeting time or declaring a dividend. The term "necessary" is almost never associated with such timing rules. Instead, we find terms like "[when] convenient,"[91] when they "shall judge proper,"[92] "when they shall think proper,"[93] "when they may think it expedient,"[94] "as they may think proper,"[95] "at any time or times they may think proper,"[96] "as they may judge expedient,"[97] "when they shall think fit,"[98] and "as they shall deem most

[91] An Act to Establish a Seminary of Learning in the County of Montgomery, North Carolina Laws of 1797, ch. XLVII (Stokes Academy).

[92] An Act to Incorporate the Bridgeport Bank, Connecticut Acts & Laws 742 (1806).

[93] An Act to Erect an Academy at the Town of Edenton, in the County of Chowes, North Carolina Laws of 1800, ch. XXXIX.

[94] An Act for the Government of Elizabeth City, North Carolina Laws of 1816, ch. XLIII.

[95] An Act to Establish an Academy in the County of Buncombe, North Carolina Laws of 1801, ch. XLIII (Union Hill Academy).

[96] An Act for the Government of Elizabeth City, North Carolina Laws of 1816, ch. XLIII.

[97] An Act to Incorporate the Aetna Insurance Company, Connecticut Laws, May Session, 1819, ch. XXXIV.

[98] An Act to Incorporate the Newbern Steam Boat Company, North Carolina Laws of 1817, ch. XCIII (Newbern Steam Boat Company) (timing of dividends).

convenient."[99] It is evident that the use of scope terms in these timing rules is not accidental. They are employed for the purpose of conveying a broad degree of discretion to agents over matters that are not fundamental to the achievement of the enterprise's goals.

Another example concerns actions undertaken with respect to the corporate seal. Many charters of the era give the company being formed the right to a common seal and specifying a wide range of actions that the managers may undertake with respect to the seal, including changing, altering, breaking, or re-creating it. The charters almost never use the scope term "necessary" with respect to these actions, instead specifying that the managers may act at "pleasure"[100] or as they shall think "proper"[101] or "fit."[102] Here again, the use of scope terms is not accidental.

[99] An Act to Incorporate the American Geological Society, Connecticut Laws, May Session, 1819, ch. XXXII. In the rare cases where the term "necessary" is used in this context, its effect is usually to enlarge rather than reduce the agent's scope of discretion – the company may be instructed, for example, to publish notice of a meeting in newspapers other than the one specified in the statute if "necessary." An Act to Incorporate the New Haven Bank, Connecticut Acts & Laws 431 (1792); An Act to Incorporate the Middletown Fire Insurance Company, Connecticut Laws, May Session, 1813, ch. I; An Act to Incorporate the New-Haven Fire Insurance Company, Connecticut Laws, May Session, 1813, ch. XVIII.

[100] An Act to Incorporate the Newbern Marine Insurance Company, and to Establish a Bank in Said Town, North Carolina Laws of 1804, ch. XXII (Newbern Marine Insurance Company); An Act to Incorporate the Newbern Marine Insurance Company, and to Establish a Bank in Said Town, North Carolina Laws of 1804, ch. XXII (Bank of Newbern); An Act to Incorporate the New Haven Bank, Connecticut Acts & Laws 431 (1792); An Act to Incorporate the Norwich Bank, Connecticut Acts & Laws 443 (1796); An Act to Incorporate the New Haven Insurance Company, Connecticut Acts & Laws 478 (1797); An Act to Incorporate the Trustees of the Missionary Society of Connecticut, Connecticut Acts & Laws 602 (1802); An Act to Incorporate the Hartford Insurance Company, Connecticut Acts & Laws 650 (1802); An Act to Incorporate the Middletown Insurance Company, Connecticut Acts & Laws 654 (1802); An Act to Incorporate the Union Insurance Company at New-London, Connecticut Acts & Laws 709 (1805); An Act to Incorporate the Hartford Fire Insurance Company, Connecticut Laws, May Session 1810, ch. I; An Act to Incorporate the New-Haven Fire Insurance Company, Connecticut Laws, May Session, 1813, ch. XVIII; An Act for Incorporating Part of the Town of Guilford, Connecticut Laws, October Session, 1815, ch. XVII; An Act to Incorporate the Ocean Insurance Company of New-Haven, Connecticut Laws, October Session, 1818, ch. VI; An Act to Incorporate the American Geological Society, Connecticut Laws, May Session, 1819, ch. XXXII; An Act to Incorporate a Saving Society in the City of Hartford, Connecticut Laws, May Session, 1819, ch. XXXIII.

[101] An Act to Erect an Academy at the Town of Edenton, in the County of Chowan, North Carolina Laws of 1800, ch. XXXIX; An Act to Establish an Academy at Williamston, in the County of Martin, North Carolina Laws of 1816, ch. XLV (Williamston Academy).

[102] Connecticut Public Records, Vol. 9, p. 115 (1745) (Yale College).

Actions with respect to the seal are ministerial, technical, and not fundamental to the realization of the institution's goals or purposes. It is not surprising, therefore, that the scope terms used with respect to such actions convey a broad degree of freedom on the part of the corporation and its managers.

We may also consider clauses going to conditions of employment or salaries of officers. Charter provisions conferring these authorities typically employ terms such as "as they may deem proper,"[103] "if they think proper,"[104] as they "shall think fit,"[105] "as they may think proper,"[106] as they may or shall "judge reasonable,"[107] "as shall appear to them reasonable,"[108] "as they may think proper,"[109] or "as they judge reasonable."[110] Again, it appears that the omission of the term "necessary" from such clauses is not accidental. Decisions setting terms and conditions of employment for officers or establishing salaries are obviously ones that need to be committed to the broad discretion of the managers of a company.

Consider also actions by corporate directors with respect to dividends. Charters of this period typically authorize directors to declare

[103] An Act to Establish an Academy in the Upper Part of Pasquotank County, North Carolina Laws of 1809, ch. LXXVIII (Newland Academy); An Act to Establish an Academy in Camden County, North Carolina Laws of 1810, ch. LXXIV (Jonesborough Academy); An Act to Establish an Academy at Plymouth, in Washington County, North Carolina Laws of 1810, ch. LXXIII (Plymouth Academy).

[104] An Act to Establish a Seminary of Learning in Elizabeth Town, in Bladen County, North Carolina Laws of 1810, ch. LXXII (Elizabeth Town Academy).

[105] An Act to Incorporate the North River and Adams Creek Canal Company, Laws of North Carolina, 1816, ch. XL.

[106] An Act to Establish an Academy in the Town of Snow-Hill, in the County of Greene, North Carolina Laws of 1812, ch. CIV (Snow-Hill Academy).

[107] An Act to Incorporate the New Haven Bank, Connecticut Acts & Laws 431 (1792); An Act to Incorporate the Bridgeport Bank, Connecticut Acts & Laws 742 (1806); An Act to Incorporate the Ocean Insurance Company of New-Haven, Connecticut Laws, October Session, 1818, ch. VI; An Act to Incorporate the Middlesex Fishing Company, Connecticut Acts & Laws 774 (1807); An Act to Incorporate the Derby Bank, Connecticut Laws, October Session, 1809, ch. 1; An Act to Incorporate the Eagle Bank, Connecticut Laws, October Session, 1811, ch. I; An Act to Incorporate the Phoenix Bank, Connecticut Laws, May Session, 1814, ch. II.

[108] An Act to Incorporate the Norwich Bank, Connecticut Acts & Laws 443 (1796).

[109] An Act to Incorporate the Union Insurance Company at New-London, Connecticut Acts & Laws 709 (1805); An Act to Incorporate the Ocean Insurance Company of New-Haven, Connecticut Laws, October Session, 1818, ch. VI; An Act to Incorporate the Thames Insurance Company at New London, Connecticut Laws, October Session, 1818, ch. VIII.

[110] An Act Incorporating the Humpreysville Manufacturing Company, Connecticut Laws, May Session, 1810, ch. II; An Act Incorporating the Middletown Manufacturing Company, Connecticut Laws, October Session, 1810, ch. I.

dividends "as they shall think proper,"[111] "as shall appear to the directors advisable,"[112] "as to them shall appear fit and proper,"[113] "as shall appear to them proper,"[114] and as they "may judge proper."[115] Once again, the omission of the term "necessary" from most of these clauses appears to have been intentional. Like the other powers just discussed, the decision whether to declare a dividend is a matter requiring judgment, but not one that is fundamental to achieving the goals of the enterprise (it would be odd to say that the directors found it "necessary" to declare a dividend).

What about clauses conferring general executive authority on directors, commissioners, or trustees? Here again, the scope clauses only rarely contain the term "necessary."[116] Instead, terms used in this context include: "to do all other acts matters and things proper to be done,"[117] to exercise "such other powers, as shall be by them deemed for the best interest of the company,"[118] to act "according to their best discretion,"[119] to do that "which to them shall or may appertain to do,"[120] to "do and execute all

111 An Act to Incorporate the New Haven Insurance Company, Connecticut Acts & Laws 479 (1797); An Act to Incorporate the Bridgeport Bank, Connecticut Acts & Laws 741 (1806); An Act to Incorporate the Middletown Fire Insurance Company, Connecticut Laws, May Session, 1813, ch. I; An Act to Incorporate the New-Haven Fire Insurance Company, Connecticut Laws, May Session, 1813, ch. XVIII; An Act to Incorporate the Ocean Insurance Company of New-Haven, Connecticut Laws, October Session, 1818, ch. VI; An Act to Incorporate the Thames Insurance Company at New London, Connecticut Laws, October Session, 1818, ch. VIII.

112 An Act to Incorporate the Middlesex Fishing Company, Connecticut Acts & Laws 776 (1807).

113 An Act Incorporating the Humpreysville Manufacturing Company, Connecticut Laws, May Session, 1810, ch. II.

114 An Act Incorporating the Middletown Manufacturing Company, Connecticut Laws, October Session, 1810, ch. I.

115 An Act to Incorporate the Eagle Bank, Connecticut Laws, October Session, 1811, ch. I; An Act to Incorporate the Phoenix Bank, Connecticut Laws, May Session, 1814, ch. II.

116 For an exception, see An Act to Incorporate the Trustees of the Missionary Society of Connecticut, Connecticut Acts & Laws 602 (1802) ("to transact all business necessary to attain the ends of the society").

117 An Act to Incorporate a Company for Mutual Assurance Against Fire, Connecticut Acts & Laws 550 (1801).

118 An Act to Incorporate the Aetna Insurance Company, Connecticut Laws, May Session, 1819, ch. XXXIV.

119 Connecticut Public Records, Vol. 4, p. 370 (1701) (Collegiate School).

120 An Act to Incorporate the New Haven Bank, Connecticut Acts & Laws 431 (1792); An Act to Incorporate the Middletown Insurance Company, Connecticut Acts & Laws 654 (1802); An Act to Incorporate the Union Insurance Company at New-London, Connecticut Acts & Laws 709 (1805).

acts and things to them appertaining,"[121] to "put in execution whatever they may judge to be for the benefit of the Company,"[122] "to do and cause to be executed all such acts and things as to them may appertain,"[123] "to do and execute all and singular the matters, and things, which to them shall or may appertain,"[124] and to "do and act in all things whatever that may tend to the profit" of the corporation.[125] We may infer that the omission of "necessary" from these clauses sprang from a wish on the part of the drafters not to unduly saddle the ability of the managers to undertake useful but unforeseeable actions on behalf of their organizations.[126] At least for these statutes, the drafters apparently felt that the word "necessary" would impose undesirable limitations on the exercise of executive discretion.

Contrast the foregoing powers with ones where the word "necessary" *does* appear in corporate charters. The most prominent example is the decision whether to hire employees. When power to hire employees is conferred, it is typically qualified by the scope terms such as "as they may deem necessary,"[127] "as they shall judge necessary,"[128] "which shall be necessary,"[129] "as shall be necessary,"[130] as they may or shall "find

[121] An Act to Incorporate the Derby Fishing Company, Connecticut Acts & Laws 737 (1806).

[122] An Act to Incorporate the Middlesex Fishing Company, Connecticut Acts & Laws 776 (1807).

[123] An Act to Incorporate the New-London Bank, Connecticut Acts & Records 781 (1807); An Act to Incorporate the Eagle Bank, Connecticut Laws, October Session, 1811, ch. I.

[124] An Act to Incorporate the Middletown Fire Insurance Company, Connecticut Laws, May Session, 1813, ch. I; An Act to Incorporate the Thames Insurance Company at New London, Connecticut Laws, October Session, 1818, ch. VIII.

[125] An Act Establishing an Academy at Laurel Hill, in Richmond County, North Carolina Laws of 1809, ch. LXXVII (Laurel Hill Academy).

[126] The word "necessary" is used in An Act Concerning Library Companies, Connecticut Laws, October Session, 1818, ch. IX (granting general executive authority to "do all acts necessary and proper for the well ordering of the affairs of such corporation.")

[127] An Act to Establish a Seminary of Learning in the County of Montgomery, North Carolina Laws of 1797, ch. XLVII (Stokes Academy).

[128] An Act to Incorporate the Bridgeport Bank, Connecticut Acts & Laws 743 (1806); An Act to Incorporate the Hartford Fire Insurance Company, Connecticut Laws, May Session, 1810, ch. I; An Act to Incorporate the New-Haven Fire Insurance Company, Connecticut Laws, May Session, 1813, ch. XVIII; An Act to Incorporate The Aetna Insurance Company, Connecticut Laws, May Session, 1819, ch. XXXIV; An Act Incorporating the Humpreysville Manufacturing Company, Connecticut Laws, May Session, 1810, ch. II; An Act Incorporating the Middletown Manufacturing Company, Connecticut Laws, October Session, 1810, ch. I.

[129] An Act for Incorporating Part of the Town of Guilford, Connecticut Laws, October Session, 1815, ch. XVII.

[130] An Act to Incorporate the Phoenix Bank, Connecticut Laws, May Session, 1814, ch. II.

necessary or convenient,"[131] "as to them shall appear necessary,"[132] "as to them shall appear necessary and proper,"[133] "as to them shall deem necessary,"[134] "as to them shall appear necessary,"[135] "as shall be necessary for executing the business of said corporation,"[136] or "as shall appear necessary."[137]

The pattern here is far too strong to be accidental. Why is the scope term "necessary" heavily favored in the employment context while being absent or virtually absent in the other contexts just discussed? We may

131 An Act to Incorporate the Connecticut Assylum [sic] for the Education and Instruction of DEAF and DUMB Persons, Connecticut Laws, May Session, 1816, ch. III; An Act to Incorporate the American Geological Society, Connecticut Laws, May Session, 1819, ch. XXXII.

132 An Act to Incorporate a Saving Society in the City of Hartford, Connecticut Laws, May Session, 1819, ch. XXXIII.

133 An Act to Establish the Smithville Academy, North Carolina Laws of 1798, ch. LV (Smithville Academy); An Act to Incorporate the Trustees of the Springfield Academy, in the County of Halifax, North Carolina Laws of 1810, ch. LXII (Springfield Academy); An Act to Incorporate the Trustees of the Milton Female Academy, North Carolina Laws of 1818, ch. CIV (Milton Female Academy).

134 An Act to Establish a Seminary of Learning at Spring-Hill, in the County of Lenoir, North Carolina Laws of 1802, ch. XXXVI (Spring Hill Seminary).

135 An Act to Establish an Academy in Nixonton, in the County of Pasquotank, North Carolina Laws of 1803, ch. XXVI (Nixonton Academy); An Act to Establish an Academy in Beaufort County, North Carolina Laws of 1808, ch. LXXV (Washington Academy); An Act to Establish an Academy in the Upper Part of Pasquotank County, North Carolina Laws of 1809, ch. LXXVIII (Newland Academy); An Act to Establish an Academy at Plymouth, in Washington County, North Carolina Laws of 1810, ch. LXXIII (Plymouth Academy); An Act to Establish an Academy in Camden County, North Carolina Laws of 1810, ch. LXXIV (Jonesborough Academy); An Act to Establish an Academy at Plymouth, in Washington County, North Carolina Laws of 1810, ch. LXXIII (Plymouth Academy); An Act to Establish an Academy in the Town of Snow-Hill, in the County of Greene, North Carolina Laws of 1812, ch. CIV (Snow-Hill Academy); An Act to Incorporate the Town of Clinton and to Appoint Commissioners for the Said Town, North Carolina Laws of 1818, ch. LXXXIV (town of Clinton).

136 An Act to Incorporate the Newbern Marine Insurance Company, and to Establish a Bank in Said Town, North Carolina Laws of 1804, ch. XXII (Bank of Newbern).

137 An Act to Incorporate the Town of Plymouth, North Carolina Laws of 1807, ch. XLVIII (town of Plymouth). Even when "necessary" is not used in grants of hiring authority, the scope term employed tends to indicate a demanding standard: "as they may deem proper," An Act to Establish an Academy in Onslow County, North Carolina Laws of 1809, ch. LXXXIII (Onslow Academy); An Act to Establish an Academy in Carteret County, North Carolina Laws of 1810, ch. LXIV (Carteret Academy); An Act to Establish an Academy at Enfield, North Carolina Laws of 1818, ch. LI (Enfield Academy), or "as they shall judge requisite," An Act to Incorporate the North River and Adams Creek Canal Company, Laws of North Carolina, 1816, ch. XL; An Act to Incorporate the Newbern Steam Boat Company, North Carolina Laws of 1817, ch. XCIII (Newbern Steam Boat Company).

surmise that for a small corporation – one just being formed – the decision on whether to hire an employee and who to hire *is* fundamental to achieving the goals of the enterprise.

The other context in which the word "necessary" frequently appears is the one most analogous to the Necessary and Proper Clause of the Constitution – clauses conferring general lawmaking or rulemaking power on the corporation or its directors, commissioners, or trustees. This context displays the widest variance of scope terms, but the word "necessary" appears more frequently than any other.[138] Typical usages here include as may "appear necessary,"[139] "as to them shall

[138] The second most common scope term found in grants of rulemaking authority is "proper." Other scope terms evidenced in this context include as to them may or shall "seem meet," An Act to Erect a Poor House in the County of Lincoln, North Carolina Laws of 1818, ch. CXX; An Act to Erect an Academy at the Town of Edenton, in the County of Chowan, North Carolina Laws of 1800, ch. XLVII (Edenton Academy); An Act to Establish a Seminary of Learning at Spring-Hill, in the County of Lenoir, North Carolina Laws of 1802 ch. XXXVI (Spring Hill Seminary); "as the directors may deem fit and expedient," An Act to Incorporate a Company to Build a Bridge Across the Yadkin River, North Carolina Laws of 1816, ch. XXXIX (Yadkin Toll Bridge Company); "as they shall judge most convenient," An Act to Establish a Town at the Place Fixed Upon for the Court House in the County of Surry, North Carolina Laws of 1789, ch. LVIII; "as they may deem expedient," An Act to Incorporate the Town of Plymouth, North Carolina Laws of 1807, ch. XLVIII (town of Plymouth); An Act to Establish an Academy in Waynesborough, North Carolina Laws of 1810, ch. LXVIII (Waynesborough Academy); An Act to Incorporate a Company for the Purpose of Clearing Out and Rendering Navigable Newport River, North Carolina Laws of 1811, ch. XXX (Newport Navigation Company); "as may be deemed expedient," An Act to Incorporate the New-London Bank, Connecticut Acts & Laws 781 (1807); An Act to Incorporate the Derby Bank, Connecticut Laws, October Session, 1809, ch. 1; An Act to Incorporate the Eagle Bank, Connecticut Laws, October Session, 1811, ch. I; An Act to Incorporate the New-Haven Fire Insurance Company, Connecticut Laws, May Session, 1813, ch. XVIII; "as shall be convenient," An Act to Incorporate the New Haven Bank, Connecticut Acts & Laws 431 (1792); "as to them shall seem meet and most conducive to the aforesaid end thereof," Connecticut Public Records, Vol. 4, p. 370 (1701) (Collegiate School); and "as are usually made" in such institutions, An Act to Incorporate the Trustees of the Milton Female Academy, North Carolina Laws of 1818, ch. CIV (Milton Female Academy).

[139] An Act to Establish the Smithville Academy, North Carolina Laws of 1798, ch. LV (Smithville Academy); An Act to Establish an Academy in the County of Wilkes, North Carolina Laws of 1801, ch. XLII (Philomathia Academy); An Act to Establish an Academy in the Town of Wadesborough, in Anson County, North Carolina Laws of 1802, ch. XXXV (Wadesborough Academy); An Act to Establish an Academy at the Court-House in Caswell County, North Carolina Laws of 1802, ch. XXXVII (Caswell Academy); An Act to Establish an Academy in the County of Greene, North Carolina Laws of 1804, ch. XLIII (Greene Academy); An Act to Establish an Academy in Trenton, in the County of Jones, North Carolina Laws of 1807, ch. LXVI (Trenton Academy); An Act to Establish an Academy on Richland Swamp, in Robeson County,

appear right and necessary,"[140] as they may or shall "deem proper and necessary,"[141] which or as "they may deem necessary,"[142] as they "may

North Carolina Laws of 1808, ch. LXXIV (Zion Parnassus Academy); An Act for the Promotion of Learning and Scientific Knowledge in the County of Stokes, North Carolina Laws of 1809, ch. LXXX (Germantown Academy); An Act to Incorporate the Trustees of the Springfield Academy, in the County of Halifax, North Carolina Laws of 1810, ch. LXII (Springfield Academy); An Act to Revive and Amend an Act to Establish an Academy in the County of Currituck, North Carolina Laws of 1810, ch. LXX (Currituck Academy); An Act to Establish a Seminary of Learning in the County of Moore, by the Name of the "Euphronean Academy," North Carolina Laws of 1811, ch. XLIII (Euphronean Academy); An Act to Establish a Seminary of Learning in Robeson County, by the Name of Philadelphus Academy), North Carolina Laws of 1812, ch. CV (Philadelphus Academy); An Act to Incorporate the Town of Oxford in the County of Granville, North Carolina Laws of 1816, ch. XLV (town of Oxford); An Act to Establish Wayne Academy, North Carolina Laws of 1818, ch. CXI (Wayne Academy); An Act to Establish a Seminary of Learning in the Town of Hertford, in Perquimons County, North Carolina Laws of 1818, ch. XLVIII (Hertford Academy); An Act to Establish Pike Academy in the County of Tyrrell, North Carolina Laws of 1818, ch. XLVIII (Pike Academy); An Act to Establish an Academy on or Near the Lands of Stephen S. Snowdon, in Camden County, North Carolina Laws of 1818, ch. LV (Camden Academy); An Act to Establish an Academy at Swainsborough, in Onslow County, North Carolina Laws of 1810, ch. LXVII (Swainsborough Academy); An Act to Incorporate the Town of Charlotte in the County of Mecklenberg, North Carolina Laws of 1815, ch. XVII (town of Charlotte); An Act to Establish a Seminary of Learning on the Lands of James Hilliard in the County of Nash by the Name of Hilliardston Academy, North Carolina Laws of 1818, ch. CVIII (Hilliardston Academy); An Act to Establish a Seminary of Learning on the Lands of John Martin, in the County of Wake, by the Name of Forest Hill Academy, North Carolina Laws of 1818, ch. CVII (Forest Hill Academy).

140 An Act to Establish a Turnpike Road from Mattamuskeet Lake to the Main Public Road on the East Side of Pungo River, North Carolina Laws of 1818, ch. LXXI I (Pungo River Turnpike Company).

141 An Act to Establish an Academy in the Town of Wadesborough, North Carolina Laws of 1802, ch. XXXV (Wadesborough Academy); An Act to Establish an Academy in Mecklenberg County, North Carolina Laws of 1811, ch. XLIV (New Providence Academy).

142 An Act to Incorporate the Connecticut Assylum [sic] for the Education and Instruction of DEAF and DUMB Persons, Connecticut Laws, May Session, 1816, ch. III; An Act to Incorporate the American Geological Society, Connecticut Laws, May Session, 1819, ch. XXXII; An Act to Authorize the Trustees of the Lumberton Academy, to Raise a Certain Sum by Way of Lottery to Complete the Building of Said Academy, North Carolina Laws of 1802, ch. XXXIX (Lumberton Academy); An Act to Establish an Academy in Nixonton, in the County of Pasquotank, North Carolina Laws of 1803 XXVI (Nixonton Academy); An Act to Establish an Academy in Beaufort County, Adjoining Washington, North Carolina Laws of 1808 LXXV (Washington Academy); An Act to Establish an Academy at Plymouth, in Washington County, North Carolina Laws of 1810, ch. LXXIII (Plymouth Academy); An Act to Establish an Academy in the Town of Snow-Hill, in the County of Greene, North Carolina Laws of 1812, ch. CIV (Snow-Hill Academy); An Act to Establish a Female Academy in the County of Orange, Laws of North Carolina, 1818, ch. CX (Female Academy in County of

consider necessary and proper,"[143] "necessary and proper;"[144] "as may or shall be necessary and proper;"[145] as shall "seem necessary,"[146] as shall or may "be necessary,"[147] as shall seem "necessary and convenient,"[148] "as they shall judge necessary and convenient,"[149] "as shall be necessary or convenient,"[150] "as shall be deemed necessary and convenient,"[151] "as

Orange); An Act to Incorporate the Camden Bible Society, Laws of North Carolina of 1819, ch. CXXVIII.

143 An Act to Establish an Academy in the Town of Wilmington, North Carolina Laws of 1803, ch. XXXVII (Wilmington Academy).

144 An Act to Incorporate a Company to Improve, Clear Out and Render Navigable Tranter's Creek, North Carolina Laws of 1818, ch. LI (Tranter's Creek Navigation Company).

145 An Act to Incorporate the New Haven Insurance Company, Connecticut Acts & Laws 478 (1797); An Act to Incorporate the Hartford Insurance Company, Connecticut Acts & Laws 650 (1802); An Act to Incorporate the New Haven Insurance Company, Connecticut Acts & Laws 479 (1797); An Act to Incorporate the Union Insurance Company at New-London, Connecticut Acts & Laws 709 (1805); An Act to Incorporate the Ocean Insurance Company of New-Haven, Connecticut Laws, October Session, 1818, Ch. VI.

146 An Act to Incorporate the Norwich Bank, Connecticut Acts & Laws 443 (1796); An Act to Incorporate the Town of Plymouth, North Carolina Laws of 1807, ch. XLVIII (town of Plymouth); An Act to Incorporate the Town of Charlotte in the County of Mecklenberg, North Carolina Laws of 1815, ch. XVII (town of Charlotte); An Act for the Governance of Elizabeth City, North Carolina Laws of 1816, ch. XLIII (town of Elizabeth City); An Act to Incorporate the Trustees of the Milton Female Academy, North Carolina Laws of 1818, ch. CIV (Milton Female Academy).

147 An Act to Incorporate an Aqueduct Company in the City of Norwich, Connecticut Laws, October Session, 1808, ch. VIII; An Act Establishing an Academy in the County of Granville, For Appointing Trustees, and for Other Purposes, North Carolina Laws of 1779, ch. XXV; An Act to Incorporate the Town of Williamsborough in the County of Granville, North Carolina Laws of 1808, ch. LXVII (town of Williamsborough); An Act to Establish an Academy in Onslow County, North Carolina Laws of 1809, ch. LXXXXIII (Onslow Academy); An Act to Establish an Academy in Cataret County, North Carolina Laws of 1810, ch. LXIV (Carteret Academy); An Act to Establish an Academy in the Town of Haywood in Chatham County, and to Incorporate the Trustees Thereof, Laws of North Carolina, 1818, ch. CIX (Haywood Academy); An Act to Establish the Laurencville Academy [sic] in the County of Montgomery, North Carolina Laws of 1818, ch. XXXIV (Laurenceville Academy); An Act to Incorporate the Leaksville Male and Female Academies, North Carolina Laws of 1818, ch. XLIX; An Act to Establish an Academy at Enfield, North Carolina Laws of 1818, ch. LI (Enfield Academy).

148 An Act to Incorporate the Newbern Marine Insurance Company, and to Establish a Bank in Said Town, North Carolina Laws of 1804, ch. XXII (Bank of Newbern).

149 An Act to Incorporate the Thames Insurance Company at New London, Connecticut Laws, October Session, 1818, ch. VIII.

150 An Act to Incorporate the Bridgeport Bank, Connecticut Acts & Laws 741 (1806).

151 An Act for Incorporating a Company to Clear the Channel of Connecticut River, Connecticut Acts & Laws 542 (1800); An Act to Incorporate a Company for

they shall deem necessary and convenient,"[152] "as shall appear necessary or expedient,"[153] "as shall be thought necessary;"[154] "suitable and necessary,"[155] and "by them deemed necessary."[156]

Why does the term "necessary" appear so frequently in grants of rulemaking authority? It appears likely that the scope restriction, where it appears in these clauses, was a response to the perceived breadth of the authority being conferred. Legislatures commonly manifested misgivings about broad grants of rulemaking power, often stipulating that the exercise of such powers could not be repugnant to state or federal law.[157] Because the authority conferred by a grant of rulemaking power was so extensive, legislatures also appear, in many cases, to have imposed relatively stringent limits on the exercise of that authority by utilizing "necessary" as a scope term. The term "necessary," when used as a limitation on legislative authority in corporate charters, thus apparently required that

Mutual Assurance Against Fire, Connecticut Acts & Laws 550 (1801); An Act to Incorporate the Hartford Insurance Company, Connecticut Acts & Laws 650 (1802); An Act to Incorporate the Middletown Insurance Company, Connecticut Acts & Laws 654 (1802); An Act to Incorporate the Hartford Fire Insurance Company, Connecticut Laws, May Session 1810, Ch. I ; An Act to Incorporate the Middletown Fire Insurance Company, Connecticut Laws, May Session, 1813, ch. I; An Act to Incorporate the New-Haven Fire Insurance Company, Connecticut Laws, May Session, 1813, ch. XVIII; An Act to Incorporate the Ocean Insurance Company of New-Haven, Connecticut Laws, October Session, 1818, ch. VI; An Act Incorporating the Humpreysville Manufacturing Company, Connecticut Laws, May Session, 1810, ch. II ("as shall be deemed necessary and convenient"); An Act Incorporating the Middletown Manufacturing Company, Connecticut Laws, October Session, 1810, ch. I ("as shall be deemed necessary and convenient").

[152] An Act to Incorporate the Trustees of the Missionary Society of Connecticut, Connecticut Acts & Laws 602 (1802); An Act to Incorporate the Derby Fishing Company, Connecticut Acts & Laws 737 (1806); An Act to Incorporate the New Haven Insurance Company, Connecticut Acts & Laws 478 (1797); An Act to Incorporate Chauncy Gleaford, Elias Cowles, and their Associates, Connecticut Acts & Laws 583 (1801); An Act to Incorporate the Union Insurance Company at New-London, Connecticut Acts & Laws 709 (1805).

[153] An Act to Amend an Act, Entitled "an Act to Establish a Seminary of Learning in the Town of Fayetteville, and to Amend the Law for the Regulation of the Towns of Fayetteville and Hillsborough," North Carolina Laws of 1809, ch. LXXXI (Fayetteville Academy).

[154] An Act to Incorporate the Windham Aqueduct Company, Connecticut Acts & Laws 778 (1807).

[155] An Act for Incorporating Part of the Town of Guilford, Connecticut Laws, October Session, 1815, ch. XVII.

[156] An Act to Incorporate the Aetna Insurance Company, Connecticut Laws, May Session, 1819, ch. XXXIV.

[157] *See* note 67–70, *supra*.

rules enacted for the governance of the institution be reasonably closely adapted to achieving the goals for which the institution was formed.

6. Finally, the corporate law background may provide information about the meaning of the term "proper." We have already seen that "necessary" and "proper" had different meanings in corporate charters: The former is used within distinctive contexts that do not overlap with the usage of "proper." We now investigate whether the term "proper" has a distinctive context of its own independent of other scope terms.

"Proper" is the second most common scope term (after "necessary") in general grants of legislative authority to corporations or their directors, commissioners, or trustees. In addition to the usages together with "necessary" just described, these include "as to them may appear proper,"[158] as they may or shall "deem proper,"[159] "as to them may seem proper,"[160] "as they shall think fit and proper;"[161] as they shall or may "think proper,"[162] as they may "think expedient and proper,"[163] "as

158 An Act to Establish a Seminary of Learning in the County of Montgomery, at or Near the Town of Henderson, North Carolina Laws of 1797, ch. XLVII (Stokes Academy).

159 An Act to Incorporate the Middletown Insurance Company, Connecticut Acts & Laws 656 (1802); An Act to Establish an Academy in the Town of Wadesborough, North Carolina Laws of 1802, ch. XXXV (Wadesborough Academy); An Act to Establish an Academy in Nixonton, in the County of Pasquotank, North Carolina Laws of 1803, ch. XXVI (Nixonton Academy).

160 An Act to Incorporate the Trustees of the Nutbush Mineral Springs Academy, on the Land of John Simms, in the County of Warren, North Carolina Laws of 1810, ch. LXV (Mineral Springs Academy).

161 Connecticut Public Records, Vol. 9, p. 117 (1745) (Yale College).

162 An Act to Incorporate a Company for the Purpose of Rendering Navigable Great and Little Contentnea Creeks, North Carolina Laws of 1815, ch. XVI (Great and Little Contentnea Creeks Navigation Company); An Act to Establish a Turnpike Road from Mattamuskeet Lake to the Main Public Road on the East Side of Pungo River, North Carolina Laws of 1818, ch. LXXI I (Pungo River Turnpike Company); An Act to Establish an Academy on the Land of William M. Sneed, in the County of Granville, North Carolina Laws of 1810, ch LXVI (Montpelier Academy); An Act to Establish an Academy on the Lands of Thomas B. Littlejohn, Adjoining the Court-house in Granville County, North Carolina Laws of 1811, ch. XLVI (Oxford Academy); An Act to Incorporate the Broad River Navigation Company, and Also the Inhabitants of Rutherfordton, of the County of Rutherford, North Carolina Laws of 1811, ch. XXXII (Broad River Navigation Company); An Act to Establish a School by the Name of New Prospect in Perquimons County, North Carolina Laws of 1817, ch. LXXIV (New Prospect Academy); An Act to Appoint Commissioners for the Town of Chapel Hill, in Orange County, North Carolina Laws of 1818, ch. LXXX (town of Chapel Hill).

163 An Act to Incorporate the Allemance Library Society in the County of Guilford, North Carolina Laws of 1819, ch. CVII.

may seem requisite and proper,"[164] and "as to them may appear just and proper."[165]

The term "proper" also appears distinctively in scope clauses where the term "necessary" is largely absent. It is the dominant term conditioning grants of authority to declare a dividend: "as they shall think proper,"[166] "as to them shall appear fit and proper,"[167] "as shall appear to them proper,"[168] and as they "may judge proper."[169] The term "proper" appears with reasonable frequency in clauses authorizing managers to determine salaries or conditions of employment; usages here include "as they may deem proper"[170] and if or as "they think proper."[171] The

[164] An Act to Incorporate a Company to Build a Bridge Across the Yadkin River, North Carolina Laws of 1816, ch. XXXIX (Yadkin Toll Bridge Company); An Act to Incorporate the Leaksville Toll Bridge Company, and For Other Purposes, North Carolina Laws of 1818, ch. LXXXIII (Leaksville Toll Bridge Company); An Act to Incorporate the Clinton Toll Bridge Company, and to Appoint Commissioners for the Same, North Carolina Laws of 1818, ch. LXXIII (Clinton Toll Bridge Company).

[165] An Act to Incorporate the Town of Hookerton in Greene County, North Carolina Laws of 1817, ch. LII (town of Hookerton); An Act to Incorporate the Town of Clinton and to Appoint Commissioners for the Said Town, North Carolina Laws of 1818, ch. LXXXIV (town of Clinton).

[166] An Act to Incorporate the New Haven Insurance Company, Connecticut Acts & Laws 479 (1797); An Act to Incorporate the Bridgeport Bank, Connecticut Acts & Laws 741 (1806); An Act to Incorporate the Middletown Fire Insurance Company, Connecticut Laws, May Session, 1813, ch. I; An Act to Incorporate the New-Haven Fire Insurance Company, Connecticut Laws, May Session, 1813, ch. XVIII; An Act to Incorporate the Ocean Insurance Company of New-Haven, Connecticut Laws, October Session, 1818, ch. VI; An Act to Incorporate the Thames Insurance Company at New London, Connecticut Laws, October Session, 1818, ch. VIII.

[167] An Act Incorporating the Humpreysville Manufacturing Company, Connecticut Laws, May Session, 1810, ch. II.

[168] An Act Incorporating the Middletown Manufacturing Company, Connecticut Laws, October Session, 1810, ch. I.

[169] An Act to Incorporate the Eagle Bank, Connecticut Laws, October Session, 1811, ch. I; An Act to Incorporate the Phoenix Bank, Connecticut Laws, May Session, 1814, ch. II.Only rarely do we find other scope terms in grants of dividend authority: "as shall appear to the directors advisable," An Act to Incorporate the Middlesex Fishing Company, Connecticut Acts & Laws 776 (1807), or as the directors "shall judge necessary," An Act to Incorporate the North River and Adams Creek Canal Company, Laws of North Carolina, 1816, ch. XL.

[170] An Act to Establish an Academy in the Upper Part of Pasquotank County, North Carolina Laws of 1809, ch. LXXVIII (Newland Academy); An Act to Establish an Academy in Camden County, North Carolina Laws of 1810, ch. LXXIV (Jonesborough Academy); An Act to Establish an Academy at Plymouth, in Washington County, North Carolina Laws of 1810, ch. LXXIII (Plymouth Academy).

[171] An Act to Amend an Act to Establish a Seminary of Learning in Elizabeth Town, in Bladen County, North Carolina Laws of 1810, ch. LXXII (Elizabeth Town Academy); An Act to Incorporate the Union Insurance Company at New-London, Connecticut

term also appears in grants of authority to set times for discretionary acts such as setting a meeting time, declaring dividends, or levying a tax. Usages here include as they may or shall "think proper,"[172] as they "judge proper,"[173] or as they "deem proper."[174]

Each of these contexts where "proper" plays a distinctive role is one affecting the interests of corporate stakeholders other than the managers

Acts & Laws 709 (1805); An Act to Incorporate the Ocean Insurance Company of New-Haven, Connecticut Laws, October Session, 1818, ch. VI; An Act to Incorporate the Thames Insurance Company at New London, Connecticut Laws, October Session, 1818, ch. VIII.

Scope terms other than "proper" found in this context include "fit," An Act to Incorporate the North River and Adams Creek Canal Company, Laws of North Carolina, 1816, ch. XL, and "reasonable, " An Act to Incorporate the New Haven Bank, Connecticut Acts & Laws 431 (1792); An Act to Incorporate the Bridgeport Bank, Connecticut Acts & Laws 742 (1806); An Act to Incorporate the Ocean Insurance Company of New-Haven, Connecticut Laws, October Session, 1818, ch. VI; An Act to Incorporate the Middlesex Fishing Company, Connecticut Acts & Laws 774 (1807); An Act to Incorporate the Derby Bank, Connecticut Laws, October Session, 1809, ch. 1; An Act to Incorporate the Eagle Bank, Connecticut Laws, October Session, 1811, ch. I; An Act to Incorporate the Phoenix Bank, Connecticut Laws, May Session, 1814, ch. II; An Act to Incorporate the Norwich Bank, Connecticut Acts & Laws 443 (1796); An Act Incorporating the Humpreysville Manufacturing Company, Connecticut Laws, May Session, 1810, ch. II; An Act Incorporating the Middletown Manufacturing Company, Connecticut Laws, October Session, 1810, ch. I.

172 An Act to Incorporate the New-London Bank, Connecticut Acts & Laws 782 (1807); An Act to Incorporate the Eagle Bank, Connecticut Laws, October Session, 1811, ch. I; An Act to Incorporate the Phoenix Bank, Connecticut Laws, May Session, 1814, ch. II; An Act to Incorporate the Derby Bank, Connecticut Laws, October Session, 1809, ch. 1; An Act to Establish an Academy in the Town of Buncombe, North Carolina Laws of 1801, ch. XLIII (Union Hill Academy); An Act to Establish an Academy at Williamston in the County of Martin, North Carolina Laws of 1816, ch. XLV (Williamston Academy); An Act for the Governance of Elizabeth City, North Carolina Laws of 1816, ch. XLIII (Elizabeth City) (when to levy a tax).

173 An Act to Incorporate the Bridgeport Bank, Connecticut Acts & Laws 745 (1806).

174 An Act to Incorporate the Eagle Bank, Connecticut Laws, October Session, 1811, ch. I; An Act to Incorporate the Phoenix Bank, Connecticut Laws, May Session, 1814, ch. II.

Other scope terms associated with discretionary timing authority include "shall judge necessary," An Act to Incorporate the New Haven Bank, Connecticut Acts & Laws 431 (1792); An Act to Incorporate the Middletown Fire Insurance Company, Connecticut Laws, May Session, 1813, ch. I; An Act to Incorporate the New-Haven Fire Insurance Company, Connecticut Laws, May Session, 1813, ch. XVIII, "as they may judge expedient," An Act to Incorporate the Aetna Insurance Company, Connecticut Laws, May Session, 1819, ch. XXXIV, "as they shall deem most convenient," An Act to Incorporate the American Geological Society, Connecticut Laws, May Session, 1819, ch. XXXII, "when they may think it expedient," An Act for the Governance of Elizabeth City, North Carolina Laws of 1816, ch. XLIII (Elizabeth City), "when they shall think fit," An Act to Incorporate the Newbern Steam Boat

who are charged with making the decision in question. The decision to declare a dividend affects the interest of shareholders; the decision as to when to call a meeting or levy a tax affects the interests of those who are supposed to attend the meeting or pay the tax; the decision to set salaries or conditions of employment affects the interests of the employee; the decision to adopt rules for the governance of an institution affects the interests of everyone who is subject to the rules. Where the term "proper" is absent or rare – contexts such as hiring employees, purchasing property and erecting buildings, appointing or electing new trustees, or general spending authority – the relevant relationships are not between the corporation and its stakeholders but rather between the corporation and a third party acting at arm's length (job candidates, people who might sell property or provide services to the company, nominees for managerial positions, vendors).

The term "proper" might therefore convey the idea that in carrying out a given authority, the company or its managers should design the actions taken so as to consider the effect on stakeholders in the firm. As applied to the Constitution's Necessary and Proper Clause, the message could be that laws must not only serve the general interest of the country as a whole, but must also take into account the individual interests of particular citizens. Thus, even if a law qualifies as "necessary," it could still be outside congressional authority if, without adequate justification, it discriminates against or disproportionately affects the interests of individual citizens vis-à-vis others.[175]

Company, North Carolina Laws of 1817, ch. XCIII (Newbern Steam Boat Company) (timing of dividends), "convenient," An Act to Establish a Seminary of Learning in the County of Montgomery, at or Near the Town of Henderson, North Carolina Laws of 1797, ch. XLVII (Stokes Academy), and "as often as circumstances shall render it necessary,") An Act to Incorporate the Town of Hamilton, North Carolina Laws of 1804, ch. XLV (town of Hamilton).

175 This interpretation of "proper" advanced here has points of similarity with the view expounded by Gary Lawson and Patricia Granger in their insightful article, *The "Proper" Scope of Federal Power: A Jurisdictional Interpretation of the Sweeping Clause*· 43 Duke L. J. 267 (1993). Based on historical, linguistic, and structural analysis, Lawson and Granger argue that the term "proper" requires that laws must be "peculiarly within Congress's domain or jurisdiction" and must not infringe upon the retained rights of the states or of individuals. The results of Lawson and Granger's analysis are potentially congruent with the view expressed here, since legislation that interferes with the retained rights of individuals is also likely to discriminate against or disproportionately affect the interests of particular people without adequate justification or excuse.

IV. CONCLUSION

This chapter has investigated the corporate law background of the Necessary and Proper Clause. The remarkable incidence of scope clauses in corporate charters of the era – including many using the terms "necessary," "proper," and "necessary and proper" – suggests that these documents could have been a source of the constitutional provision, or at least that similar interpretative principles might apply in both contexts. Justice Marshall, for one, appears to have understood the analogy. When he famously pronounced that "we must never forget that it is a *constitution* we are expounding,"[176] he was contrasting the appropriate methodology for interpreting the Constitution with an approach that would be appropriate for another, unnamed type of legal document. The obvious candidate is the corporate charter. Although Marshall rejected the salience of the parallel, his apparent reference to corporate charters highlights the importance of these instruments as part of the legal background of America's fundamental law.

An examination of corporate charters of the founding era provides guidance on questions of interpretation. The corporate law background suggests that the Necessary and Proper Clause does not grant independent lawmaking competence does not grant general legislative power, and does not delegate unilateral discretion to Congress to define whether a given action is or is not constitutionally authorized. The use of the doublet "necessary and proper" is probably meaningful, and suggests that Congress must stay within the scope of delegated power across all dimensions of the decision being taken. For a law to be "necessary," there must be a reasonably close connection between constitutionally recognized legislative ends and the means chosen to accomplish those ends. To be "proper," a law must not without adequate justification discriminate against or otherwise disproportionately affect the interests of individual citizens.[177]

As noted at the outset, these results should be viewed with caution. The key terms "necessary" and "proper" have no definite meaning in

[176] *McCulloch v. Maryland*, 17 U.S. (4 Wheat.) 316, 406 (1819) (emphasis in original).

[177] This interpretation of the term "necessary and proper" derived from the corporate law background appears to be generally consistent with Gary Lawson and Guy Seidman's account of the clause as referring to a principle of reasonableness requiring delegated authority to be exercised in a measured, proportionate, and rights-regarding fashion. *See* Gary Lawson and Guy Seidman, *The Jeffersonian Treaty Clause*, 2006 U. Ill. L. Rev. 1, 48–54.

corporate practice, although I have argued that a rough or approximate meaning can be attributed to them. Even if the data I have examined – principally North Carolina and Connecticut corporate charters of the colonial and early federal periods – are representative of early American legal practice, there is no proof that the wording of the Necessary and Proper Clause was borrowed from corporate charters or that the corporate law background had any influence on the members of the Committee of Detail, much less on the other delegates at the Convention or the participants in the ratifying debates. The interpretation of the Constitution, moreover, is not necessarily constrained by how similar words would be understood in a different legal context – a point stressed in the clearest possible terms in *McCulloch v. Maryland.* And the meaning of the Necessary and Proper Clause today is not necessarily governed by inferences about original understanding. These caveats notwithstanding, the analysis presented here offers perspective and adds texture to the historical understanding of this most important constitutional provision.

Index